GAVIN YOUNG

From Sea to Shining Sea

A Present-Day Journey Through America's Past

America! America!
  God shed His grace on thee
And crown thy good with brotherhood
  From Sea to Shining Sea!

<small>KATHERINE LEE BATES:</small> *America the Beautiful*

PENGUIN BOOKS

PENGUIN BOOKS

Published by the Penguin Group
Penguin Books Ltd, 27 Wrights Lane, London W8 5TZ, England
Penguin Books USA Inc., 375 Hudson Street, New York, New York 10014, USA
Penguin Books Australia Ltd, Ringwood, Victoria, Australia
Penguin Books Canada Ltd, 10 Alcorn Avenue, Toronto, Ontario, Canada M4V 3B2
Penguin Books (NZ) Ltd, 182–190 Wairau Road, Auckland 10, New Zealand

Penguin Books Ltd, Registered Offices: Harmondsworth, Middlesex, England

First published by Hutchinson 1995
Published in Penguin Books 1996
1 3 5 7 9 10 8 6 4 2

Copyright © Gavin Young, 1995
Maps by Rodney Paull © Hutchinson, 1995
All rights reserved

The moral right of the author has been asserted

Printed in England by Clays Ltd, St Ives plc

The author and publishers wish to thank the following for permission to reproduce
copyright material: William Heinemann, part of Reed International Books, Curtis
Brown Ltd and the Estate of John Steinbeck, for extracts from *The Grapes of Wrath*,
Cannery Row, *Travels with Charley* and *The Winter of Our Discontent* by John Steinbeck;
Hamish Hamilton Ltd and the Estate of Raymond Chandler for extracts from *Farewell My
Lovely* (© Raymond Chandler 1940), *The High Window* (© Raymond Chandler 1943),
The Long Goodbye (© Raymond Chandler 1953), *The Little Sister* (© Raymond Chandler
1949) and 'The Simple Art of Murder' from *Pearls are a Nuisance* (© Raymond Chandler
1950); The University of Chicago Press for an extract from *A River Runs Through It* by
Norman Maclean; Faber and Faber Ltd and the Estate of T. S. Eliot for the lines from
'Burnt Norton', from *Collected Poems 1909–1962*; Faber and Faber Ltd for the extract from
Great Plains by Ian Frazier; and Macmillan Inc for extracts from *Gone with the Wind* by
Margaret Mitchell. Every effort has been made to contact copyright holders and the
publishers apologise for any inadvertent omissions.

To

Alexandra and Arthur Schlesinger, Jnr.
and
Tara and Ted Conklin

With thanks

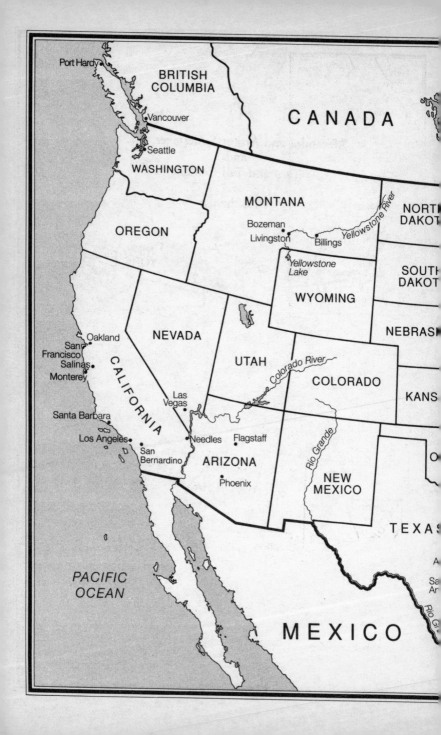

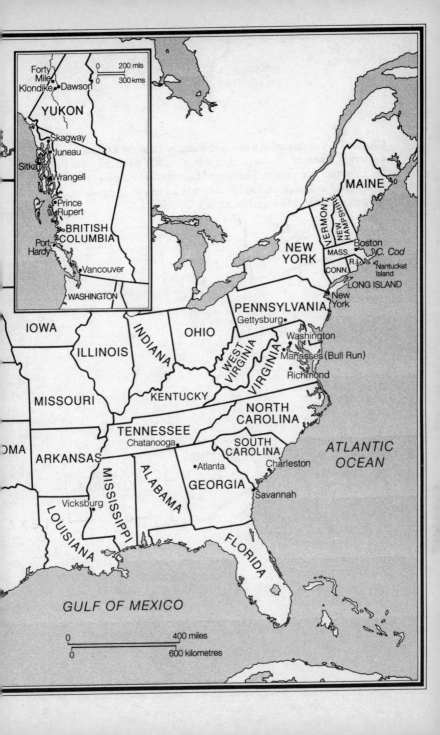

NOTE

Chapters 1-4 appeared in a much reduced form in the London *Observer*. Chapter 11 was published in a slightly different form in the *Observer* and then in *Discovery* Magazine in Hong Kong. Chapter 13 also appeared in *Discovery* in a somewhat cut down version, and with photographs by Nik Wheeler.

The Past – the dark unfathom'd retrospect!
The teeming gulf – the sleepers and the shadows!
The past – the infinite greatness of the past!
For what is the present after all but a growth out of the past?

WALT WHITMAN: 'Passage to India'

Go, go, go, said the bird: human kind
Cannot bear very much reality.
Time past and time future
What might have been and what has been
Point to one end, which is always present.

T. S. ELIOT: 'Burnt Norton'

Contents

Acknowledgements

Any thanks must start with Arthur Schlesinger, who, while having nothing to do with this book's shortcomings, was a very accessible and reassuring point of reference for much of the time it was being put together.

Colin Campbell and Deborah Scroggins (now Colin's wife) were both of great help while I was investigating the battlefields of Georgia, and Colin actually walked over some of them (often in driving rain) and then drove me down the route General Sherman took on his way to burn Atlanta and to 'make Georgia howl'. My old friend Norman Sherry turned up in San Antonio, Texas, where he was busy preparing the second volume of his life of Graham Greene, but not too busy to put me in touch with the one and only Maury Maverick – and a good thing, too, because, among much else, Maury disabused me of my absurd illusion that the Alamo was a *river*.

Another old friend, Nik Wheeler, the photographer with whom I once did two books about Iraq, accompanied me to Arizona and the Mojave Desert, travelling with me down Route 66 on the trail of the Okies in Steinbeck's *Grapes of Wrath*. And of course he went with me, too, in the footsteps of Chandler's Philip Marlowe through the sad streets of Los Angeles and Santa Monica. I have Nik's son, Adam, to thank for driving me up to Big Sur and Carmel where Joan Fontaine, yet another friend from way back, had me to stay while I investigated 'Cannery Row', as Nik's wife Pamela had put me up in the Wheelers' house in Los Angeles.

I was lucky in Carmel, too. There I found a wonderful contact with John Steinbeck's early life. John Thompson took me to see Bruce Ariss, an artist and once a close friend of Steinbeck, who moved to Pacific Grove, Monterey, as early as 1934.

As for my time in Montana, it would not have been half as enjoyable without the arrangements made on my behalf by Bill and Pam Bryan, founders and owners of a splendid organisation in Bozeman called Off The Beaten Path. Among other things, they put me in touch with two first-class naturalists and ideal trekking companions, Ken Sinay and John Good, a former director of Yellowstone Park, who since I wrote this account of my visit there has actually gone back to live in the Yellowstone, his favourite park of all.

As for the Yukon, that chilly adventure was made possible by Dick North, a humorous and warm-hearted man who has given up a good deal of his life to preserving the name of the writer Jack London. (Dick admires London immensely and so he chose to be associated with him. Yet I have a sneaking idea he would have been almost equally happy with Mark Twain.) It was Dick who reintroduced me to Robert Service, whose poems I had hardly thought about since I was a very small boy. Service's Yukon poems – 'The Shooting of Dan McGrew', for example – I now find wholly delightful.

Most important of all, for me, Dick put me in touch with Paul and Cathy Wylie – an action that somehow changed my life. Now, I simply cannot imagine never having seen Forty Mile River, or never having mushed the Wylies' dogs, or never having slept in that cabin in the frozen clearing – in that tiny log hut with no running water or electricity.

I will never forget flying through a snow blizzard with 'Custer' in the tiny Cessna he had had mounted on skis. I cannot imagine never having set foot in Duncan Sprigg's wonderful 'Snake Pit' bar in Dawson City – the Malamute Saloon, I sometimes call it; or never having seen the Klondike; or not having walked up Bonanza Creek or strolled in a cloud of insects by the 'marge of Lake Lebarge'. How could I have missed sailing past Sitka or crossing over Dead Horse Gulch above little Skagway? All those things, I thank God, I have done. I have Dick North to thank, though he would modestly deny it, for having been able to do them.

Finally there is Ted Conklin. Owner of the venerable American Hotel in Sag Harbor, Ted allowed me to stay in the hotel's annexe for a long time and, out of sheer goodness of heart, charged me virtually nothing for it. On top of which, he invited me to his wedding celebrations. No one can do more.

Of course, many others helped me in this long adventure. I hope I may be forgiven for not naming them all but I am immensely grateful to them none the less.

At the London end of things, I must of course mention with gratitude Anthony Whittome, my cheerful and expert editor; and, above all, my 'sea anchor' Gritta Weil who, despite ill health, put my typescript together as swiftly and competently as ever.

Introduction

Like many voyages round America, this one starts in New York City. I got to know New York well in the 1960s and have visited it regularly ever since. I came to love the city then, so that every time I came back to it later – as I frequently still do – I could not help agreeing with E. B. White, a favourite writer of mine, when he wrote years ago in the *New Yorker*: 'the two moments when New York seems most desirable, when the splendour falls all round about and the city looks like a girl with leaves in her hair, are just as you are leaving and must say goodbye and just as you return and can say hello . . . .'

White, in another piece, also compared New York to a girl – a different one but equally charming – 'a wonderful brisk girl whose arm you want to take on the way home'.

And a good deal later, I remember reading in a story by Scott Fitzgerald:

> It was dark outside and Broadway was a blazing forest fire as [he] walked slowly towards the point of brightest light. He looked up at the greatest intersecting planes of radiation with a vague sense of approval and possession. He would see it a lot now, lay his restless heart upon this greater restlessness . . . .

Of course, as far as I was concerned, I was the 'he' in that passage.

I have to admit that New York isn't *quite* what it was to me years ago. For one thing, too many people I knew in the old days are dead; so it is too much a city full of ghosts. Nevertheless, it still has its magical moments, and it is certainly true that 'I like', as the Lorenz Hart song said, 'New York in June'. To be precise, *early* June, when the temperature is pleasantly high (but not *too* high), long holidays lie ahead, and the trees in Central Park are fat again with the leaves of summer. Early June is the season in New York when those magical moments are most likely to occur.

To take one example: often at around noon at this time of year I wander into the wonderfully cool air of the Oak Bar of the Plaza Hotel to gaze from a high bar-stool out of its broad windows at the sunlit park and happy passers-by. As often as not I do so with a Bullshot to hand – that light and mildly enlivening concoction of vodka and bouillon – expertly mixed by one of the two cheerful barmen on duty: Ruben from St Thomas in the American Virgin Islands, or Malcolm, a Jamaican from Port Antonio, who for some reason has developed an ambition to become a Highway Patrol cop in Maryland.

At about this time, the magical highlight of the day arrives. I stroll from the Plaza's entrance, turning half-left through drying horse-dung and twittering sparrows, to visit Corina, the oldest mare in the ranks of buggy-horses that wait for customers on 59th Street. This is close to the great statue, over-gilded by Mr Donald Trump, of General William Tecumseh Sherman. The terrible general who burned Atlanta sits astride his favourite charger, Ontario, and stares so imperiously down 5th Avenue that he looks as if he was seriously considering burning that too.

Before each visit to Corina, I usually have filled my pockets with candy, or even a carrot or two. For although the old grey mare is twenty years old, her appetite is unimpaired by age, and as she waits to bear a smiling couple or even a whole happy family off for a tour in the park, she likes something to munch on.

Corina is looked after by her driver, a jolly, reddish-haired young lady in a very old top-hat called Theresa, and the two of them are to be found on 59th Street in the sunshine most days of the week. I make a point of greeting them.

'Hello, Theresa.'

'Hi. How ya doin'?' Theresa says with a smile.

'Hello, Corina.' And Corina nods her old grey head up and down and says nothing.

If the two of them are not there they are in the park with a buggyful of laughing children, or simply taking a day off. But you will most likely find Corina with her forefeet up on the sidewalk and her hindfeet in the road, waiting patiently between her shafts for the next lot of customers. Her nose may be deep in her feeding-bag; or she may simply be gazing round her to see what the other horses or the passers-by are up to. And Theresa will be standing nearby, touting for custom and keeping a weather eye on her old friend.

As for General Sherman, he looks far too military and fierce to be capable of reciting *Hamlet* or *Coriolanus* by heart (although, in life, he could actually do so). And it seems unlikely that that grim-faced soldier would ever have co-founded the Players' Club in the tree-shaded peace of Gramercy Square with Edwin Booth, the actor whose brother had assassinated Abraham Lincoln, who was at that time his boss. Nevertheless he did that, too. Sherman had a soft spot for actors. He felt that they were a cruelly despised class of people; he wanted them to be able to mix with their betters – by which he meant high society.

Sherman died at home in his rocking chair rereading for the umpteenth time Charles Dickens's *Great Expectations*, a favourite novel. It was a sympathic end to the ruthless soldier who had cruelly fulfilled the promise he made to his superior, General Grant, to 'make Georgia howl'.

In the pages that follow I track 'Uncle Billy' Sherman and his battles on the long devastating march through Georgia to the sea at Savannah passing through (a totally rebuilt) Atlanta. As a matter of fact, Sherman's shade seemed to follow me about. I ran into it again several months later (and many miles further west) hovering around the battlefield of the Little Bighorn where Custer got his comeuppance at the hands of Crazy Horse.

Before Little Bighorn I travelled to places a good deal closer to Central Park. In search, for example, of the old whalers of Melville's time, I visited Sag Harbor, New Bedford and Nantucket, 'quitting the good city of Manhatto'' for those old whale-haunted Atlantic ports as Ishmael had done in *Moby Dick* – and Melville himself did in real life.

In succeeding months my trail took me very far from Central Park: to the Alamo at San Antonio, Texas; to Los Angeles in pursuit of Raymond Chandler's Philip Marlowe, and Arizona in the tracks of Steinbeck's Okies; from Carmel and Oakland I followed Jack London all the way to Dawson City and the Klondike in the frozen Yukon Territory of Canada; and from there to the home of the grizzlies, and the ranges where once millions of buffaloes roamed, and the scene of Custer's Last Stand on the plains of Montana.

So a long time elapsed before I saw Corina again. Then I was back in New York, it was June a year later – late afternoon in Central Park – and Corina's buggy once again had a complement of laughing customers aboard, and Theresa was in the driving seat.

Standing thankfully in that sunlit corner near the trees, I watched Corina, her ears jauntily pricked, with Theresa wearing her battered top-hat, as she happily trotted away into the park to be lost to view among the wonderful green leaves of summer.

From that comforting view of the old grey mare, I turned at last towards the glowing, golden statue of 'Uncle Cump' – great, Shakespeare-obsessed General Sherman – who had had more than one chance to be President of the United States, and had preferred not to be any such thing. He still looked sternly – perhaps even wistfully – down 5th Avenue as if he longed to see it in flames like the Atlanta he had once so deliberately and ruthlessly set ablaze. And, by a strange chance, the downtown flare of afternoon sun gave me an odd impression that Lower Manhattan was indeed, as Fitzgerald had said, a flaming forest fire.

I had travelled a long way; all round America, in fact. It had taken a long time. I was glad to be back in New York, in the exciting city in which it has always seemed that anything can happen.

New York City, 1992 –
Sag Harbor, Long Island, 1994

From Sea to Shining Sea

Part One

The Broken Mast

Sail forth, steer for the deep waters only,
And we will risk the ship, ourselves and all . . .
O daring joy, but safe! are they not all the seas of God?

WALT WHITMAN: 'Sea-Drift'

The excessive length of whaling voyages has always been the
outstanding fact of a whaleman's life, the fact that marked him
apart from all other seamen.

CLIFFORD W. ASHLEY: *The Yankee Whaler*

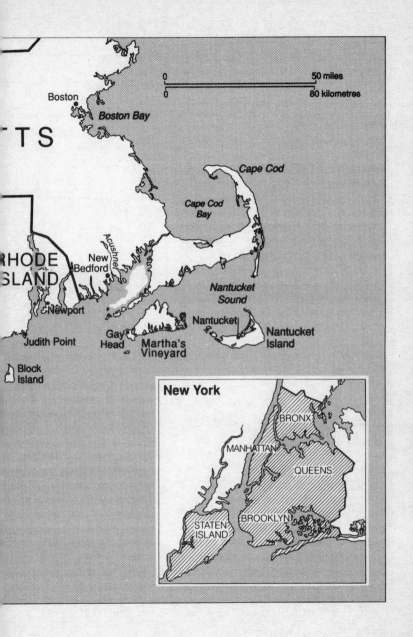

Boston

Boston Bay

TTS

50 miles

80 kilometres

Cape Cod

Cape Cod Bay

Acushnet

RHODE ISLAND

New Bedford

Newport

Judith Point

Nantucket Sound

Nantucket

Nantucket Island

Gay Head

Martha's Vineyard

Block Island

New York

BRONX

MANHATTAN

QUEENS

STATEN ISLAND

BROOKLYN

Chapter 1

I too Paumanok,
I too have . . . been washed on your shores, you fish-shaped island.

WALT WHITMAN

About two months after the burning of Los Angeles that followed the acquittal of the police officers in the Rodney King beating case, and about a month before quite serious racial violence in the Washington Heights district of Manhattan, I set off with a sense of excited relief from New York for the little port of Sag Harbor that lies on an eastern arm of Long Island Sound.

Not that I was fleeing the violence which pessimistic friends predicted might engulf some cities of America, as the hot summer weather began to inflame tempers and diminish patience all round. Or even trying to escape the gloomy predictions of the imminent dissolution of America that drifted at that time like choking clouds of cigarette smoke across the dinner tables of New York. A harsh period of recession seemed to be going to continue for quite a time, and just at that moment America was in the middle of a particularly uninspiring presidential election year. The violence, often drug-induced, was a brutal and mindless extra.

Actually, though, I went regardless of this grimness, according to a schedule I had set myself sometime before. My plan was to start a voyage round the United States by spending the early summer in a search for the Golden Age of American whaling. What was left to see, I wondered, of the world of Moby Dick, Captain Ahab, and brave (or foolhardy) men like Ishmael, Starbuck, Stubb and Queequeg, and their ship, the *Pequod*? The old whaling port of Sag Harbor was my first stop.

I had no idea if racial obsessions had spread to places like Sag Harbor, New London, New Bedford and Nantucket. In the eighteenth and nineteenth centuries whalemen of many races and colours had put to sea in more or less perfect harmony from these towns to find fortune or death as comrades together. So first of all I went east to little Sag Harbor; to Long Island – or Paumanok, as the Indians called it: the fish-shaped island.

Before doing so I called at a favourite bookshop, the Burlington on Madison Avenue, and bought the Library of America edition of *Moby Dick*. I had read it years before, and I had forgotten that, as well as being a novel, it was in itself a goodish guidebook to whaling, whales and whalers.

Rereading it now, I found that Ishmael, the 'I' of Melville's masterpiece, had not visited Sag Harbor – but Queequeg, the tattooed harpooneer from the South Seas, certainly had. Having smuggled himself aboard a Sag Harbor whaler near his Pacific native island, Queequeg had first set foot on American soil at Sag Harbor itself, before making his way to New Bedford and his rendezvous with an astonished Ishmael in a bed at the Spouter Inn there.

It was a relief to leave the mugginess of New York in June. The minute you arrive in Sag Harbor, there is no mistaking the fresh feel and healthy smell of a fishing port. There is a special cleanness and clearness in the air; even from a fair distance you smell the salt of the sea and fancy you can smell fish, too. I was brought up partly in an English fishing port in the West Country on the other side of the Atlantic Ocean, and the spring-of-the-year feeling in such places is unmistakable and unvarying. It is with Sag Harbor as it is with Cornwall.

The map shows Sag Harbor elusively tucked away near the eastern end of Long Island, where the land divides into two forks and starts to resemble the claw of a lobster. Hidden behind a point of land called Cedar Point and an offshore island called, appropriately, Shelter Island, it is a small port not completely protected from the hurricanes that periodically rush in from the Atlantic and hammer it. With its wide bay and protective island you can see why Sag Harbor, settled in 1730, was well situated to become in the next hundred years or so America's fourth biggest whaling port – after New Bedford, Nantucket and New London.

Atlantic whales were hunted for decades, but the boom period of whaling was relatively short. In those early days whales of all sorts were slaughtered in virtually all the seas of the world, but the years from 1828 to 1848 were the flush times. In 1839, for example, Sag Harbor could put thirty-one vessels to sea; all of them jointly owned by several local families. Consequently at that time just about the entire community shared, directly or indirectly, in the amazingly lucrative business of blubber hunting. For just about every lamp of the Western world was fuelled by whale oil from Sag Harbor and the New England whale ports; the West's candles were made of sperm oil from Sag Harbor, and Western corsets were stiffened with Sag Harbor whalebone. There were few paupers and little unemployment in Sag Harbor, thanks to the whales and handsome old houses of rich whalemen are still to be seen there.

This prosperity had to end. In 1859 when petroleum was discovered, the whaling merchants didn't pay much attention. They should have done so, because that discovery signalled the beginning of the end of the whaling boom. After it Sag Harbor's extraordinary prosperity began to wilt and a succession of disastrous fires – the ever potential hazard of wooden-built towns – did nothing to revive it.

The exploitation of whales goes back a long way and started small. The Long Island Indians introduced the early white settlers to whaling and riches. The Indians of Paumanok, the fish-shaped island, are gone now, but driving to the far end of the Island from New York you become aware of their former presence.

A little bus comes bouncing out from central Manhattan, bumping and weaving through the potholed, littered streets of Queens, through the shadowy avenues of rusty girders that hold up the overhead railroad, then on through the creeping ugliness of an ever expanding city, until finally the rural island greenness crawls out to embrace the highways.

Now at last the character of the place names changes. You leave Hicksville and Levittown and are happy to find yourself in the vicinity of Patchoque, Yaphank and Quoque: all Indian names. Sag Harbor itself took its name from the Indian word for a groundnut. Beyond Sag Harbor the road speeds on across flat sandy ridges, through pines and the fresh salt air to Amagansett and Montauk. After that all you can do is dive into the Atlantic Ocean.

The Indians were the first ones to start cutting up the bodies of whales washed up on the Atlantic beaches by chance. Later the settlers, cottoning on to the potential profits, began dividing the better part of each whale between them, while continuing to give the fins and tails to the Indians.

A bit later, when settlers and Indians took to the sea together after whales, the Indians came into their own. They made first-class harpooneers. Tashtego, the Gay Head harpooneer in *Moby Dick*, was an Indian from Martha's Vineyard not far from Nantucket. And the whales they aimed to 'dart their irons' into (harpoons were never 'thrown' or 'tossed', any more than 'harpooneers' were called 'harpooners') were North Atlantic Right Whales. The blubber of the Right Whales, when rendered down by boiling in large iron kettles called 'try-pots', produced a great quantity of oil as well as whalebone – otherwise called 'baleen' – which in those stiff-backed days of stays, umbrella frames, corsets and crinoline hoops, was in much demand. Most of the stranded whales in the early days were washed up on the southern shores of Long Island facing the Atlantic. There, in the area round East Hampton and Southampton, nature nowadays is kept very much in its place by rich people who really live and work in New York. Sag Harbor, on the other hand, where the whaling masters landed whales caught at sea, still manages to retain the unpretentious look of a small but genuine fishing port, even if there is relatively little fishing there.

I say 'small' because, emerging at Main Street from a few short minor streets lined by fine trees, lawns and wooden buildings made of clapboard and cedar shingles, almost before you know it you are facing the wharf and the boats and feeling the fresh cool wind from the bay. Small, the place certainly is.

That first morning the bus from Manhattan stopped just short of the wharf to drop me at the American Hotel, a warm red brick building standing on the site of a much older one. The hotel's terrace bordered Main Street, and next door was the fire station and opposite a bookstore and a movie house showing *Howards End*. A friendly lady receptionist was seated at a desk situated between a large and lugubrious moose's head that thrust out of one rose-papered wall and a print of General Washington's triumphal entry into New York in 1788 on another. She assigned me to a room in the hotel's annexe. The hotel had few rooms, she said apologetically; they tended to get booked up during summer weekends.

That was all right with me. I carried my bag to the annexe, an old and rather pretty house with a fanlight and framed doorways that looked as if it had been there since before the Revolution. The wooden staircase creaked like an octogenarian with an artificial leg, and my bed looked old enough for General and Mrs Washington to have slept in it after their entry into New York; its high wooden bedhead rose against the wall like a wave. An attractive desk that was probably early American but had echoes of Napoleon III about it, stood in a corner, and there was a television set on a white rattan table. Two marble-topped bedside tables, with reading lamps, reminded me that I was going to need something lighter than *Moby Dick* to read during the next week or two. I dumped my bags and went out to do something about it.

The bookstore on Main Street had a good selection. It had one guide to Sag Harbor that was clearly essential: *East Hampton, A History and Guide*, written with a great deal of loving care, and partly compiled, as it happened, by an old friend and enthusiastic part-time Sag Harbor resident, Jason Epstein, a vice-president of a New York publishing company. With it I bought a paperback reissue of jottings from Harold Ross's *The New Yorker* covering the years 1927 to 1976 and written by one of its finest writers, the late E. B. White. About to travel round America myself, I added to these a book of travels round the United States by John Steinbeck in the early Sixties. It was a book I had read when I first arrived in America, and I remembered it with affection thirty years later. Called *Travels with Charley* – Charley was Steinbeck's ageing French poodle – the book had an extraordinary unforced charm, and seeing it again now was like unexpectedly running into a friend one had half forgotten or thought had died.

Happily clutching these precious books, I strolled on down Main Street to the wharf. It was still quite early and a mist hung over the calm blue water of the bay so that I seemed to see everything through breathed-on glass. Motor launches pottered about the entrance to the little marina, and a two-masted beauty with a sleek black hull was silhouetted against the green finger of Cedar Point. In the whaling days, from a lighthouse on that point, an American flag was raised to welcome returning ships. The lookoutmen of Sag Harbor, watching for locally registered square-riggers rounding it, heavy with barrels of the whale oil that were the rich reward of perhaps three years' desperate labour in the Pacific, lost no time in announcing their arrival to the families of the crewmen. In some cases, those families would have trouble recognising them after such a long separation.

In the calm of a late twentieth-century summer morning, it took an effort on my part to imagine those agitated days.

Sightseers from New York, unattractive in T-shirts and cotton shorts, strolled slackly about hand in hand inspecting the yachts grouped near the Dockmaster's office. The office was conveniently situated over the Village of Sag Harbor Comfort Station, 'constructed' – a plaque said – 'in 1987 by Mayor George E. Butts, Jnr.'. Two swans calmly preened themselves near wharves on which in the old whaling days people had welcomed the return of the long-absent ships; where the taverns and whorehouses had awaited the thirsty rush of lascivious sailors ashore; and where the whalemen, free at last, riotously relaxing after tedious months at sea – Fijians, Kanakas from the New Hebrides, Sandwich Islanders, Portuguese, Malays, Chinese and Montauk Indians from the far eastern end of Long Island – brawled, drank and otherwise let off wild steam after the hardships of their seemingly endless voyages. Hardships – and considerable danger, too, for literally hundreds of Sag Harbor men and boys were lost at sea.

For the money: what else but the thought of money made it worth risking their lives? After all, between 1820 and 1850 about $15 million in sperm oil, whale oil and whalebone flowed into Sag Harbor pockets. Someone has said the little port was the 'Kuwait of its time' – at least, that is, until 1870 by which time new-fangled kerosene had wholly replaced the whale oil in the lamps of the Western world.

By noon it was hot in the sun and near the American Hotel I went into a restaurant called Spinnakers which had a pleasant bar. I asked for a beer and the Irish barman said he had an unusual draught beer called Fuller's which he personally recommended.

'It's an English or maybe a Welsh beer,' he said.

'That'll do fine.'

'It's better than American beer.'

'American beer is a little watery for me.'

'Well, you know what they say,' he said, grinning. 'American beer is like making love in a canoe. It's not bad. But it's too darn close to water.'

His grin induced me to have another one.

By the time I had finished the beer it was still early, so I wandered further down the street to a smaller place near the waterfront. There I perched on a counter stool and opened *Travels with Charley*.

Quite soon I found something I had missed on first reading, or had simply forgotten in the intervening thirty years. This was that Steinbeck had set out on his voyage in search of America in a specially made camper, which he called Rocinante after Don Quixote's horse, from his waterside house in – of all places – Sag Harbor. In fact, in a very early chapter he describes in vivid detail a hurricane named Donna which came tromping her way out of the Caribbean and struck the little harbour which I could see fair and square from where I sat, nearly sinking his 22-foot cabin boat in the middle of the bay. 'Our little bay', he wrote, 'is fairly well protected, but not that well.'

I ordered a bowl of chili and when he brought it the barman leaned across the counter to see what I was reading.

'*Travels with Charley*, eh?' he said with interest.

'Steinbeck lived somewhere here, did you know? Say thirty years ago. About the time he won the Nobel Prize.'

'Yeah, I remember,' he said, 'I was given that book to read when I was at school.'

'Lucky to be given a book like this at school.'

'Yeah, lucky, huh?' he smiled, and added, 'Steinbeck wrote another one – about Sag Harbor, I think. I never read it though. Called *The Winter of Discontent*, something like that.'

This was news to me. After paying for lunch I went straight back to the Main Street bookstore, bought the second Steinbeck – a novel called, as a matter of fact, *The Winter of Our Discontent* – and then, like a squirrel with a particularly fat nut, scurried off with it to the terrace of the hotel. Skimming through it, almost at once I found this passage:

> Our town of Baytown [as Steinbeck called Sag Harbour] is a handsome town, an old town, one of the first clear and defined whole towns in America. Its first settlers . . . were sons of those restless, treacherous, quarrelsome, avaricious seafaring men who were a headache to Europe under Elizabeth, took the West Indies for their own under Cromwell, and finally came to roost on the northern coast, holding charters from the returned Stuarts. They successfully combined piracy and puritanism, which aren't so unalike when you come right down to it. Both had a strong dislike for opposition and both had a roving eye for other people's property.

A page or two further on I saw his description of Sag Harbor's glorious and distinctive architecture.

> Some of those old captain-owners had good taste too. With all their money, they brought in English architects to build their houses. That's why you see so much Adam influence and Greek revival architecture . . . . It was that period in England. But with all the fanlights and fluted columns and Greek keys, they never neglected to put a widow's walk on the roof. The idea was that the faithful home-bound wives could go up there to watch for returning ships, and maybe some of them did.

Some other houses, he said, were what is called Early Federal American; peak roofs and clapboard siding. And the giant elms, he added, are as old as the houses; those, that is, that periodic gales have left upright.

You walk for about ten minutes between just such old houses and old trees to get to Sag Harbor's Oakland Cemetery. There's no ignoring the little town's whaling past there. Oakland is not as old as the town's Old Burial Ground, next to the 'Whaling Church', which goes back to at least 1767, but it is much larger and still used.

And it contains the Broken Mast monument.

Stepping through its gates I found myself surrounded by graves of former ships' captains, most of them whalingmen and some of them victims of fatal accidents in remote seas. Oakland is a well ordered place; its wide paths are carefully weeded and brushed and the graves are arranged in rectangular plots like detached houses in neat suburban blocks. When I arrived on a sunny afternoon, gardeners were there, working in various parts of the cemetery; and its high trees, fat now with the leaves of summer, were full of the cawing and whistles of birds.

A large, jolly-looking grey-haired woman was on her knees planting pink hydrangea bushes in four plots round a tombstone. The tombstone looked newer than the others, and its inscription said: 'George Balanchine (1904–1983). Ballet Master.'

'He had four wives, I believe,' said the woman smiling. 'They are not here, though.'

When I asked her the whereabouts of the Broken Mast monument, she pointed behind me with an earthy finger.

'Most of the earliest graves are down that way,' she said. 'You can't miss it.'

Indeed there was no mistaking it. The mast stood on a plinth that stood about seven-foot high. The marble replica of a broken mast towered about another eight-foot above that. The mast was in marble and had a marble coil of rope round its base.

An inscription on the plinth said that the memorial had been erected in 1856 by the brothers of John E. Howell, who died 23 July 1840, 'while engaged in the Whale Fishery in the Pacific Ocean, in command of the ship *France*. He lost his life in an encounter with a Sperm Whale in the 28th year of his age'.

The most interesting aspect of the mast was, of course, the way it had been fashioned to represent a *broken* mast. The top of the marble column looks exactly as if it had been snapped off in a gale: jagged slivers of mast stuck up into the air like the sharp uneven ends of a snapped matchstick. It would not be difficult to see in it a giant replica of Captain Ahab's ivory leg – the second one, broken off in his penultimate encounter with Moby Dick, the whale as 'big and white as a snowhill' Ahab had vowed to hunt and kill, a huge creature which, the moment before he succeeded, destroyed his ship the *Pequod*, and, except for Ishmael, all of her crew. Broken mast or snapped ivory leg, no symbol could be more chillingly appropriate in a former whaling town's cemetery.

And there is more than that to the memorial. Under a harpoon and an oar, a bas-relief depicts a whaling tragedy – perhaps the death of John E. Howell himself. A limp body is being hauled by crewmen on to a capsized boat while a whale spouts triumphantly and the whaling ship – perhaps it's the *France* – hovers apprehensively in the background. The names of three other captains who died in the Atlantic or Pacific Oceans 'in actual encounters with the monsters of the deep' are engraved there, too; and scattered through this part of the graveyard are numerous ships' masters similarly lost and mostly quite young – no more than twenty-nine or thirty, although one is a mere twenty-seven. A Captain David Hand, a famous privateer and hero of the American Revolution, lies near the Broken Mast, his five wives around him. His grave is marked with a small Stars and Stripes on a stick presumably as a tribute to his outstanding patriotism.

That night, after dinner in the American Hotel, I creaked up the stairs of the annexe and began to riffle through the pages of *Moby Dick*. I wanted to see what Melville had to say about Queequeg's arrival here.

> Queequeg was a native of Kokovoko, an island far away from the West and South. It is not down in any map; true places never are . . . .
> A Sag Harbor ship visited his father's bay, and Queequeg sought a passage to Christian lands . . . . The captain at first threatened to throw him overboard . . . but at last relented.

For Queequeg was persistent. This son of a South Pacific king was – he told Ishmael – 'actuated by a profound desire to learn among the Christians, the arts whereby to make his people still happier than they were; and more than that, still better than they were'.

> But, alas! the practices of whalemen soon convinced him that even Christians could be both miserable and wicked; infinitely more so than all his father's heathens. Arrived at last in old Sag Harbor; and seeing what the sailors did there; and then going on to Nantucket, and seeing how they spent their wages in *that* place also, poor Queequeg gave it up for lost. Thought he, it's a wicked world in all meridians; I'll die a pagan.

Poor Queequeg. I took to him, particularly after reading a few pages, on to the description of his confrontation with the first wheelbarrow he had ever seen. That had been in Sag Harbor, too. Not knowing how to manage the strange thing, he had lashed his heavy sea-chest to it, shouldered the whole caboodle, and marched with it up the wharf to his boarding house. Not surprisingly he caused quite a stir.

As far as I knew I was alone in the annexe. But soon I heard creakings on the stairs and began to listen for footsteps too. There was no sound of footsteps, or of doors opening or closing. Just the creaking – then silence. Strange, I thought. It was one of the oldest houses in an old town, though. Could it be the ghost of Queequeg heaving his barrow aloft? I hoped it was not someone on the prowl like the Tony Perkins character in the Hitchcock film *Psycho*. Or, worse still, his mother. I thought the best thing to do was to turn out the light and go to sleep.

Chapter 2

Now bend to your oars, boys,
And make the boat fly,
And mind just one thing now,
Keep clear of his eye.

OLD WHALING SONG

The entrance to the Sag Harbor Whaling Museum is unusual. You pass through the jawbones of a Right Whale – curving white ones that meet nine feet or so over your head. You could almost feel like Jonah as you slip under them.

Take comfort from the fact that a Right Whale has a throat so small that it could barely swallow a herring. One old whaleman of Sag Harbor scoffed to Melville, 'A penny roll would choke him.' Well, it's possible, Melville argues facetiously, that Jonah might not have been *swallowed* but merely lodged temporarily in some part of the whale's mouth – 'For truly, the Right Whale's *mouth* would accommodate a couple of whist-tables, and comfortably seat all the players. Possibly, too, Jonah might have ensconced himself in a hollow tooth.' But no: on second thoughts, he adds, the Right Whale is toothless.

Sperm Whales – even white ones like Moby Dick – are the largest whales possessing a lower jawbone full of big and very sharp teeth. Unlike Right Whales they would have no difficulty whatsoever in swallowing a man or, for that matter, crunching up a whole whaling boat like a shrimp. In fact, Sperm Whales depend on their teeth for nourishment. They live partly on the giant squids that lurk on the ocean floor, chewing them up into chunks like soft rubber before swallowing them.

For whalemen the most frightening thing about Sperm Whales was that they often turned – with what seemed like deliberate malice – on a boatful of the men tormenting them with harpoons and, rolling on their backs to give their great underjaw maximum play, snapped it greedily up. At other times infuriated whales would simply ignore the whaling boats around them and in a frenzy head straight for the whale ship itself, ram it with full force of their enormous heads,

14

shivering its timbers and sending it straight to the bottom – which is what Moby Dick did to Ahab's *Pequod*. Sperm Whales seemed disconcertingly able to *think*.

A chart in the museum showed the largest whale in the world to be a Blue Whale: it said it could grow to 102 feet. Sperm Whales can be a mere 70 feet or so, but they dive further and are far more aggressive. (On the other hand, Melville reported seeing specimens of 90 feet and more. One wonders: Have the larger whales been greedily wiped out over the years?)

All whales must dive, the chart pointed out, to find food: plankton not far below the surface, in the case of Baleen Whales; giant squids in the case of Sperm Whales, which sometimes dive two miles down to find them – the only living things there as big as themselves.

Wandering round the splendid Greek Revival museum, it was hard to rid one's mind of horrific images of battles to the death between these two monstrous sea creatures – Sperm Whales and squids; nightmare struggles in the dark depths of the ocean; the swirl of black waters; the savagely chomping lower jaw of the whale, the severed, but still wriggling, tentacles of the huge squids . . . .

With relief I turn to a manifesto signed in 1803 by Thomas Jefferson, 'requiring whoever it might concern' to allow the ship *Nancy*, John Godlie master, 'to pass without any hindrance, seizure or molestation'. There were other such manifestoes, one signed with the shaky scrawl of George Washington, another with the bold thick-nibbed pen strokes of John Adams.

A 30-foot whaling boat lay in a shed in the garden; it looked wider and shallower than I had imagined, and the oars were unusually long with unusually narrow blades. It must have taken uncommon strength to pull them once the chase for a whale was on.

A chase began without any warning at the very moment that a 'pod' of whales spouting in mid-ocean was sighted.

From the lookout in the crosstrees came the awaited cry. 'There she blows! There! There! There she blows! There – there – *thar* she blows – bowes – bo-o-o-s!'

'Where away?'

'Three points off the lee bow, sir.'

'How far off?'

'Two miles and a half.'

'Thunder and lightning!' the captain shouts. 'Call all hands! Lower away!'

Three boats are launched in a wild commotion; the crews dropping into their places among the tangled gear; the boats rocking and pitching, as the mates grasping the steering oars in their sterns begin shouting encouragement to get under way, double-quick.

Stubb, the happy-go-lucky, good-humoured, second mate of the *Pequod*, a Cape Cod man, has his own mock-bullying style.

'Pull, pull, my fine hearts-alive . . . . Why don't you break your backbones, my boys? The devil fetch you, you ragamuffin rapscallions; you are all asleep. Stop snoring, ye sleepers and pull! Pull, will ye?' he shouts through the smoke of his pipe.

With their long skinny oars thrashing, the boats spread out, heading for the puffs of vapour made by the spouting whales, the excited oarsmen quite forgetful of their parched throats and bleeding hands, 'the waves curling and hissing around them like the erected crests of enraged serpents'.

All the while Stubb keeps urging the rowers on.

'Start her, now; give 'em the long and strong stroke, Tashtego. Start her, Tash, my boy – start her, all; but keep cool – cucumbers is the word – easy, easy – only start her like grim death and grinning devils, and raise the buried dead perpendicular out of their graves, boys – that's all. Start her!'

Several times Tashtego is almost within 'darting distance' but each time the whale tips up his tail – 'turns flukes' – and dives. When it came up again to breathe, the oarsmen, who were facing away from it towards the stern, could only hear the enormous creature spouting and wallowing nearby and the long-drawn whistle of his exhaust, catch a sidelong glimpse of something like a black, glistening hillside lapped by waves. They felt the humid vapour of his lungs drift like a mist over the boat and their necks; and smelt the rankness of it in their nostrils. Now and then, with a roar of displaced waters, the monster would rise clear of the sea, and for a moment became a terrifying silhouette arched against the sky.

This was the moment the harpooneer was waiting for.

'Stand up, Tash!' Stubb shouted, and Tashtego sprang up, harpoon in a huge hand. There was an 'enormous wallowing sound like fifty elephants stirring in their litter' and then Stubb's urgent whisper. 'There! There! Give it to him!'

Tashtego raised his wrestler's arm, and seemed to lean into something with all the force of his bowed body. Something shot hot and hissing along every one of their wrists: the harpoon line. It leaped out of the boat with a short, rushing sound; and Tashtego's darted iron buried itself deep in the whale's side. 'Fast, by God!'

With a frantic lunge that almost took Tashtego over the bows and into the water, the boat shot off with the speed of light over the waves; drawn behind the fleeing whale it was anchored to the harpoon. (The purpose of a harpoon, by the way, was not to kill a whale, but to attach the boat to it. The whale would then be lanced to death.)

The pursuit could be very long or comparatively short, but in the end, as the whale tired, it became slower and slower. 'Stand by to haul in line!' called Stubb; and inch by painful inch the crew hauled it in, closing with the whale. Stubb changed places with Tashtego, from the bows quickly driving in his own six feet of steel and churning it around in the whale's side. Four times more he lanced it; and at last the blood flowed and the great body weakened. Soon the great black mass lay awash – a huge, dark, helpless object, fin up, lapped by the sea, a prey now for any shark. Passing a line through a hole cut in his blowhole, the boat's crews slowly and with great effort rowed the hulk to the ship – for the cutting, and for the oil rendering ritual of the try-pots.

After three years or more of this, who would begrudge a whaleman all the riches whale oil could bring him – and a good deal of respect, too?

Just before leaving Sag Harbor with Charley, John Steinbeck wrote that he had been approached by a well-known and highly respected political reporter: a completely honest man. He had been grass-rooting with the then presidential candidates, and when Steinbeck saw him he was not happy, because, as he said, he loved his country, and he felt a sickness in it. To Steinbeck, he said bitterly:

> 'If anywhere in your travels you come on a man with guts, mark the place. I want to go to see him. I haven't seen anything but cowardice and expediency. This used to be a nation of giants. Where have they gone? You can't defend a nation with a board of directors. That takes men. Where are they?'
> 'Must be somewhere,' I said.

Surely some of these people did inhabit the earth once upon a time. In the persons, for one thing, of brave and unpretentious men with names like Stubb and Tashtego.

As I have said, I hadn't left New York simply to escape the general malaise over the nation's economy with the alleged inability of its politicians to pull it together. Yet, it had been in 1960 that Steinbeck's 'respected reporter' had told him to find a man with guts. So it sounded as though history was repeating itself. The *New York Times* had followed me to the American Hotel; and because it is difficult to ignore newspapers in an election year, I read it.

At lunch at Spinnakers, over Fuller's Ale and clam chowder, I learned about the efforts of Ross Perot, the feisty, if mystifying, billionaire from Texas, to win the votes of anyone fed up with America's orthodox politicians – run-of-the-mill politicians, he implied, like aspiring Democrat presidential candidate Bill Clinton and reigning Republican President George Bush. Perot seemed to be appealing to some voters, even if I had yet to meet anyone who knew what he truly represented. Perhaps he was simply a voice in the land, saying what a good many people wanted to hear.

When I turned from the newspaper to the E. B. White book I had just bought, I came upon a piece he had written in 1948 apropos Henry A. Wallace, then the Progressive Party's candidate for President; a piece that seemed uncannily applicable to Perot. White had received from a group calling itself the Businessmen for Wallace an invitation to attend a dinner.

> The invitation shows a picture of Mr Wallace in the act of delivering a speech, and there seems to be shining around him (and coming from above) a wonderful radiance. It is probably a Consolidated Edison radiance, but there is nothing in the photograph to indicate that . . . . Halfway down the shaft of light is a caption that says, 'And a voice was heard in the land'. The question that naturally arises, of course, is whether this land wants a voice. A distinguishing feature of America is that it has never had a voice; it has a lot of hoopdedoo but no voice, and that's the way we like it. Frankie Sinatra can handle the country's voice requirements, and the political candidates can handle the hoopdedoo, and we'll take ours without radiance, please.

As I write this, Mr Perot – who, incidentally, is no leftwinger like Henry Wallace – seems to have withdrawn from the contest and his supporters will have to get on as best they can without his voice in the land. They are unhappy. They and other Americans are now stuck with the hoopdedoo, whether they like it or not. And, what's more, without any radiance to speak of.

Sag Harbor's Whaler Church is by far the most extraordinary building in the place. Once more I walked between the old wooden houses and old trees up the slope to Union Street where it stands, wholly incongruously, looking like a temple in Old Egypt; perhaps in Karnak, although at its dedication, Jason Epstein's guidebook said, the officiating priest had compared it, for some reason, to the temple of Solomon. At any rate, it was built at the height of Sag Harbor's whaling boom in 1844, and it is officially known as the First Presbyterian Church.

It had a locked-up look when I approached its main tower; the high doors in it were firmly closed and showed no sign of having recently been opened. Round to the left I found another door, and even a man in shirt-sleeves and old trousers.

'I'm the sexton,' he said, warily, and when I asked if I could look round, he added, 'Follow me, then.'

The inside of the church is enormous. 'We can seat about a thousand in here,' said the sexton. It was high and wide and light, with an organ loft and galleries, Corinthian columns and mahogany pews. Rather fancifully, the guide said that 'on a bright day, with light filtering through the softly tinted windows, you can almost feel the room rocking on a gentle sea.' It was a fine day now, but I didn't feel in the least bit at sea, although the whole auditorium was the opposite of austere and I could see why the old whalers had been so proud of the unusual temple-church they had built themselves. Nor was I surprised when the sexton said,

'Julie Andrews came here the other day. She sang a couple of things from *My Fair Lady. The Sound of Music*, things like that. The place was packed out. Oh, yes. Packed.'

His name was Larry Gay, he said, his reserve giving way with this talk of Julie Andrews. He came, he went on, from Niagara Falls, 'Born there. I was into landscaping – for too long, I suppose. I began to go back to church.'

When I asked him if, as sexton, he had ever had to dig graves in the Old Burial Ground next-door, he said,

'Jeez, no. We don't use the Old Burial Ground, too many stones and rocks. We had to move some graves to Oakland. They have guys digging there. Well, not exactly digging, using machines now, of course.'

He tapped a Corinthian column, which made an unexpectedly dull sound. 'All solid wood,' he said proudly. His wife was a Methodist, 'But she comes here with me. It's all the same, really. We have a nice woman pastor here. Nice church, too, as you can see.'

I shook his hand and went outside. The church had once had a great steeple, built 135 feet high so that sailors could see it as they rounded Cedar Point or even Montauk. It was a strange addition to the strange Egyptian temple façade – part Christopher Wren, part soaring pagoda. But a hurricane carried it off in 1938, and it crashed down into the Old Burial Ground, among the weather-stained gravestones of Sag Harbor's oldest whalemen. Among them was one mildewed stone dating from 1801. It commemorated Sally, wife of one Job Halsey, and someone had inscribed on it the following happy lines:

19

> I bid adieu to all below
> I go where Angels dwell.
> Since 'tis God's wish it shall be so,
> I bid you all farewell.

The following morning I took a hired car to Orient Point, crossing by the Shelter Island Ferry to a second ferry to Greenport, and then, as John Steinbeck and Charley had done, drove to the ferry which crosses Long Island Sound to New London.

It was a beautiful day and the mainland of Connecticut, only an hour or so away, was bright and shimmering ahead. Passengers stretched out on the benches on the sundeck in T-shirts and the baggy, flowery cotton shorts that everyone seemed to be wearing this year: older ones stayed in the bar, watching a TV soap opera – *The Golden Girls*, I think. I ordered myself a hot dog and a Beck's beer and opened that day's *New York Times*. As if we hadn't had enough already, there were fresh revelations of someone's financial machinations involving the Bank of Credit and Commerce International. The filing of criminal charges against important Americans of the utmost probity – or so they had previously been presumed to be – would probably follow. There were other stories too about fraudulent goings-on in the business world.

Once more history seemed to be repeating itself. E. B. White, as usual, had a relevant comment – in a short piece he wrote as long ago as 1933:

> Most imperative of recent missives was a letter from *Forbes*, reminding us that we are not a bluebird. 'You are not a bluebird,' the letter said, gruffly, and then added, 'You are a business man .... Business is a hard, cold-blooded game today. Survival of the fittest. Dog eat Dog. Produce or get out. A hundred men are after your job ....'
>
> We are not, as they say, a bluebird .... As for business, we agree that it is a hard, cold-blooded game. Survival of the fittest. Dog eat Dog. The fact that about eighty-five per cent of the dogs have recently been eaten by the other dogs perhaps explains what long ago we noticed about business: that it had a strong smell of boloney. If dog continues to eat dog, there will be only one dog left, and he will be sick to his stomach.

When I read that I felt a mysterious surge of sympathetic joy. Mr White had, with those few words, made a sunny day seem sunnier; my humble fellow passengers in their flowery shorts, watching *The Golden Girls*, were all at once the most admirable people I had ever seen.

I sprang up and ordered another hot dog (no boloney here) and another Beck's. Then I threw the *New York Times* and the crooked financiers into a trashcan, and took E. B. White up to the sundeck to admire the view; hand in hand with him, so to speak.

Chapter 3

Mad with the agonies he endures from these fresh attacks, the infuriated Sperm Whale ... rushes at the boats with his head; they are propelled before him with vast swiftness, and sometimes utterly destroyed.

THOMAS BEALE: *History of the Sperm Whale*, 1839

The most immediately astonishing thing about New Bedford was not the blast of pop music that issued from the bar of Durrant's Sail Loft Inn where I was staying, but the fact that it was in Portuguese.

Sure enough, when I went into the bar to investigate, an ear-splitting cacophony of strange sounds came out to meet me. A huge record machine was going full-blast, on a large TV screen Spain was playing Portugal at soccer to the accompaniment of a raucous full-volumed commentary in Portuguese, and a good many short tough-looking men with hairy arms and black unshaven chins were yelling at each other, also in Portuguese, across glasses of beer and wine. Apart from beer and wine, they smelled vaguely of fish. Signs on the walls said things like 'Sinta Prazer Sinta Portugal', 'Beba Cerveja Super Bock', and '*Leitao todas as segundas e quintasfereiras*'. Had I suddenly been transported to Lisbon?

Actually I had already been warned. At the piers that stretched along the Acushnet River at the back of the Sail Loft Inn, I had seen fishing smacks with names like *Maria Angela*, *Jaime M*, and *Kimbawa*, and it didn't take much power of deduction to conclude that the men shouting at each other in the bar were their crewmen. Several of them glanced at me curiously when I pushed my way in and ordered myself (in English) a Super Bock, just as fishermen in, say, Oporto might have idly eyed a foreign tourist there.

At the entrance of Durrant's Sail Loft Inn a sign said, 'Where the City meets the Sea'; and it stood right up against the Acushnet at 'One Merrill's Wharf' at 'Lat. 41° 38′ Long. 70° 55″', a position the sign pointed out. The young manager in the front office confirmed that the men in the bar were indeed fishermen. They lived here, he said; New Bedford had a sizeable Portuguese population; a good many from the Azores, the others from Cape Verde, off the west coast of Africa.

It had always been so – well, at least since the whaling boom of the early 1800s. Nantucket and New Bedford whalers crossed the Atlantic and augmented their crews with men from the Azores and hunted whales off Cape Verde. The original Sail Loft was built at that time, in 1847, by a whaling master, Captain Edward Merrill, and later became a place where sails were made in the days when New Bedford whalers alone owned 329 sailing ships.

Not all the ships in the huddle of masts along Cold Pocket Pier and Steamship Pier near the Inn had Portuguese names. I saw a boat called *Playtime* and another called *Sea Lion* next to *Beira Litoral* and a big trawler called *Portugal*. Fish-heads with bulging eyes lay about the piers' wooden planks and the air reeked of fish round the *Maria Angela* as her crew offloaded their catch into a warehouse. A number of black crewmen – probably originally from the Azores – were busy with baskets and lobster traps, and when they shouted to each other over the sound of the winches, they shouted in Portuguese. But whatever the names of the boats, English or Portuguese, they were all registered in New Bedford, Massachusetts. According to the Sail Loft's manager, their crews were a good lot. They were very hard-working men. It paid them to be, he said: they could earn $60,000 'in a good year'. The only thing he worried about was that local waters were being *over*-fished.

'That's a serious problem. You should watch that.'

'Damn right,' he said.

All along, from the moment I left New York, I had intended to telephone from New Bedford to Virginia, where two families of Vietnamese refugee 'boat people' that I had taken under my wing were patiently waiting for their American citizenship. I had wanted to invite one or two of the younger ones to join me here for a day or two in the sun of the New England summer. I called them now – and found, to my disappointment, that none of them could afford to take even half a day away from school or job. The four adults had two jobs apiece – day and night. They were sorry but they couldn't risk those jobs by taking time off.

As for the six younger ones, aged from nine to twenty-five, they studied in the daytime, then, having finished their homework, went off to night jobs; when they slept, heaven knows.

'Not this year, Dad,' said Cun, the eldest, aged twenty-five. 'Next year, perhaps, after I graduate.'

Cun's brother, aged twenty-two, was off to a US Marine Corps camp in a week's time. The Marines helped to pay for his tuition. His younger brother Hao was about to follow him to Boot Camp.

'Sorry,' said Bao, aged seventeen. 'I have exams next week.'

Lastly, Ly, aged twenty-four, was firmest of all. 'Perhaps I will have time off in seven or eight years' time, Dad. Not before.' That is when he will qualify as a doctor.

The youngest, aged nine, had to go to school and apart from that is not allowed to go anywhere alone.

So that was that.

It was a pity. These Vietnamese additions to the American 'melting pot' might have got on well with the Portuguese; after all, they shared a dream whether they knew it or not. And they would have seen a part of America that they had never seen since they arrived, as some of America's newest immigrants. What they had seen of their new land so far, they had seen almost exclusively on television. They had been appalled by the pictures of burning of the stores of other Asians – Koreans mostly – in Los Angeles. Since then, the country had been flooded with talk about the importance of the Family – as the *sine qua non* of law, order, thrift, hard work, and above all resistance to the drug peddlers who ravaged the land, luring urban youngsters from schools and workplaces into addiction to 'crack' and thereafter to crime. Politicians, stumping the states in this election year, harped on the need to restore family life, 'the old values'. One couldn't deny there seemed to be something urgent in what they said.

Here in New Bedford, black and white Portuguese-speaking family men from the other side of the Atlantic chose to work hard for a good living without recourse to drugs or brawling. Working is what they were happy doing: it was their version – and a time-honoured one – of the American dream.

It was the same with 'my' Vietnamese. I had befriended them long ago in Hué and Saigon during the war. After the communist victory, when the males had spent eight years shut away in 're-education' camps, the two families had arrived in America, having experienced unimaginably hair-raising escapades and with barely two cents to rub together. There they waited patiently for their children to join them, and one by one over several years those children escaped, risking their teenage lives in one leaky boat after another, braving the danger of storms and pirates – to find sometimes precarious refuge in Filipino, Malaysian or Thai refugee camps. At last – phew! – they were in Virginia, studying by day and relentlessly working by night to pay their way.

What lives they have had! What a hell of a past! So that now their sights are fixed unswervingly ahead. The future: that's where *their* dream lies.

Because of all that, I was deeply disappointed that they couldn't join me in New Bedford.

'I stuffed a shirt or two into my old carpet-bag, tucked it under my arm, and started for Cape Horn and the Pacific. Quitting the good city of Manhatto, I duly arrived in New Bedford.' So Melville wrote in *Moby Dick*.

Melville himself sailed from New Bedford in 1841 in the whaling ship *Acushnet* of Fairhaven – 358 tons, three masts, two decks; Master, Valentine Pease. Fifteen months later the *Acushnet* arrived at Nuka Hiva in the Marquesas and there Melville deserted her to begin the adventure he later described in *Typee*.

On the other hand, Ishmael in *Moby Dick* arrived in New Bedford and at once began searching for a suitable place to stay until he could take a packet boat to Nantucket. It must have been very near Merrill's Wharf that he eventually came across the creaking sign swinging over the door with a painting of a tall, straight jet of spray, and the words – 'The Spouter Inn: – Peter Coffin' on it. The entrance to the inn, he thought, was like the bulwarks of some condemned old craft, and inside was a wallful of rusty old whaling lances and harpoons – one of which Coffin, the innkeeper, said dramatically had had a bloody history: it had been used many years ago to kill fifteen whales between sunrise and sunset.

Coffin regretted that there was not a single bed unoccupied since that very day a number of whaling ships had arrived in port.

'But avast,' he added, 'you hain't no objections to sharing a harpooneer's blanket, have ye?'

The harpooneer, the innkeeper said in an offhand way, was a 'dark complexioned chap . . . [who] eats nothing but steaks and likes 'em rare'. He did not mention the harpooneer's odd habit of taking his harpoon to bed with him; nor that his name was Queequeg and that he was a wild pagan from some far-off part of the South Seas. Ishmael was left to find out for himself that this 'dark complexioned chap' – with a head like George Washington's – was a hulking, grotesque fellow with a bald, purplish skull and a small scalp-knot on his forehead. More than that, he was covered from foot to topknot with the most strange tattoos – a patchwork of 'odd little parti-colored squares and triangles' so that he looked as if he had been dreadfully cut about in a fight. He seemed to Ishmael to have been in a Thirty Years' War, and to have barely escaped from it. This apparition compounded Ishmael's astonishment by producing an embalmed head from a bag and a pipe in the shape of a tomahawk which he proceeded to smoke in bed.

There were more surprises to come. Queequeg's idea of a morning shave was to prop a bit of mirror against the wall, lather his face with a piece of hard soap and then, with his harpoon, begin a vigorous scraping (or rather, as Melville said, harpooning) of his cheeks. Then he wrapped himself up in a great monkey jacket and strode out carrying his harpoon before him like a marshal's baton. Later, at table, he used the harpoon to grapple the beefsteaks – done rare – towards him.

New Bedford's streets in those days were as full of strange creatures like Queequeg and 'wild specimens of the whaling craft', reeling drunkenly about the place, as they were now of sober Portuguese and Cape Verdeans. On top of them, every week scores of Vermonters and New Hampshire men arrived, 'all athirst for gain and glory in the fishery'. They were mostly young and stalwart of frame, Melville said. 'Fellows who have felled forests, and now seek to drop the axe and snatch the whale-lance. Many are as green as the Green Mountains whence they came.'

New Bedford had benefited, like Sag Harbor, from whaling. It was full of patrician houses, and parks and gardens which, Melville said fancifully, had been harpooned and dragged up from the Atlantic, Pacific, and Indian Oceans.

It is impossible even now to ignore New Bedford's whaling past. Much of the old riverside district has been preserved. As in Sag Harbor, the walls of its inns and restaurants are covered with vivid reminders; paintings and prints of whales and ships and tossing seas. The whaling museum has several magnificent ones: most impressive of which are one or two of Sperm Whales deliberately attacking whale boats, throwing their crews bodily into the waves – 'kill scenes' by an artist called Garnarey, who Herman Melville himself said painted 'the finest presentation of whales and whaling' he had seen. The waves 'curl and hiss' in the paintings around the whale and the terrified men 'like the erected crests of enraged serpents', just as he had described.

And the Portuguese connection, as well as whaling, keeps cropping up. Near the Sail Loft Inn, where the seagulls screamed and fought for scraps, is moored a fine two-master, the *Ernestina*, once the *Effie M. Morissey*. She is still capable, I was told by her watchman, of going to sea although launched as long ago as 1894. From her masthead she flies the Stars and Stripes and the yellow, red and green flag of Cape Verde with its black star. That is because the people of Cape Verde gave her to the United States as a gift some years ago, since for twenty-eight years of her active life the *Ernestina* had hauled cargo and Cape Verdean immigrants from Africa to New Bedford.

As for the Cape Verde whaling connection, a chart in the whaling museum informed all and sundry that Cape Verde was one of the American whalers' principal haunts – with Tonga, the Solomon Islands, the Falklands, Galapagos, Brazil, Western Australia and Hawaii. (A corresponding chart showed Right Whales were often to be found in east New Zealand, the Sea of Japan, and north to Kamchatka, and the Okhotsk Sea.)

A memorial inscription on the wall of the Seamen's Bethel – the old whaleman's chapel that still stands on Johnny Cake Hill in New Bedford – says:

> To the memory of Nathaniel E. Cole, 24, Boat steerer of Fall river, Mass, Edward Laffrey, 27, of Burlington, Vermont, and Frank Kanacka, 19, all lost by the upsetting of their boat July 15th 1854 in the Okhotsk Sea.

'Few are the moody fishermen, shortly bound for the Indian Ocean or Pacific,' wrote Melville in *Moby Dick*, 'who fail to make a Sunday visit to the spot. I am sure I did not.

Inside the door of the chapel is a portrait of the chaplain who preached the day Melville attended a service in December 1840. It shows Father Enoch Mudge to have been quite a handsome man, burly and jowly. Melville, who gave him a fictional name, Chaplain Mapple, in his novel, said he had a certain 'venerable robustness' and went on to describe the curious interior of the chapel itself. The outstanding feature was its pulpit, built like the prow of a ship thrusting out towards the congregation, with its lectern resting on the bowsprit. The pulpit is still like that, though in 1866 a fire damaged the building somewhat. But the chapel is simple, well proportioned and – well, shipshape. In Melville's time the pulpit was constructed without stairs, and instead a rope ladder hung down its side like those which sailors used to mount a ship from a boat at sea.

A great favourite of the whalemen, Father Mapple, like Father Mudge, had been a sailor – and even a harpooneer – in his distant youth. Now in healthy old age he clambered grimly into the pulpit by the rope ladder 'as if ascending the maintop of his vessel', and once aloft, turned round and hauled the rope ladder up after him. Then, slowly opening the leaves of the Bible, isolated 'in his self-containing stronghold', he began his sermon. The strange pulpit seemed quite fitting. For, Melville says, after all 'the world's a ship on its passage out, and not a voyage complete; and the pulpit is its prow'.

The church's walls are lined with memorial plaques. Some of the epitaphs were light-hearted:

> The sea curls o'er him and the foaming billow,
> As his head now rests upon a watery pillow.

And others were less so, in particular the one under a memorial to Captain William Swain, Master of the *Christopher Mitchell* of Nantucket, who 'after fastening to a whale, was carried overboard by the line, and drowned in the 45th year of his age'. As a matter of fact, Swain was an old man compared to most whaling victims, and his epitaph,

> Be ye also ready; for, in such an hour as ye think not, the Son of Man cometh

has about it a forbidding note.

The voice of Father Mudge/Mapple had reverberated round the plaques in his day — thirty-one in all — as he pinpointed his sermon's text: 'Beloved shipmates, clinch the last verse of the first chapter of Jonah — "And God prepared a great fish to swallow up Jonah." '

His deep rolling voice rose above the noise of a violent storm outside, and the sermon, in language wonderfully attuned to a congregation of sailors inclined to shuffle their heavy sea-boots impatiently among the pews, kept every eye on the preacher.

> Shipmates, this book . . . is one of the smallest strands in the mighty cable of the Scriptures. Yet what depths of the soul does Jonah's deep sea-line sound! . . . . We feel the floods surging over us; we sound with him to the kelpy bottom of the waters; seaweed and all the slime of the sea is about us! . . . it is a two-stranded lesson; a lesson to us all as sinful men, and a lesson to me as a pilot of the living God.

Father Mapple was a wise old sea-parson and his sermon sensibly kept to familiar features of a seaman's life; so that, according to Mapple, when Jonah goes aboard a ship seeking passage to escape God's wrath —

' "Who's there?" cries the Captain at his busy desk, hurriedly making out his papers for the Customs — "Who's there?" '

The whalemen listening intently in their pews would have pricked up their ears at the reference to Customs papers: every ship's officer has had trouble with *them*. Despite the fearful images of storms at sea and the insides of a whale, the lesson of Jonah, Father Mapple concluded, is relatively consoling: 'Sin not; but if you do, take heed to repent of it like Jonah.' It is a lesson offering hope even to a sinner, after all. And hope, I imagine, is what whaling men would have needed a great deal of.

There was a good deal of religion about in the whaling boom period; and no doubt there was a good deal of devilry, too. Many of the whaling captains were deep-dyed Quakers from Nantucket – the island had been settled by that sect – pious but sometimes hard-hearted men, Melville thought. But it cannot have been easy to divert from temptation men of several races who for months – maybe years – had eaten the same food, looked at the same faces, at the same sea, heard the same jokes, endured the same routine day after day, seemingly endlessly; particularly in port at last with money in their pockets and a snug bar open ahead of them ready to serve them with all the gin-and-molasses – a favourite drink – they could possibly desire.

Typical of the hard breed of God-fearing ex-whalers were the two part-owners of Captain Ahab's ship the *Pequod*, old Captains Peleg and Bildad, both grizzled, brown and brawny Quakers, 'insulated Nantucketers' (you might say), distrustful of all aliens unless they hailed from Cape Cod or Martha's Vineyard. One can learn something of the sea-going New England character from the mixture of piety, parsimony and pragmatism in the gruff farewell words of advice old Bildad vouchsafed the *Pequod*'s crew. 'Don't stave the boats needlessly, ye harpooneers .... Don't whale too much a' Lord's days, men; but don't miss a fair chance either, that's rejecting Heaven's good gifts.' Did he fix his eye pointedly on poor Flask, the third mate and a Martha's Vineyard man, to admonish him 'If ye touch at the islands, Mr Flask, beware of fornication'? Then a final dismissive wave of the hand. 'Good-bye. Good-bye! ...'

Before leaving for Nantucket, I strolled once more by the Acushnet River. More fishing boats were unloading their catches, and a large trawler was put-putting up from the river's mouth. Crewmen, both white-skinned and black, in T-shirts and jeans, one or two wearing tiny crucifixes on chains round their necks, stood chatting in Portuguese among the fish-heads on the reeking piers.

What a pity my Vietnamese family had not been able to witness all this sun and activity. They had been, I knew, profoundly disturbed and disappointed by the violent, shameful scenes from the West Coast on television. Here they would have been comforted. They, like the Portuguese fishermen going calmly and determinedly about their business, only wanted to follow in the successful tradition of earlier immigrants – the Jews, for example, and the Italians. They had already learned from hard experience that nothing came to anyone without risk and hard work – and that self-discipline was the other side to the American Dream.

Here in New Bedford was a hard-working world that had sprung directly from that of Ishmael, Queequeg, Stubb, Starbuck — and Melville himself. Central Los Angeles, as New Yorkers would say, it wasn't.

Chapter 4

'My God! Mr Chase, what is the matter?'
'We have been stove by a whale.'

Narrative of the shipwreck of the whale ship
Essex of Nantucket, destroyed by a Sperm Whale
in the Pacific Ocean: by Owen Chase, first mate.
New York, 1821

> Nantucket! Take out your map and look at it. See what a real corner of
> the world it occupies; how it stands there, away offshore, more lonely
> than the Eddystone lighthouse. Look at it – a mere hillock, and elbow
> of sand; all beach, without a background. There is more sand there
> than you would use in twenty years as a substitute for blotting paper.

That is how Herman Melville described this little hummocky island
30 miles out in the Atlantic.

Ishmael and Queequeg took a packet boat to it from New
Bedford. I flew in a small plane, across the blue water that covers
innumerable shifting sand shoals, above little Cuttyhunk Island, the
Sow and Pigs Reef, and over Gay Head on Martha's Vineyard, once
the home of Tashtego the *Pequod*'s harpooneer. It is deceptively
placid water that covers not merely sand shoals but things much
more deadly. Shortly after my visit the Cunard giant, the *Queen
Elizabeth 2*, steaming back to New York from a Canadian cruise,
a local pilot in her wheelhouse, had a 74-foot gash torn in her hull
by an apparently uncharted rock lurking below the surface a short
distance southwest of the Sow and Pigs Reef. On future charts I
shall look for a rock marked 'Queen Elizabeth Ledge'.

From the air Nantucket Island certainly looked just as Melville
had described it – all hillocks and plenty of sand over which the
little plane skimmed in to land.

A man in a check shirt and nondescript trousers was waiting for
me at the airport gate. A bulky man, wearing a cap with an extra
large peak that jutted downwards rather like a penguin's beak over
his wide glasses and a chin and cheeks covered with a thick fringe of
heavy grey beard. A mutual friend in New York had told me he was
'just the man for me'; he had adopted Nantucket, or been adopted

by it, since arriving here from New York in 1958. He had become an enthusiastic fisherman by now, a boat owner, too, a marine artist and a maritime historian. He had come here from New York 'to get away from it all', and had clearly done so. His name was Paul Morris. He shook my hand in a friendly way, and loading my small bag into his rattling station-wagon, drove off at speed to his house on the edge of the small port of Nantucket which lies on the north side of the island.

Paul Morris lived with his wife, Signe, in a fine grey-shingled house backed by tall trees, that, although quite big, contrived to seem smaller than it was by reason of the astonishing amount of pictures of sailing ships on its walls and rooms full of a clutter of antique American furniture, books on fishing and sailing and general bric-à-brac. The kitchen-living room, though more or less uncluttered, was a fine big light room with a wide fireplace and a large table at which we sat, and in a moment his wife joined us there, bustling in from the workshop where she turned out 'scrimshaw' – hand-carvings on ivory or bone. In the old days, Paul explained, scrimshaw had been the special art of whalingmen who, with nothing better to do on long voyages, occupied their time by carving whales' teeth and bones with intricate ornamental patterns. Often, by shaping them with saws and files, they made them into useful things: walking sticks, spurs, rolling pins, knives and forks, rulers, clothes pegs, pegs for scoring in games like picquet, and numerous other objects – sometimes of the most elaborate kind. A harmless way to keep idle hands busy; profitable, too. Paul Morris himself had had to give up carving. 'I've got emphysema,' he said. 'The dust did me no good.'

His first question, after establishing that I was booked into the Jared Coffin House – one of the oldest hotels in this old town – was, 'Do you like lobsters, Mr Young?' and when I said yes, he surprised me by jumping up, snatching a newly caught, cooked lobster from his icebox, deftly dissecting it with a pair of claw-crackers and a sharp knife, laying a small dish of butter and a Budweiser beer beside it, and telling me to help myself. 'Never mind us,' he grinned. 'We've had lunch.'

It was the second-best meal – and the most striking example of New England hospitality – I had encountered since setting out from New York. I suppose the best meal had been at Finn's Restaurant on the waterfront at Block Island off the Rhode Island coast: a 'chicken' lobster, about one pound in weight (small for America), with a green salad. There wasn't much to choose between that lobster and this one.

Talking of food, even John Steinbeck, travelling with Charley, found that by the roadsides of America he never had a really *good* dinner or a really *bad* breakfast. 'You could never tell with American food,' Ian Fleming's James Bond had once said. 'As long as they got their steaks and seafood right, the rest could go to hell.' Fleming was certainly right about the steaks, and the rightness of seafood. And even though since Bond's time (about thirty-five or forty years ago), the 'rest' no longer went automatically to hell, gastronomic excellence in America, as I was to find in due course, was rather elusive.

As for whales, whalebone is utterly worthless today, but in the Second World War Britons got more or less used to whalemeat processed into something called 'snoek'. And Melville had had a few words to say about whales as food: 'The fact is that among his hunters at least, the whale would by all hands be considered a noble dish, were there not so much of him; but when you come to sit down before a meat pie nearly over a hundred feet long, it takes away your appetite.'

Paul Morris and his wife laughed loudly when I repeated this, and laughed again when I told them a story of W. C. Fields I had heard years before. The gist of this was that Fields had been invited to attend a gala banquet for a famous explorer recently returned from the South Seas. What, the intrepid guest was asked, sort of food had he had to face on those remote islands?

'Oh, quite wonderful,' he replied. 'The natives would spread down great mats on the sand and lay on them dish after marvellous dish. Let's see, there would be shark's fin and paw-paw and tuna fish and squid and deer meat and lobster and crab and breadfruit and whale – '

'*Whale?*' Fields's loud and distinctive boom interrupted him. 'Why, that sounds like a meal in itself.'

'When I first came here,' Paul said, 'we used to go looking for Indian arrowheads or the heads of the small spears the Indians once used. A long time ago, of course. After all, the last Nantucket Indian died in 1854. They couldn't take the white man's diseases.'

'The same story in the Pacific, Tierra del Fuego, and just about all over the world. The fatal impact of the white man.'

'Yeah, I'm afraid so.'

What actually happened on Nantucket to its already dwindling Algonquin Indian population – by 1763 only 358 Indians survived, in a wigwam village near a pond not too far from where the Morrises now live – was the consequence of the arrival in August of that year of a strange ship off the island's north shore. The name of the ship might appropriately have been Nemesis, and the two men who rowed ashore to ask for food might, as far as the Indians were concerned, have been skeletal representatives of Death itself. The wretched Indian woman who kindly washed their clothes for them, while they explained that their ship was carrying Irish immigrants to the American colonies, was the first victim. She became ill almost at once, and soon died. By the time she was buried, more and more Indians of her village had succumbed to the white men's strange disease. Two hundred and twenty-two of them never recovered. The clue to the outbreak – and to the true plight of those aboard that sinister ship – was revealed when two female Irish corpses, obviously buried a short distance out to sea, were washed ashore. They had both died of smallpox.

The last Nantucket Indian of all, Abram Quarry, died peacefully and with dignity, aged eighty-four, and the place where his little cottage once stood is named Abram's Point in his memory.

Paul Morris has a collection of hollowed-out stone pots, stone axeheads and, he says, igneous rocks – small boulders of the sort that you find in the South Pacific: Gauguin's grave on Nuka Hiva in the Marquesas is made of them. Can there have been volcanoes *here*? It seems unlikely. In any case, the isolated island has no rivers and very few large trees – they are regularly swept away by the violent storms that roar in from the ocean. The island is also frequently enveloped, as I saw when Paul took me around the south and west of it, in some of the densest fogs I have ever seen.

The French-born middle-aged sea-dog, whom Paul Morris laughingly calls 'his chief officer', came breezing into the Morrises' parlour a little later.

'Oh, British, eh?' he cried, when he had been introduced, and he had a few fingers of vodka from Paul's quart bottle. 'Well, what's the news of Charles and Princess Di?' he laughed. He was not a bit put out when I said I hadn't the faintest idea. He did, however, have something to add about the Portuguese fishermen of New England.

'I was recently in Fayal in the Azores,' – he pronounced it 'Ay-zores' – 'and there in Peter's bar Peter told me *he* has relatives in *Nantucket*. They get around, those Portuguese mariners.'

The Jared Coffin House, at the meeting of Broad and Centre Streets, had been a hotel since about 1846. The Coffin who had built it had moved at his wife's insistence to Boston – she found Nantucket too isolated. It is an extremely handsome three-storey brick building with a grand entrance at the top of some steepish steps. Peter Coffin had been the fictional owner of the Spouter Inn in New Bedford, the one who obliged Ishmael to share a blanket with the oddly tattooed harpooneer, Queequeg. Names like Coffin were locally persistent: Nantucket had had a great many prominent Coffins in its history, and Starbucks as well. There was still a Starbuck Street, and once a Mary Starbuck had been the doyenne of the early settlers; she had welcomed the first Quakers to the island – they were for long the dominant sect there, and she became a Quaker herself. And there had been a lot more Starbucks after them.

The Starbuck who was the First Mate of the *Pequod* in *Moby Dick* was a Nantucket Quaker, too. He was a long, earnest man and, 'looking into his eyes,' said Melville, 'you seemed to see there the yet lingering images of the thousand-fold perils he had calmly confronted through life.' Cautious and honest-hearted, Melville's Starbuck was, like most professionals in dangerous trades, 'no crusader after perils'; that is, he didn't court unnecessary danger. He used to say: 'I will have no man in my boat who is not afraid of a whale,' – meaning that the most reliable and useful courage arises from the fair estimation of the encountered peril. Joseph Conrad had written that his Captain William Lingard had the wise fear of a brave man, and that could have been applied to Starbuck, the Nantucket whaleman, too.

This Starbuck was perhaps the most loyal officer on board the *Pequod*. But, in his 'wise fear', he knew Ahab was mad.

'Vengeance on a dumb brute, Captain Ahab,' he ventured, with Quakerly boldness, to tell him, 'seems blasphemous.'

And Ahab, the obsessed megalomaniac, responded furiously. 'Talk not to me of blasphemy, man; I'd strike the sun if it insulted me.'

Starbuck bravely persisted: 'Shall we keep chasing this murderous fish till he swamps the last man? Shall we be dragged by him to the bottom of the sea?'

But Ahab shook him off again. 'Starbuck, I am old,' he said impatiently. And, turning his back, 'Lower away!' he shouted to his men, 'Stand by the crew!'

And so he led all of them to their predestined doom.

'Hey,' said Paul Morris next day, 'do you know what a hen frigate is?' He laughed. 'Well, you know what a chicken lobster is, I know that.' The peak of his cap that was shaped like a penguin's beak poked forward over the bearded face of what could have been a gentle pirate.

'A small ship?'

'Hell, no. A hen frigate is a ship with a woman aboard. That's all it is. See, some captains took their wives along with them.'

We were sitting in the downstairs grill of the Jared Coffin House with Signe.

'They didn't *always* take their wives with them,' said Paul, 'although some voyages, as you know, were very long. Actually, the longest on record went on for eleven years. Eleven years at sea – imagine that!'

An excellent handbook to whaling I had bought, *The Yankee Whaler* by Clifford W. Ashley, says of those exceedingly long absences from the home port:

> The length of whaling voyages has always been the outstanding fact of a whaleman's life, the fact that marked him apart from all other seamen . . . .
>
> The same food, the same faces, the same sea, the same routine, day after day without end . . . . Every man knew the uttermost thoughts of all his shipmates; there was nothing further of interest to be heard from any one of them . . . . All hands brooded over misfortunes and wrongs that rapidly magnified themselves into formidable proportions. This was the time to bring out the leadership of the officers. The situation was one that it was then their duty to anticipate.

Eleven years at sea! As Paul Morris had said, imagine that! No wonder some late-returning whalers were no longer recognised by their own wives.

As it happened I had visited the Nantucket Whaling Museum that morning and made some notes. I read out to the Morrises extracts I had copied down from letters exchanged, at very long intervals, between a whaling captain in the Pacific and his wife back in Nantucket.

'Dear Ezra, where did you put the axe? Love Martha.'

Fourteen months later: 'Dear Martha, What do you want with the axe? Love Ezra.'

One year later: 'Forget about the axe, what did you do with the hammer? Love Martha.'

Signe laughed. 'I can just imagine Paul writing to me: "Hey, what do you want with the credit card?" '

'Yeah. Except I wouldn't be crazy enough to leave it behind. Not even hidden.'

Later, we walked down Broad Street towards Steamboat Wharf. It was a pretty town all right, even if Paul did complain about what he called 'the Mickey Mousing' of Nantucket. The 'gentrifying' of it for the tourists, he meant. By now less a fishing town than a holiday place for weekenders, the threat of an 'epidemic of quaintness' in Nantucket had led to a column in the *New York Times* by the humorous writer Russell Baker, who himself owned a summer house there.

There had already been, Baker wrote, 'a severe outbreak of cobblestones' in Nantucket, and a 'tell-tale rash' of electrified fake gas streetlamps was beginning to spread along the sidewalks. The onset of gas lamps, Baker warned, was always a bad sign, presaging an imminent, raging epidemic of quaintness. He had, he admitted, seen these plagues before. 'In the worst cases,' he said, 'inhabitants find themselves dressed in wigs, hoop skirts, knee britches and such, while standing in public places stirring boiling vats of candle wax for tourist snapshots.'

It had not come to that, of course, although it may do yet – quaintness is considerably more of a threat to Nantucket than to little Sag Harbor. After all, Nantucket is more of a popular tourist resort and bigger, even though it seems bigger than it really is. You start walking round the actual town of Nantucket, and even before you have a chance to turn an ankle on those new-laid cobblestones, you find you have seen it all.

'Now I am going to drive you round the island,' Paul Morris said, and in his big, ramshackle car we set off across the hummocks that make the Atlantic-bound island resemble a huge sea-girt golf course full of unkempt bunkers. From an incongruous windmill with creaking sails still grinding corn to the harbour whose entrance is still wide enough to permit the Hyannis tourist ferry to reach the terminal behind Brant Point, we seemed to cover the whole island in next to no time.

I had to leave for New York. As I told the Morrises, I was sorry to go. People had said that New Englanders could be dour, even xenophobic. I certainly hadn't found that. And into the bargain I had been spared the dreary New York chit-chat about a dreary election. Certainly I had seen no strife, racial or otherwise.

One incident had struck me above all as significant. It occurred to me soon after my ferry had left Orient Point on its way to New London that in *Travels with Charley*, as *his* ferry approached New London all those years ago, something had seriously disturbed Steinbeck. Near the river's mouth he had seen the dark shape of a submarine slipping to the surface. Shortly after that another similar shape had appeared – and a moment later yet another. New London, Steinbeck knew, was one of the homes of America's submarine fleet, and he supposed, resignedly, they were obliged to keep the world's peace with what he termed 'this venom'. 'I wish,' he thought, 'I could like submarines, for then I might find them beautiful, but

they are designed for destruction and their main purpose is threat.'
He remembered crossing the Atlantic in a troopship during the Second World War, and 'somehow the light goes bleak for me when I remember burned men pulled out from the oil-slicked sea'.

I kept an eye open on the sundeck for those sinister black shapes slashing through the water like spoutless whales. But we saw nothing until the ferry pushed up into the river, and there on a slipway were two monstrous tubes, skeletons of (presumably nuclear) submarines, high out of the water, perhaps half-built or under repair.

The middle-aged man in checkered shorts on the seat beside me became quite agitated. He touched my wrist, pointed to the shipyard, and cried excitedly, 'Say, isn't that a heart-warming sight?'

'Reinforcements for the Navy? Heart-warming?'

'No, no,' he shook his head impatiently. 'Just think. Either those subs will never be launched because the need for them is gone, or they will be launched, and just lay around idle because they will never be needed to defend us from those god-damned Russians. And there's nobody else left with a navy big enough to attack us – that's what I mean.' He turned to me, beaming. 'The way I see it, that thought should make this June holiday a good deal happier one for all of us.'

I saw what he meant; and he was right. Despite the looting in Los Angeles, plunging standards of education, misery in the inner cities, an ailing economy, the alleged supremacy of Japanese cars over American ones, and the uninspiring look of the presidential candidates – despite everything that seemed incurably bad or merely gloomy on the American horizon – at least, for now, a Third World War seemed a minor threat. For the moment, at least. That *was* something.

I sat on the sundeck looking at the harmless shells of those unfinished submarines on their ramps, and the sun's rays did feel hotter and the breeze fresher. I knew that tomorrow my nose and forehead would start to peel. Frankly, I didn't give a damn.

At Nantucket's little airport, half hidden among the hummocks, Paul Morris had pressed two books on me. The first was his history of a famous American windjammer called the *Benjamin F. Packard*, copiously and splendidly illustrated with Paul's photographs of her. The second was a book of his own maritime sketches. Both books will remain among my most prized possessions; souvenirs of yesterday's world of brave whales and whalers: of Nantucket, of men like Starbuck, Stubb, Tashtego and Queequeg – as well as the Portuguese fishermen of today's New Bedford. And of course of the hospitality of Paul and Signe Morris.

Soon I and my sunburnt nose descended sadly towards New York's La Guardia airport and there my north-east adventure came to an end. Next week the Democrats would be holding their Party Convention in New York City, separating me from a sun-soaked world where people lived and actually enjoyed working together in peace. I would be transported back to what suddenly seemed a quite unreal place, where frenetic talk of an unravelling country, drugs, unemployment and lobbyists propagating the rights of vociferous 'minorities' dominated the newspaper headlines.

From that unreal place would I begin to think of Starbuck and Stubb shouting 'Stand up!' from a whaleboat's stern? Would I wonder if Tashtego and Queequeg, braced as a 60-foot whale arched against the sky above them to fall back into the sea with the sound of 'fifty elephants stirring in their litter' – would I wonder if they paused to consider their ethnic origins? Were these two staunch whalemen, the giant Indian and the tattooed Polynesian – as they darted their irons into some gleaming monster's black side – ever frozen motionless in a sudden preoccupation with their rights?

More likely, I suspected, they simply concentrated on doing their duty. I am reminded of what André Gide wrote about men (or women) of action in his preface to *Night Flight* (*Vol de Nuit*) by Antoine de Saint-Exupéry. 'The author [said Gide] brings out a paradoxical truth of considerable psychological importance: that man's happiness lies not in freedom but in acceptance of a duty.' Joseph Conrad was another writer and man of action who subscribed to this important paradoxical truth.

So blessings on you both, loyal Tashtego and dutiful Queequeg, doomed immigrant from the South Pacific.

Part Two

Making Georgia Howl

I can make the march and make Georgia howl!

GEN. WILLIAM TECUMSEH SHERMAN

Hurrah, hurrah! We bring the Jubilee!
Hurrah, hurrah! The flag that makes you free!
So we sang the chorus from Atlanta to the sea,
While we were marching through Georgia.

'Marching Through Georgia':
words and music by HENRY C. WORK

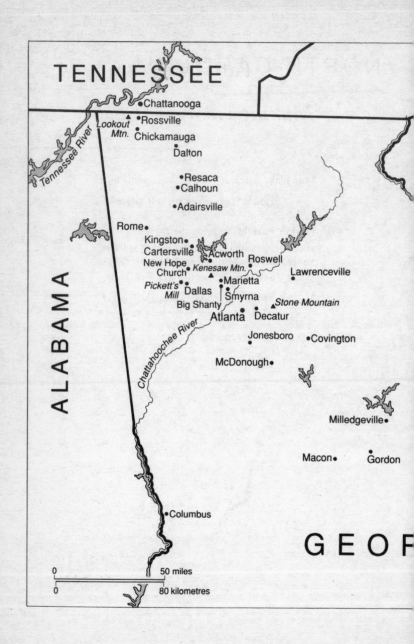

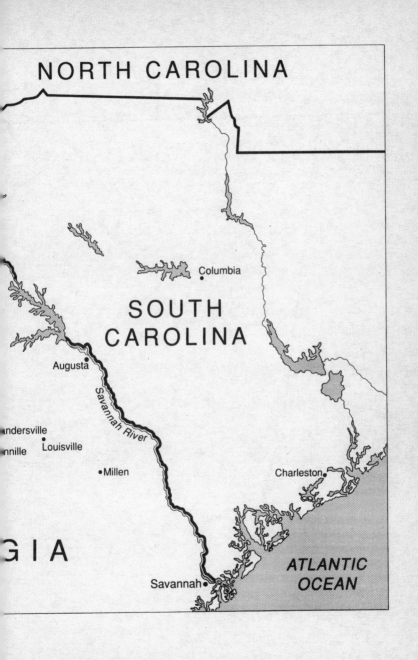

Chapter 5

The famous, war-winning march of the Union Army under General William Tecumseh Sherman through Georgia to the sea really began in Chickamauga. The bloodthirsty tone of the march was set there; and the extraordinarily bloody nature of its engagements were certainly foreshadowed in this terrible battle.

Extracts from letters, journals and books can tell only a little of the horror:

> Bullets whack against tree trunks, solid shot cracks skulls like eggshells .... Men went down as the grass falls before the scythe. One captain was gasping in death within a foot of another man's head, his bowels all torn out .... The only visible wound was a wide, ragged opening in the abdomen. It was defiled with earth and dead leaves .... He moved his limbs; he moaned at every breath. In his great agony he had torn up the ground on which he lay ....

Reminiscences speak of: 'Shots, shrieks, curses, shouts and yells: a devilish uproar. Men are fighting with clubbed muskets, rifles, pistols, bayonets, and color staffs. ...'

Others talk of the fate of animals: 'Horses lie still or hobble about pathetically with one or two legs shot off at the hock.'

In some books there are photographs of the aftermath of Civil War battles with captions like 'Blue and Gray lie together in peace'. The bodies are usually on their backs and horribly swollen; their hands clutch air; sometimes parts of their faces are missing. They have been photographed in trenches at Petersburg; in a sunken road at Antietam; in the woods at Chancellorville. Today, it is true, Blue and Gray do indeed lie together in peace. Six hundred and twenty thousand men all told died in the four years of the Civil War – as many American lives as were lost in all the nation's other wars, including Vietnam.

'Boys,' General William Tecumseh Sherman, lecturing survivors later, used to say, 'war is all hell.' They – and he – should have known what he was talking about.

'Uncle Billy' is what his men called Sherman; and his relatives called him 'Uncle Cump'. They both regarded him with affection, even if he certainly knew what hell war was. After all, in 1864 he himself waged it with a vengeance by launching his devastating march through Georgia to the sea – and the beginning of that hellish episode came at the battle of Chickamauga on the borders of Georgia and Tennessee, one of the bloodiest set-tos of the whole four years of the war.

Walking the battlefield of Chickamauga with Colin Campbell, a friend from Atlanta, it was the trees that astonished me. Acres of them covered the field, screening large areas of it from every other part. How on earth, I wondered, had the Confederate General James Longstreet – the giant with the big beard – known that the woods in front of his men were momentarily denuded of Unionist troops? Surely he couldn't see that for himself? He couldn't have seen a thing. Yet his veterans of the Army of Northern Virginia crashed through, putting the Unionist Army to abject flight, and Longstreet had nearly won the Civil War on his own.

If he *had* won it there would have been no march by Sherman to the sea at Savannah; nor would Atlanta have been burned; *Gone With The Wind* would never have been written or filmed; and William Tecumseh Sherman's golden statue would not stand outside the Plaza Hotel in New York City at the corner of 59th Street and 5th Avenue.

Colin and I contrived to arrive at the site of the Chickamauga battlefield on Veterans' Day (a holiday for certain federal officials), so we had no right to be surprised to find the battlefield's historian had taken the day off, in any case we were quite content to walk over the battlefield on our own. We would move on to Chattanooga next day, we told ourselves, when the holiday would be over and that the battlefield's historian-on-the-spot – we had already arranged to meet him – would lead us to the places that mattered.

Colin was a young journalist, ex-*New York Times*, now the leading columnist of the *Atlanta Constitution*. A mutual colleague in New York had recommended him as a possibly willing guide to at least part of Sherman's invasion-path through Georgia. He turned out to be much more than that.

After investigating some of Melville's old haunts I had turned to the grim-faced general with the Indian name, who loved Dickens and Shakespeare and probably won the war by his ruthless 'scorched earth' march through Georgia from Chattanooga to Savannah on the Atlantic Ocean. 'I can make Georgia howl!' he had said. Not only Georgia howled because of him, all the South did as well.

The fascination of Chickamauga, it seemed to me, was that, if the Confederate commander, General Braxton Bragg, had followed up Longstreet's shattering of the Unionist line here – *if* he had done so – Sherman, as I say, might just as well have gone back to his Dickens there and then and left Georgia severely alone.

In a gentle cool breeze Colin and I tramped the field on which up to about 35,000 men had been reduced to red pulp. I only hoped that, in return for driving me here and agreeing to spend the next day on the heights of Chattanooga, Colin would find enough material for his weekly column. I wondered, too, at odd moments what had become of that famous old train, the 'Chattanooga Choo-Choo'.

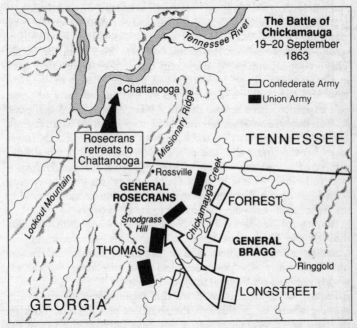

A small wooden shack marks the spot where Longstreet's men under the immediate command of General Hood found their breakthrough point. The shack stands on a wide piece of open grassy ground, and it is called Brotherton's Cabin. A few Civil War cannons have been placed decoratively round it. Ahead of me as I stood with my back to the cabin, a field sloped down to thick woods, dense with the leaves of early autumn now – the battle had taken place in late September. In that tangled undergrowth, among the terrifying hiss and ring of bullets on tree bark, the whisper of stray shots and the rush of round shot, the Unionist infantry had striven in vain to halt the yelling onrush of Hood's three divisions. I tried to imagine the scene, and decided that the last thing I would have liked to have been in life was a Unionist infantryman on that day.

'To my astonishment I saw the entire country in front swarming with Confederates,' Ambrose Bierce wrote, describing exactly what he saw that day. Bierce, one of the few American writers actually to take part in the Civil War, was a topographical engineer with General Hazen's brigade. That day what he witnessed was nothing less than the Union army of General William Rosecrans in which he served being cut clean in two. 'We had barely time to turn tail and gallop down the hill and away. All was bickering confusion.'

Rosecrans himself galloped away; and so did his corps commanders, General McCook and General Crittenden (two evident second-raters to whom Rosecrans had remained absurdly loyal). They galloped and hardly drew rein before they were safely back in Chattanooga. There, red-faced and puffing, Rosecrans had the mournful duty to wire his superiors in Washington the bad news: 'We have met with a serious disaster.' Next day he wired again that he even doubted whether he could hold his position in Chattanooga, *the* important rail junction and a gateway to the lower South. It was lucky for the Union that one part of Rosecrans's army stood firm: a force of a few brigades under Major-General George Thomas – later to be dubbed 'the Rock of Chickamauga' for obvious reasons – held out on a hill on the other side of the woods and the field to my right: a hill with the Dickensian name of Snodgrass.

Aiming for Snodgrass Hill, Colin and I pressed with difficulty through the barriers of leaves and branches. Confederates and Unionists must have been almost hopelessly constricted by the limited visibility – a good deal less than rifle range – that the woods imposed on both infantry and artillery.

From time to time I could see the vague shapes of small deer slipping ahead of us through the shadows of the trees. Both on the field of Chickamauga and a few days later on the site of the massacre of Unionist soldiers at Pickett's Mill just before Sherman entered Atlanta itself, I was forcibly reminded, as large whippy branches sprang back to catch me stinging swipes across the face, of how nearly impossible it had been for a general to see where on earth his own men had got to, leave alone where the enemy troops were. How was it possible to conduct a battle at all? Leave alone the visibility – what of the appalling din? It must have been like waging war in a dark room with the *1812 Overture* roaring out of loudspeakers turned up full blast. In such conditions, terrible accidents could happen, beyond the usual tragedies of war. After all, trees and poor visibility had caused the accidental shooting to death by his own troops of the Confederacy's hero, Stonewall Jackson, at Chancellorville.

In a short piece on his experiences at the Pickett's Mill holocaust a little later, Bierce wrote:

> The civilian reader must not suppose when he reads accounts of military operations in which relative positions of forces are defined . . . that these were matters of general knowledge to those engaged . . . . It is seldom, indeed, that a subordinate officer knows anything about the disposition of the enemies force – except that it is unamiable – or precisely whom he is fighting. As to the rank and file, they can know nothing more of the matter than the arms they carry. They hardly know what troops are upon their own right or left the length of a regiment away. If it is a cloudy day they are ignorant even of the points of the compass . . . . What is going on in front of him [a soldier] does not know at all until he learns it afterwards.

Even I – and I suspect Colin, too – hemmed in by trees as we soon were, had no idea of whether we were facing north, south, east or west. In which direction Chattanooga lay I had no idea. Whereabouts was Atlanta? Sherman may have known; I certainly did not.

Struggling our way from field to field, we fought our way at last to the Snodgrass House, a wooden hut with stone slabs serving as steps to its entrance and, nearby, a blasted tree stretching bare branches like the burnt arms of a hideously wounded war casualty. Here Thomas, 'the Rock of Chickamauga', had held out and rescued some Northern pride from the abject defeat. The wooden hut stood in a commonplace field; and again the field was fenced in by seemingly impenetrable woods.

Standing here, how could one not cast one's mind back to Bierce's terrible story of the boy at Chickamauga? – the story of the innocent little boy who had strayed from home in these very woods and, by a horrible mischance, had wandered into the middle of the battlefield. Lost in these woods, his first impression came when he was suddenly conscious of a shambling, awkward object, about which there was something horribly familiar. It was neither a deer nor a bear. Yet it was followed by another and another and yet another, every one creeping or stumbling towards a brook.

> They were men. They crept upon their hands and knees. They used their hands only, dragging their legs. They used their knees only, their arms hanging idle at their sides. They strove to rise to their feet, but fell prone in the attempt . . . . Singly and in pairs and in little groups, they came on through the gloom . . . . They came by dozens and by hundreds. The very ground seemed in motion toward the creek. Occasionally one who had paused did not again go on, but

lay motionless. He was dead. Some, pausing, made strange gestures with their hands, erected their arms and lowered them again, clasped their hands; spread their palms upward, as men are sometimes seen to do in public prayer . . . .

The boy – not more than six years old – edged nearer to them and peered into their faces with innocent childish curiosity. All their faces, he suddenly saw, were 'singularly white and many were streaked and gouted with red'. Something in this – 'something too, perhaps, in their grotesque attitudes and movements' – reminded him of a painted clown he had once seen in a circus. And he laughed as he watched them.

The worst image in this terrible vision of battle comes when a wounded soldier turns upon the child a face that lacked a lower jaw – 'from the upper teeth to the throat was a great red gap, fringed with hanging shreds of flesh and splinters of bone . . . .' No wonder that Bierce himself, having seen such things more than once – he was at Shiloh, too, as well as Pickett's Mill and Chickamauga – never in all his long life recovered completely from the sight of these shattered men.

The feeling of claustrophobia; the sense of those bloody-faced creeping things dragging smashed limbs through the trees; above all, the idea of that creature with half a face moving clumsily along on all fours as in a hideous pantomime – it was all too much to think about. I was glad when we burst out into daylight and on to a broad footpath. We followed it past monument after monument raised to commemorate the 145,000 troops who had fought here nearly 130 years ago. To the 1st Ohio Cavalry, for example; and to Long's Brigade ('Lt Col Valentine Cupp commanding'); to the Pennsylvanian contingent of the 1st Cavalry Division of Rosecrans's Army of the Cumberland. On one monument, the statue of a young soldier in a posture of noble defiance raised the standard of the 2nd Minnesota. Yet there was no statue to a creeping soldier – Federal or Confederate – on all fours with his lower jaw missing.

Quoted in *Voices of the Civil War*, the Confederate General D. H. Hill, speaking of the shambles on Chattanooga road north from the Chickamauga battlefield, claimed never to have seen 'the Federal dead lie so thickly on the ground'. And he emphasised the fratricidal nature of the whole struggle with his next remark: 'That indomitable Virginian soldier, George H. Thomas [who had remained loyal to the Union] was there . . . confronting . . . the forces of Braxton Bragg [the Confederate commander-in-chief], his friend and captain in the Mexican war.'

A rebel yell of triumph sounds in the voice of Major William Owen, another Confederate officer on the spot: 'It is glorious to have these fellows out here.' He was talking about Lee's 'old war horse' General James Longstreet, and General John Hood, who carried one arm in a sling as a result of a wound he had received at Gettysburg, who was to lose a leg at Chickamauga – and, even after all that, come back into the war once again. 'It recalls our old fights,' Hill exulted. 'I feel certain we will have a victory today.'

He was right. The South did have a victory; indeed, it very nearly had a victory, even at this late stage, significant enough to win the entire war.

At the time Bragg clashed with Rosecrans at Chickamauga, the fortunes of the North were at a low ebb. People longed for peace; and a popular song, 'When This Cruel War Is Over', best reflected this longing. Federal losses under General Grant had mounted appallingly. Lincoln was up for re-election in 1864, and partly because of the casualties his re-election was doubtful. One trouble for him was that many Northerners were utterly fed up with what seemed to be pointless slaughter without an end in sight. General George McClelland, the Democratic Party's rival candidate for President, was thought to advocate immediate peace on the simple condition that the Union must be restored and preserved. Lincoln, on the other hand, had felt obliged to add a second condition: the emancipation by the South of its slaves. Yet an enormous number of potential Northern voters, even now, could not stomach that. Not even men like William Tecumseh Sherman, although he intended to do his soldierly duty whoever won the presidential campaign. Like many other Unionists, Sherman's principal obsession was that the Union – or 'Nation' in Lincoln's preferred word – must be preserved.

The crisis in Lincoln's Republican Party grew so intense that there was even a call from some Republicans to nominate a new candidate. This would have meant backing away from the abolition of slavery as a Northern condition for peace negotiations with the South. Lincoln was urged to send a letter to Jefferson Davis, his Confederate opposite number, offering simply 'to make distinct offers of peace ... on the sole condition of acknowledging the supremacy of the constitution', i.e. of agreeing to restore the Union of all the United States and so ending the rebellion.

All came out well for Lincoln, as we know. But for now, worn and exhausted after Chickamauga, Rosecrans was, as Lincoln himself said, 'confused and stunned like a duck hit on the head. ... Well, he has been whipped.'

Yet Rosecrans was still in luck. His Confederate opponent, Braxton Bragg, failed to follow up Longstreet's breakthrough, the Unionists were able to escape to Chattanooga, and there they prepared for the siege that was bound to come. At the battle of Chattanooga that followed two months after Chickamauga, the Unionists under Ulysses S. Grant, were able to put the Confederates to chaotic flight. The 'turning point' in favour of the South was past and gone. It never returned.

To my relief, Colin Campbell did get a column out of our walk through the woods at Chickamauga. Next week, he wrote under the dateline 'Chattanooga, Tenn.':

> The last time I toured these parts I not only rediscovered Chickamauga, one of the country's ghostliest Civil War battlefields, I also made a howling error.
>
> I wrote that on Sept. 20, 1863, during the battle of Chickamauga in far northern Georgia, the Union General George Thomas put up such a spirited fight against a Southern breakthrough that most of his fellow Northerners managed a safe retreat 'across the Tennessee River to Chattanooga'.
>
> Chattanooga, yes. Across the river, no. Alas, the Tennessee River was, and some say still is, *north* of Chattanooga.
>
> Gavin Young waved away my Tennessee River problem as a trifle, and proposed: 'Just report, this time, that the river has changed course since you last visited Chattanooga. It will be a *fantastic* scoop.'

The day after our walking tour of the Chickamauga battlefield, Colin and I met the Chattanooga battlefield's resident historian, James H. Ogden III. I tried my theory out on him.

'Jim, I have a feeling that at Chickamauga Braxton Bragg lost the war for the South.'

We were standing on the top of Lookout Mountain, the great crag that dominates the city to the south. We were standing in a downpour of rain, too, but Ogden looked gratifyingly interested.

'If he'd crushed the Federal forces,' I went on, 'there'd have been no possibility of the North capturing Atlanta before the 1864 election, Lincoln might have lost the vote, and the South might have become an independent, slave-owning country.'

Ogden looked thoughtful.

Spouting hypotheses and rivulets of water, we squelched about Lookout Mountain, slipping and sliding on the sodden earth, coming to no conclusions. Occasionally we stood in the downpour, studying Ogden's maps. Below us, Chattanooga was almost totally obliterated from sight by the mist of rain that lay over Moccasin Bend, the place where the Tennessee River curved dramatically round a piece of land strangely shaped like an Indian slipper.

'Rosecrans,' I went on, 'was a disaster, no? A loser, if ever there was one. He could have destroyed the Union for ever.'

Ogden – the expert – took all this well. For a moment he stopped pointing things out on his sodden map.

'Rosecrans,' he pointedly disagreed at last, with a deprecating smile, 'was an excellent general.' He smiled again, and said memorably, 'He just had *one bad day*.'

Colin evidently found this remark, as I did, strangely exhilarating, for he said in his next column, 'To be driving around in a cold rain, to pace the turf, to hear Ogden's crisp recitals, study his maps – while contemplating such tricks of fate as Bragg's paralysis and Rosecrans's "one bad day". History feels so inexorable – until it seems fragile.'

'So what happened to Rosecrans?' I asked.

'He was fired, of course,' Ogden told us, 'and got shunted off to Missouri for a while. Later he moved to Southern California – near LA. He even ran successfully for Congress.'

'So it might have been Rosecrans instead of Sherman who made Georgia howl and who found immortality in a large equestrian statue in Manhattan that Donald Trump recently had plated with gold. Or it might have been Rosecrans instead of Grant who became President of the United States. . . .' To me, the might-have-been possibilities were beginning to run on.

Colin's column in the *Atlanta Constitution* bore the headline ' "One Bad Day" south of Chattanooga'.

All these might-have-beens . . . .

'Rosecrans ended up in Southern California,' I said. 'I wonder if he became a movie producer.'

If Rosecrans got his comeuppance at Chickamauga, Bragg got his at Chattanooga. He had been less impressed by the size of his victory than he had been by the number of his losses – which amounted to 30 per cent or more of his effective force: that is, 20,000 killed, wounded and missing. Ten Confederate generals were killed or wounded, including Hood, who lost his leg. One can sympathise with Bragg in his dilemma as he surveyed the woods full of his dead or dying men. And one can also see how it was that his reluctance to pursue and achieve the final annihilation of the North's Army of the Cumberland infuriated hot-headed men like Nathan Bedford Forrest, the Confederate cavalry wizard, who demanded: 'What does he fight battles for?' A little later Forrest went a good deal further to Bragg face to face: 'I have stood your meanness as long as I intend to. You have played the part of a damned scoundrel.... If you ever again try to interfere with me or cross my path it will be at the peril of your life.' He refused to serve any longer with Bragg and went off forthwith to Mississippi. His words should have made a difference. For Forrest, the most brilliant cavalry raider the South possessed, could not be dismissed out of hand simply as an insubordinate firebrand. His activities had made him such a pest to the Northern commanders that Sherman had written to Grant, 'Forrest must be hunted down *if it costs 10,000 lives.*'

As a matter of fact, Forrest's protest was only one of several by Bragg's generals. In response to their outcry – which included a letter from Longstreet swearing that 'nothing but the hand of God can save us as long as we have our present commander' – Jefferson Davis himself came up and called the general to an urgent pow-wow to try to sort things out. It was a singularly abortive visit. Every one of Bragg's corps commanders condemned him; each one would have welcomed serving under Longstreet. He was a general, they swore, who could lick his weight in wild cats. But the upshot was that Davis left Bragg in charge.

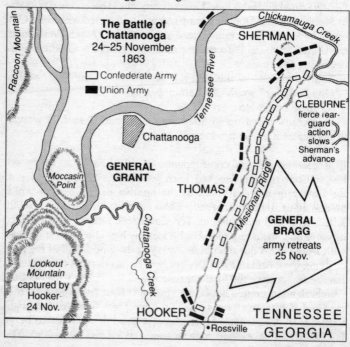

The Battle of
Chattanooga
24–25 November
1863

□ Confederate Army
■ Union Army

The effect of these pathetic shenanigans on Confederate military morale was not a happy one. And so, on this miserable note, the Confederate siege of Northern-held Chattanooga began. This time Bragg, plagued by ill health and lethargy, was up against the great Grant. The outcome, we all know.

Patient James Ogden, our guide, had gone home, soaked to his underwear after our circumnavigation of Lookout Mountain. At drink time that evening I sat waiting for Colin, in the main lobby of our Chattanooga hotel, filling in the time reading *Voices of the Civil War*. I had no further need to ask myself what had happened to the Chattanooga Choo-Choo. I was sitting in it. The old train of the song had become, as if by magic, a hotel of the same name. Over my head, midway between the old ticket office and a large bar and restaurant, a towering ceiling arched, supported by what looked very like the original railway station girders painted brown. Evening light poured down through the high station windows set in it.

The oddest thing about the hotel was the way in which the railroad tracks stretched away behind it: I moved to the coffee shop and ordered a beer. Between sips of Budweiser I saw through the coffee shop's window railway carriages on those tracks that looked ready to steam straight off to Baltimore and New York. I had already inspected those carriages and found they had been made into bedrooms; at $95 double-occupancy you could rent them for the night. One carriage had 'Dining Car' written on it and apparently still served dinner ('dinner in the diner, nothing could be finer'). There was a mock engine, too – its cabin was pink with a wide funnel, it had a cow-catcher, and the rest of it was a vivid green. It was called the 'Cincinnati Southern'. It wasn't going anywhere.

Colin and I had decided to eat in the town, so that ruled out dinner in the diner even if it did mean having to forgo the next day's 'ham and eggs in Car-ol-ina', as the song promised.

I forget where we ate dinner that night. I have an idea we emerged from the Choo-Choo, quite tired from walking across the up-and-down contours of the straggling battle area, to be considerably depressed by the streets of Chattanooga: a gutted hotel ('The Grand') looked down at us with staring, blank windows like the dead empty eyes of a corpse, and there was a second crumbling hotel down the street that carried a sign that it was for sale – a sign that showed evidence of having been there some time. In the end, as far as I remember, we walked down the road to a small corner restaurant; Italian, I think. Later, walking back to the hotel through the seedy streets of that part of Chattanooga, a description of the city under siege by a Federal war correspondent I had been reading earlier while I waited for Colin, came back to me:

> Life in Chattanooga ... was dreary enough [the reporter noted]. If there was little of beauty and elegance in the place when our troops retreated into it from Chickamauga, there was a great deal less a fortnight subsequently .... Residences were turned into block-houses; black bastions sprang up in former vineyards; rifle pits were run through graveyards.

The fall rains were beginning then, and at that stage of the war hundreds of civilians huddled together in the centre of the town as best they could. Underlining the squalor, one journalist from the North said that many of the houses they occupied surpassed in filth, the numbers of occupants and general destitution the worst tenement house in New York City. As for the besieging Confederates, their lot was no better.

> Three days rations were generally eaten at one meal, and the soldiers had to starve the next two days and a half. The soldiers ... were almost naked, and covered all over with vermin and camp-itch and filth and dirt. The men looked sick, hollow-eyed, and heartbroken .... Reviewed by Honourable Jefferson Davis – when he passed us with his great retinue of staff officers ... at full gallop, cheers greeted him with the words, 'Send us something to eat, Massa Jeff. I'm hungry! I'm hungry!'

That at least is what Private Sam Watkins of the 1st Tennessee Regiment recalled of the siege. Perhaps this deprivation was one reason for the Confederate disaster that followed very soon; a deprivation allied to the abject pessimism of many of Bragg's men. For example, one Georgia rebel wrote home, 'There is no use fighting any longer no how. For we are done gon up the Spout the Confideracy is done whiped it is useless to deny any longger.' Yet how do you balance those sombre sentiments with the incredible spirit that drove Private Ellis of the 32nd Tennessee Infantry at Chickamauga – despite having marched for six weeks without shoes – to go into battle (still without shoes) and keep up with his company at 'all times until wounded'?

Next day Colin and I had more hard walking. It was still cloudy and grey and spitting with rain. We saw the slopes up which the Union General Hooker had stormed Lookout Mountain, easily driving off the very few Confederates on it – the defending force had been fatally reduced by Bragg. And we drove to the Rossville Gap where Hooker sharply swung line north to wind up the left wing of Bragg's army that was stretched along Missionary Ridge.

Bragg's troops had a marvellous view from the top of the ridge not only of Grant's rapidly expanding force in Chattanooga below them – but also, on the far side of the valley, of Racoon Mountain and, to the south, the woods of Lookout Mountain now in Hooker's hands, beneath which the Tennessee River made its extravagant loop round Moccasin Point. At night, when the clouds dispersed, they also had a fine, if depressing, view of the massed fires of the opposing army.

Rossville Boulevard, which runs today from the Gap straight into Chattanooga, provides a dire warning of what ribbon development in America may become outside every sizeable town in the Union. All the stunning ugliness of Southeastern America seems to be concentrated here. 'Welcome to Tennessee', a sign says. And then for two or three miles, on either side of the road all you see is little but pawn shops, used car lots, piles of scrap metal, tattoo parlours, and 'adult' movie houses. It is staggeringly tawdry.

James Ogden looked at it in disgust, saying, 'We call Rossville "Ross Vegas", did you know?' And eyeing one of the many used car lots, he added, 'Don't ever buy a used car from Rossville Boulevard. You'll probably find a banana in your crank case.'

We looked up in relief at Missionary Ridge, where Bragg's units had been dug in.

'One of Bragg's mistakes,' James Ogden said, 'was not to have his defensive position up on top of the ridge. Actually it was below the crest. Some other officer would have done it better. On the Federal side Grant's men formed practically a straight line: Sherman on the left, Hooker and Lookout Mountain on the right.

'Sherman's idea was to roll up Bragg's force on Missionary Ridge from north to south. Hooker would come up the other way – south to north. It didn't quite work out like that. Mainly because the Confederate general, Pat Cleburne, put up an unexpectedly fierce resistance to Sherman, and thus blocked his advance.'

Pat Cleburne – an Irishman, nicknamed the 'Stonewall Jackson of the West', was one of the better Confederate commanders. He had attracted my own admiration since I first read about the Battle of Chattanooga. For one thing, his photograph revealed an interesting face; strong, unusual features over an unbuttoned general's tunic of Confederate grey. Cleburne had extraordinarily high cheekbones and deeply recessed eyes with a strange, sad, faraway look, and his moustache and light beard left uncovered a wide and sensitive mouth. It was an arresting face.

That sad, faraway look evidently concealed a hefty streak of toughness, and Cleburne equally evidently had the confidence of his soldiers, because when the main Federal advance up the central slopes of Missionary Ridge turned into a sort of race through the fleeing ranks of Bragg's Confederate defenders, Cleburne even counter-attacked successfully and thus made an effective rearguard for the bulk of the shattered Southern army as it fled 30 miles down the Rossville–Atlanta Road. I liked Cleburne: his looks as much as his fighting ability.

We drove along Missionary Ridge. I looked down it and, thinking of the Union advance up it, remarked that the slope looked mighty high to me.

Ogden said, 'Well, it actually is a twenty-minute walk from bottom to top on a fine day. It's really a collection of bumps and knobs.'

He went on: 'The Union victory at Chattanooga was called "a miracle", which consisted of the totally unplanned and unordered surge of General Thomas's men to chase the Confederates from the foot of the Ridge way up to the top.'

That was the miracle. No one had issued an order to advance. It was simply that, pinned down in a storm of Confederate fire from above, the Union troops had nowhere to go than up. So up they went. Someone with Grant said, 'Without further waiting, first one regiment, then another started with its colours up the ascent, until with loud hurrahs the entire line charged up the ridge.'

Private Sam Watkins, among the retreating Confederates, described it thus:

> I heard Captain Turner, who had four Napoleon guns ... halloo out the order to fire, and then a roar.
> The next order was, 'Limber to the rear!' The Yankees were cutting and slashing, and the cannoneers were running in every direction. I saw one brigade throw down their guns and break like quarter horses. Bragg was trying to rally them. I heard him say, 'Here is your commander,' and the soldiers hallooed back, 'Here is your mule'.

Grant, watching this unplanned assault with General Thomas, growled menacingly to 'the Rock of Chickamauga',

'Thomas, who ordered those men up that ridge?'

'I don't know. I didn't,' replied Thomas.

And Grant turned away still growling, 'If the assault fails, someone will pay heavily for it.'

But the assault did not fail. Confederate regiments were captured entire, and battery after Confederate battery. Braxton Bragg wrote in his report: 'No satisfactory excuse can possibly be given for the shameful conduct of our troops. . . . The position was one which ought to have been held by a line of skirmishers against any assaulting column.' And another officer said much the same thing – only more strongly:

> The scene of disorder beggars description . . . . It is difficult for those acquainted with the unflinching bravery of these same soldiers – tried and never found irresponsive to the call of duty upon every field of battle from Shiloh to Chickamauga – to understand the unaccountable, shameful panic which seized them, and for which no apology can be found.

To Jefferson Davis Bragg wrote, 'we both erred in the conclusion for me to retain command here after the clamour raised against me.' But the war, which the South could have won after Chickamauga, was already lost.

We drove on – looking down to our right, down the slopes on which the fate of the South was decided. Fine large houses stood looking down on downtown Chattanooga. Some were smaller examples of colonial mansions; others were in Tudor style; still others oddly neo-Japanese. One would have said that one Gothic monster had been built as the home of a railroad baron: it was grandly pillared and porticoed. The houses stood in groves of fine trees which were shedding their leaves now on to the lawns below them; yellow and golden leaves, damp in the autumn drizzle. The Ridge was a good spot to live on: from your windows you would be able to see the great loop in the Tennessee River that shone like a silver thread.

A total of 12,482 men were lost at Chattanooga; a relatively small number compared with Chickamauga, or Sharpsburg (23,500), or Gettysburg (43,454). That was the price the Union paid to retain its possession of the rail centre of the South.

Driving slowly along through the modern squalor of Rossville, it was impossible not to look back over the years at General Thomas's men as they moved steadily up Missionary Ridge through the storm of Confederate fire. Thomas's 'orders' had been simple – almost no orders at all.

'If they can take the Ridge,' he'd said to his officers, 'tell 'em to push ahead!' And the soldiers pushed ahead.

Because of that extraordinary, unordered 'miracle' on the Ridge, Chattanooga has been described as a soldier's battle rather than a general's victory.

'Perhaps,' I said to Ogden, 'Rosecrans had hoped that he himself would go on to capture Atlanta. But after Chickamauga, Rosecrans was fired. The battle here made Sherman's opportunity, didn't it?'

'I suppose, in a way, you could say that Sherman's march to the sea started here,' replied James Ogden cautiously. 'Yes, I suppose you could say that.'

We dropped Jim Ogden off in the car park of the Choo-Choo Hotel. Then Colin turned the car's nose down the road Sherman had taken to Atlanta and Savannah, and we shot through the Rossville Gap into Georgia. It was as if we had closed a door behind us; and at the same instant opened one on a time that somehow seemed to belong to a quite different era.

The time of the end of America's Civil War; the time of Sherman's great march through Georgia.

Chapter 6

'If you don't have my army supplied, and keep it supplied, we'll eat your mules up, sir – eat your mules up!' – that was 'Uncle Billy' Sherman standing no nonsense from an anxious quartermaster in his army who thought that he might not be able to keep up with the onrush of Sherman's march to Atlanta.

The omnipotent general would have been in an excellent position to deal with a slow-coach builder or deliberately poodle-faking engineer of today. On the way to Atlanta, when an army engineer asked Sherman for four days in which to rebuild a burned bridge, 'Uncle Billy's brusque reply was: 'Sir, I give you forty-eight hours or a position in the front ranks.'

I doubt if you could have said that to an officer in Vietnam. Certainly not in the Gulf War. The Civil War was a much rougher kettle of fish.

Sherman's crucial contribution to the North's victory truly began in Dalton in northwest Georgia in early May 1864.

The march was organised in two parts. The first part ran as far as Atlanta, and its fall on 2 September saved Abraham Lincoln's election hopes. The second ran on from Atlanta (which Sherman left on 16 November) to the Atlantic Ocean at Savannah. As Atlanta burned (Sherman, of course, had fired it), the triumphant general was asked what his next objective was. Talking and gesticulating, and impatiently shooting smoke from his cigar in his habitual way, he enigmatically snapped, 'Salt water. Salt water.'

Sherman was brutally outspoken about his intentions; nothing enigmatic there. 'I am satisfied,' he said flatly, 'and have been all the time, that the problem of this war consists in the awful fact that the present class of men who rule the South must be killed outright rather than in the conquest of territory.'

Here is the point he said: 'We are not only fighting armies, but a hostile people, and must make old and young, rich and poor, feel the hard hand of war, as well as their organised armies.'

And later, 'My aim then was to whip the Rebels, to humble their pride, to follow them to their inmost recesses, and to make them fear and dread us.'

To Grant, his superior in Washington, he stuck up for the plan which a number of people at headquarters opposed. 'This may not be war,' he said, 'but rather statesmanship, nevertheless it is overwhelming to my mind that there are thousands of people abroad and in the South who reason thus: "If the North can march an army right through the South, it is proof positive that the North can prevail." '

The plan was that Sherman's men would live off the land. They would destroy banks, storehouses, factories, and if necessary private houses. They would advance on a 60-mile front, 15 miles each day, on a deliberately erratic course to bamboozle the enemy. They would use railroads to bring up supplies; they would repair rails torn up by the enemy – repair them *instantly* with mobile crews; they would deny railroads to the enemy by tearing up the rails, heating them over fires and bending them into the knots universally called 'Sherman's ties'. All that was part of Sherman's plan for what he called his 'tour of the South'.

In the interest of 'living off the land', some of Sherman's 62,000 troops were told to function as foragers (or 'bummers' as they soon came to be called). They spread out across the land; and some of them, some of the least responsible, had the time of their lives. One Federal officer would never forget his first sight of a group of bummers returning to camp with their wagons and carts:

> At the head of the procession . . . an ancient family carriage, drawn by a goat, a cow with a bell, and a jackass. Tied behind . . . a sheep and a calf, the vehicle loaded down with pumpkins, cabbages, guinea fowls, carrots, turkeys, onions, squashes, sorghum, a looking-glass, an Italian harp, sweetmeats, a peacock, a rocking-chair, a gourd, a bass viol, sweet potatoes, a cradle, dried peaches, honey, a baby carriage, peach brandy – and every other imaginable thing a lot of fool soldiers could take in their heads to bring away.

These 'fool soldiers' were the life of Sherman's army on its long march. Three hams, a sack of meal, a peck of potatoes, a fresh bed quilt, an old coffee pot and, say, a jug of vinegar – all these things could make part of a long campaign tolerable, even reasonably enjoyable. The taste for 'bumming' got into the men's veins and some of them roamed far from their units, to avoid army discipline for one thing and to have a bit of freelance fun on their own. Freelance fun was not officially condoned by Sherman himself, but after all he had issued orders that foraging was not only permissible but vital to the success of such a freewheeling campaign.

One Georgian – fictional, but there were many real Southerners like her – who was feeling the 'hard hand of war' in 'fear and dread' of the Yankees lived in a destitute, though once grand house called Tara, a little way south of Atlanta. Scarlett O'Hara had decided that her few remaining dependants simply could no longer go on eating nothing but yams. Some of them were already moaning that they wanted their accustomed drumsticks and rice and gravy. In her despair, she had almost decided she would have to walk to the nearest town to see if she could find any food there, when she heard cautious footsteps on the gravel outside. She peered out. It was a Yankee cavalryman.

> He sat slouched in the saddle, a thick, rough-looking man with an unkempt black beard straggling over his unbuttoned blue jacket . . . . Little close-set eyes, squinting in the sun's glare, calmly surveyed the house from beneath the visor of his tight blue cap . . . . He slowly dismounted . . . .

Terrified, Scarlett's first impulse was to hide in the closet or crawl under the bed. But when she heard him making his way towards the kitchen where her household's meagre but precious meal – all they had left – stood in pots on the fire, she determined that – by God! – this was one Yankee who would do no more stealing.

Fetching her dead husband's heavy pistol and cocking it, she crept to the head of the stairs. The man was coming slowly up them with Scarlett's mother's sewing box in one hand and a pistol in the other.

> She wanted to cry: 'Put it down! Put it down, you dirty—' but the words would not come. She could only stare over the banisters at him and watch his face change from harsh tenseness to a half-contemptuous, half-ingratiating smile.
> 'So there is somebody ter home,' he said, slipping his pistol back into its holster and moving until he stood directly below her. 'All alone, little lady?'
> Like lightning, she shoved her weapon over the banisters and into the startled bearded face. Before he could even fumble at his belt, she pulled the trigger. . . . The man crashed backwards to the floor, sprawling into the dining-room with a violence that shook the furniture . . . two streams of blood crept across the shining floor, one from his face and one from the back of his head.
> Yes, he was dead. . . . She had killed a man.
> She stood there . . . every sound and scent magnified: the slight

rough rustling of the magnolia leaves, the far-off plaintive sound of a swamp bird and the sweet smell of the flowers outside the window.

A report by Sherman to Grant after the capture of Savannah shows that he was aware that sometimes his bummers had gone beyond the bounds of even the ruthless form of warfare he himself had planned. They had been 'a little loose in foraging', he admitted. They had done some things they ought not to have done. 'Yet they have supplied the wants of the army with as little violence as could be expected.'

Unfortunately, however, Scarlett was obviously not the only one to suffer. One Georgian woman begged a group of bummers who had found a few chickens under her house to leave them to her. 'No!' she wailed. 'They're all we've got left. They've been coming all day, stealing everything – but they said we could have those to keep my little ones alive!' These men were different. One of the foragers bowed and smiled when he told her, 'Madam, we're going to suppress this rebellion if it takes every last chicken in the Confederacy.' And the chickens were carted away.

Both Scarlett and the other Georgian lady were, exactly as Sherman had intended, feeling the 'hard hand of war'.

By May 1864, though Sherman's army was beginning its advance through Georgia, the invaders were still in Dalton in the northwest of the state. To people living in Atlanta Dalton was a very faraway place. Life went on much as before. In the first week of May, for example, there were eight grand balls held in Atlanta. The ladies of the capital danced all night at the balls and helped care for the wounded by day – for even then, wounded Confederate soldiers filled every hospital, every hotel and boarding house, and even many large private homes, too.

On Sundays people drove out, as if they were tourists, to see the trenches, breastworks and redoubts their slaves had built on the outskirts of the city to keep Sherman out.

Wagons and carriages full of girls and chaperones rode gaily out down Peachtree Road in search of woodland decorations for the bazaar which was to be held that evening at one of the hospitals . . . . One wagon, ahead of the others, bore four stout negroes with axes to cut evergreens and drag down the vines, and the back of this wagon was piled high with napkin-covered hampers, split-oak baskets of lunch and a dozen water-melons. Two of the black bucks were equipped with banjo and harmonica and they were rendering a spirited version of 'If You Want to Have a Good Time, Jine the Cavalry'. Everyone was riding down Peachtree Road to gather greenery and have a picnic and go melon cutting. Everybody, thought Scarlett, morosely, except me.

Still, slowly but surely, the battles Sherman fought against the Confederacy's General Joseph Johnston brought him nearer to his objective, Atlanta. No one in Atlanta believed that 'Old Joe' Johnston would ever let Sherman's Yankees into the city. That was an unthinkable nightmare.

Even so, Sherman's advance was marked with fights and skirmishes which, if small in scale, were still very bloody. They marked his progress like hideous milestones: Dalton, 9–13 May; Resaca, 14–15 May; Calhoun, 14 May; Adairsville, 17 May; Kingston, 18–19 May; New Hope Church, 25–27 May; Kenesaw Mountain, 10 June–2 July; Big Shanty, 8–9 June; Ezra Church, 20 July; Jonesboro, 31 August. Finally, the battles for Atlanta, which ended in its evacuation, began at 5 p.m. on 1 September 1864. After four months of deepening anxiety, the blissful drives down Peachtree, the picnics and the melon cutting ended in the roar of burning buildings and exploding shells. And soon Atlanta, one of the great cities of the Confederacy, evacuated by its soldiers and citizens, was dead: nothing but an abandoned, blackened shell.

Colin Campbell once again drove me erratically round northwest Georgia. We toured not only Cobb County but also a number of other counties, too: Walker County, for example, Chattooga County, Bartow and maybe Paulding as well. At any rate we seemed to be careening around the countryside of northwest Georgia for hours – one moment not far from Dalton, then passing a signpost pointing to Rome, then to Cartersville and Silver Creek; at least our contorted meanderings took us through some interesting country. Sherman, too, on his move southwest from Dalton had experienced – like us – 'much confusion'. 'We were all mixed up,' he confessed, and once he added, 'I slept on the ground, without cover, alongside of a log, got little sleep.' At daylight he resolved to renew a sharp little battle he had begun.

> I had come up in person, as my map showed that we were near an important crossroad called 'New Hope', from a Methodist meeting-house there of that name. I ordered General Hooker to secure it if possible that night . . . . The woods were so dense, and the resistance so spirited, that Hooker could not carry the position, though the battle was noisy and prolonged far into the night.

It was not far from New Hope Church that Colin and I came upon a site of a particularly appalling battle. Ambrose Bierce, who was present, was so shocked by the senseless killing that he memorialised it in a vivid piece of reporting to which he gave the title: 'The *Crime* at Pickett's Mill'.

The crime, Bierce wrote bitterly, was that imperfect accounts of an especially horrendous engagement were buried in the official reports of the victors. The battle is ignored by General Sherman in his memoirs; yet Sherman ordered it. General Howard wrote an account of the campaign of which it was a mere incident; and he dismissed it in a single sentence. Yet, as Bierce says, 'Howard planned it, and it was fought as an isolated and independent action under his eye.'

The horrific fight occurred on 27 May 1864, at a time when the armies of Generals Sherman and Johnston confronted each other near Dallas, Georgia. The place was Pickett's Mill.

When Colin and I approached Pickett's Mill on a gloomy morning 128 years later, a cold wind oozed thinly through tall bare pine trees. There was a cemetery for old cars near the battlefield, and near a dense wood of skeletal conifers was a sign that mysteriously warned, 'Intoxication Prohibited'. It was a suitably depressing site for a crime, all right.

The actual Mill was long since gone and we had to plunge down steep slopes through what was to all intents and purposes a wilderness, to arrive at the scene Bierce had described. The Union attack, he said, was to be made in column of brigades, Hazen's brigade of Wood's division leading.

> That such at least was Hazen's understanding I learned from his own lips during the movement, as I was an officer of his staff [Bierce goes on], but after a march of less than a mile an hour and a further delay of three hours at the end of it to acquaint the enemy of our intention to surprise him, our single shrunken brigade of fifteen hundred men was sent forward without support to double up the army of General Johnston. 'We will put in Hazen and see what success he has.' In the words of General Wood to General Howard we were first apprised of the true nature of the distinction about to be conferred upon us.

Hazen was a difficult commander; difficult in the sense that although he was a

> born fighter and an educated officer, his memory [says Bierce] was a terror to every unworthy soul in the service. His was a stormy life: he was in trouble all round. He was aggressive, arrogant, tyrannical, honorable, truthful, courageous – a skilful soldier, a faithful friend and one of the most exasperating of men.

'We will put in Hazen and see what success he has,' General Wood had said. He might have been talking of a terrier at the entrance to the sett of a ferocious badger.

With rising wrath Bierce went on in support of Hazen:

> For my commander and my friend, my master in the art of war, now unable to answer for himself, let this fact answer: when he heard Wood say they would put him in and see what success he would have in defeating an army – when he saw Howard assent – he uttered never a word, rose to the head of his feeble brigade and patiently awaited the command to go. Only by a look which I knew how to read did he betray his sense of the criminal blunder. The enemy had had seven hours in which to learn of the movement and prepare to meet it.

When the Union assault began, Hazen's men went in against two divisions of Confederate troops, one of which was commanded by Pat Cleburne, the outstanding Irish Confederate general whose men had blocked Sherman on Missionary Ridge at Chattanooga, when the rest of Braxton Bragg's army was dissolving in panic.

Colin and I descended carefully into the wood. And there, for the first time, although we at least had no opposing troops blasting away at us, we recognised the full horror of what Hazen's men must have experienced. For a start the terrain was a nightmare. That bleak morning we found ourselves teetering, slipping and stumbling up and down precipitous ravines; struggling uphill through almost impassable tangles of damp leaves and downhill through equally thick underwood. The field of Chickamauga had been bad enough – what with the feeling of claustrophobia induced by thick screens of trees and the actual physical pain of the stinging branches that snapped back across one's face. Here at Pickett's Mill claustrophobia was induced not only by the encircling trees, but by the menace of the dips and undulations of the ground; and by slippery earth ridges that seemed like steep muddy waves to be about to topple over and bury one beneath them.

Half the time Colin was out of my sight, hidden behind a ridge – and somehow this made my claustrophobia even worse; it certainly increased a sudden appalling sense of loneliness and isolation. It gave me plenty of time to imagine what Bierce and his wretched men had experienced.

> We moved forward [Bierce had written]. In less than one minute the trim battalions had become simply a swarm of men struggling through the undergrowth of the forest, pushing and crowding . . . . For the first two hundred yards our course lay along the left bank of a small creek in a deep ravine [perhaps the one I was now slipping

and sliding in], our left battalions sweeping along its steep slope. The general and staff and all the field officers toiled along on foot, as best they could. 'We shall halt and form when we get out of this,' said an aide-de-camp.

Then the second part of the nightmare in these woods hit Hazen's 1,500 men.

There came a ringing rattle of musketry, the familiar hissing of bullets, and before us the interspaces of the forest were all blue with smoke. Hoarse fierce [rebel] yells broke out of a thousand throats. The edge of our swarm grew dense and clearly defined as the foremost halted, and the rest pressed forward to align themselves beside them, all firing. The uproar was deafening; the air was sibilant with streams and sheets of missiles. In the steady, unvarying roar of small-arms the frequent shock of the cannon was felt rather than heard, but the gusts of grape which they blew into that populous wood were audible enough, screaming among the trees and cracking their stems and branches.

There was a field at the top of one muddy slope in the wood; it made a clear and welcome space that gently curved downhill away from these trees to others, equally dense, below it. It was curious. It reminded me of a certain field I had known in my youth in South Wales, a part of my grandfather's farm; its image printed in my mind as such familiar things are in extreme youth. It was a wide field, the haunt of hares at the right season of the year. I looked now for the telltale pairs of nervous, brown ears I could remember poking up over the short grass. But evidently there were no hares in this part of Georgia. All those decades ago, Bierce standing here had seen not hares but much worse things.

I had an unobstructed view of the open space across which the two lines fought. It was dim with smoke, but not greatly obscured: the smoke rose and spread in sheets among the branches of the trees. Most of our men fought kneeling as they fired, many of them behind trees, stones and whatever cover they could get, but there were considerable groups, which had endured the storm of missiles for moments without perceptible reduction, and would push forward, moved by a common despair, and wholly detach themselves from the line. In a second every man of the group would be down.

I could hear the cawing of crows hidden in the canopy of trees above my head, and I remembered now that Bierce had described the air as being 'full of noises'. Noises, mostly of the peculiar metallic ring of bursting shells, followed by the musical humming of their fragments; the rattle of musketry to the right and left; and the sigh and growl of it from the front. On my own, slipping and sliding on mud and wet leaves, and clambering laboriously over fallen trees that might have been deliberately laid across the path by a defending army, a great loneliness came over me.

Colin was still out of sight, although I could hear him floundering about, and the occasional snapping of a twig told me more or less where he was. And then a curious thing happened. I imagined I heard a strange rumbling. It was not unlike thunder, and it was certainly a thundery day. Yet there was no sign of rain and the wind was still quite cool. But a sound came to my ears very like the 'long deep sighing of iron lungs' which was how Bierce had described the noise of not so distant artillery.

I am not for a moment saying that somehow an echo of the old battle had returned to haunt me. I can only report that, stuck as I was in this wood, I heard a dull, distant sound, like the breathing of some great animal below the horizon, and that an absurd chill of fear mingled with the runnels of sweat that were already trickling down under my heavy wool shirt from my neck to the small of my back. 'The breathing of some great animal below the horizon': I repeated Bierce's words to myself. I had had no difficulty in memorising them – that was precisely the sound I thought I had heard.

Under my breath I told myself urgently, 'I must get out of this place.' And I lengthened my stride upward in the direction of the little museum building I had noticed as we came in. Below me, on either side of my narrow, slippery path, were deep ravines that once had been filled with frantically struggling men, some scrambling on hands and knees, their blue uniforms caked in mud and blood, desperate to climb out of those trenches of death, while in the background, behind the ring of grape and the metallic humming of ricochets, came the regular throbbing of the great guns – 'the pulse of the fever of battle'.

Bierce wrote that the horrific events at Pickett's Mill were just that – events that merged into those greater events of which they were part. Who now remembers Pickett's Mill? Who has written – apart from Bierce – about the terrible carnage of that day? What acts of heroism and devotion were performed there? Was it true, as someone has said, that you do not find courage where there is no danger and that love and compassion, too, may be products of active war? The battle occupied, after all, merely one day in four years of war in which such appalling bloodshed was a regular occurrence.

The Battle of Kenesaw Mountain was much like the Pickett's Mill, except that it was ten times worse. One hundred thousand Union troops caught in a storm of fire tried for three hours to drive about

From Sea to Shining Sea

40,000 Confederates off the ridge of a mountain that dominated the landscape for miles. The wretched Northerners, hopelessly trapped on the slopes of a heavily fortified hill, were forced to retreat in a crescendo of triumphant rebel yells, down its slippery slopes in wild disorder.

In those three hours Sherman lost more than 8,000 men to Johnston's 800, and in the end had gained not a foot of ground. Sherman was not normally one to own up to his mistakes, but he tacitly admitted he had made a terrible mistake here. 'The whole country,' he wrote, 'is one vast fort. The fighting is incessant, with a good deal of artillery fire . . . . Kenesaw is the key.' The area of the battle was called by his soldiers the 'Hell-Hole'. Sherman admitted that, too.

He could claim success, because in the single month of May he had steadily driven Johnston's Confederate army back from Dalton to Big Shanty through

> nearly a hundred miles of as difficult country as was ever fought over by civilised armies . . . . It is impossible to state accurately our loss of life and men in any one separate battle; for the fighting was continuous, almost daily, among trees and bushes, on ground where one could rarely see a hundred yards ahead.

Bierce himself was badly wounded in the head at Kenesaw Mountain. He went to hospital for a long time and later rejoined the Union army in Tennessee. Friends said that he was permanently embittered by his military experiences. It would be surprising if he had not been.

Reunited with Colin at the little museum, I felt a strange relief to be leaving that claustrophobic wood and its ravines. We drove rapidly to New Hope Church, gazed in awe from the crossroads there at the sinister saddle-shape of Kenesaw, and began a zig-zag, back-and-forth drive to follow the devious twists and turns to which Sherman's army had resorted to force Johnston back closer and closer to Sherman's objective, Atlanta. We stopped briefly at a sign advertising Gospel singing, Colin bought cigarettes at 'Billy's Convenience Store', and we sped erratically on. Marietta, Big Shanty, Smyrna, Dallas and Roswell cropped up one after the other on signposts on the way. Marietta I remember for the howling freight trains coming from Chattanooga which seemed to shunt back and forth through the centre of the town. Roswell I remember for fine mansions hiding behind formidable gates and for the muddy river called the Chattahoochee, the last natural barrier to Sherman's men on their road to Atlanta.

Sherman noted:

> We have pontoons enough for four bridges .... It is intensely hot,
> and a good many men have fallen with sunstroke .... From a hill
> just back of Vining's Station [near Smyrna where today the North-
> west Expressway crosses the Chattahoochee] I could see the houses
> of Atlanta 9 miles distant ... could observe the preparations for our
> reception the other side of the river, the camps of men and large trains
> of covered wagons ....

Here Sherman stumbled on some useful information:

> While I was with General Jeff. C. Davis, a poor negro came out,
> blanched with fright, and said he had been hidden under a log all
> day, with a perfect storm of shot, shells and musket-balls passing
> over him, until a short lull had enabled him to creep out and make
> himself known to our skirmishers, who in turn had sent him back
> to where we were. This negro explained that with about a thousand
> slaves he had been at work a month or more on these very enemy
> lines, which, as he explained, extended from the river about a mile.
> Therefore on the 5th of July we had driven our enemy to cover in
> the valley of the Chattahoochee and we held possession of the river
> for eighteen miles ....

By now, Atlanta's days were numbered.

Sherman does not mention a brutal incident at Roswell in his
memoirs, but one account of the Georgia Campaign gives the
text of Sherman's reply to a report from Brigadier-General Kenner
Garrard, the Union cavalry officer who captured Roswell and found
that retreating Confederate cavalry had burned the bridge across the
river. In revenge, Garrard had all buildings and factories in Roswell
torched in similar fashion – although he spared the fine old homes
in the place.

Sherman, hearing this, was seized with quite different ideas.
He ordered Garrard to

> arrest all people, male or female, connected with those factories,
> no matter what the clamor and let them foot it, under guard,
> to Marietta, whence I will send them by cars [railroad] to the
> North .... The women will make a howl. Let them take along all
> their children and clothing, provided they have the means of hauling
> it or you can spare them. We will retain them until they can live in
> peace and security.

Key adds that as a result, 'about four hundred Roswell citizens
were thus uprooted from the only homes they had ever known,
taken to Nashville, thence sent to Indiana. Many of them never
saw Georgia again.'

It was, as it were, a rehearsal for the forced evacuation of Atlanta a little later. In Sherman, the avid reader of Charles Dickens, there seems to have been a strong element of Bill Sykes.

Out of the blue, on our way back to Atlanta on Highway 41, Colin pointed out of my window.

'That looks worth a visit,' he said. I was surprised; all I could see on the other side of the highway was a shady-looking shack with one or two cars parked outside, and a sign which I couldn't read.

'We'll just stop there for a beer,' Colin explained.

'Fine,' I said. 'You're the boss.'

We made a U-turn as soon as we could, drove back and pulled into a narrow parking lot outside the shack. It had a wooden verandah which could have done with a lick of paint. The sign over it said 'Proud Mary's Dart Bar'. The silhouette of a dart divided the words into two.

Inside, several men stood at a long bar in semi-darkness. The Dart Bar, at first sight, had a most menacing look. You could hardly see one face before your own, for one thing, and darts seemed to be flying through the air thick and fast.

'Two Buds,' said Colin. I could have sworn he had suddenly acquired a Southern accent, a wise precaution in a dark atmosphere so thickly Georgian you could have cut it with a knife. When the bottles of Budweiser were dumped before us we took a closer look at the action.

The darts, for one thing, seemed reluctant to remain stuck into the dartboard, as most darts do. They dropped out as soon as they hit it, sometimes bouncing back menacingly towards the thrower. I began to wonder if we were going to see a player pinned to the ground by a dart through his foot. But the darts, hitting the board, lit up a numbered light; this, I saw, was how you scored. Evidently it was not a normal English dart game.

A player put his beer down on the bar.

'Y'all have a good 'un!' he said, making for the door.

Lurking in the shadows behind his counter, a barman raised a hand like a melon. 'Have a good 'un, y'heah!' he yelled in reply.

'What was that?' I asked Colin.

He repeated it, accent and all.

'Well, how do you spell it?' I asked, fumbling with my pencil and notebook in the near-dark.

'Wait till you see my column next Sunday,' he replied. 'That was pure Georgian.'

When I did see it I saw that Colin had spelt it exactly as I have written it above.

While I posed nervously for Colin's camera outside the Dart Bar, Proud Mary, a huge and determined-looking lady, followed us out. She was flexing biceps that would not have disgraced Arnold Schwarzenegger.

'Here's trouble,' I thought, and even Colin, normally cool, looked apprehensive. Mary had a massive frame, enclosed loosely in a purple sweater; also mighty forearms and jaw, and a shock of reddish hair. She looked Irish and it seemed to me she was in a fine fighting mood. I was wrong. To our relief, 'Proud Mary' Franklin turned out to be a charming person, delighted to hear that Colin was a newspaper columnist, and only too keen to point out that the darts – the ones flying apparently so lethally about the bar – were actually quite harmless. 'Y'see,' she said, 'there's absolutely no *steel* in their tips. Steel. Well, that *would* be dangerous, wouldn't it?'

'Have a good 'un, y'heah?' she roared genially as we sped away.

It had been a tough day. We had walked through Pickett's Mill, the 'Hell-Hole', and to top it all we had fearlessly entered Proud Mary's Bar. We had even risked a photograph outside it. By now it was evening, and we both thought we could do with something stronger than Budweiser beer. In Atlanta we found it.

Chapter 7

'They didn't know what they were fighting for, exactly, and they fought on anyway. That's what made them heroes.' When someone said that to me recently of the Federal troops in the Civil War, I thought: 'Well, if they were fighting under Sherman they would certainly have had a hard time finding out exactly what they were fighting for. The General himself did little to enlighten them.'

Sherman's pronouncements were legion and strongly expressed. Of course, in those days there was no TV, no video, no elaborate briefings, elucidations of policy or strategy as there were, for example, to help General Schwarzkopf explain his actions in the Gulf War more than a hundred years later.

One day, 'Cump' Sherman would say, 'If the people of the South had stood by the constitution I for one would have fought for the protection of the slave property.' And, 'I would not if I could abolish or modify slavery.'

On another, he wrote that when the war was won the problem before the country was not to 'enlarge the privilege of voting but gradually to curtail it – in order to have stability and security.'

He opposed the enrolment of blacks as soldiers, because those who held a sword would wield power at war's end. Power, he said, must be restricted to the whites. Above all, he maintained that the coloured race was different; 'A nigger is not a white man,' he said, 'and all the psalm-singing on earth won't make him so.' He had no use for abolitionists either or even John Brown. He even scorned democracy itself: '*Vox populi – Vox bunkum!*' he believed.

Yet Lincoln and the Republicans in the election of 1862 had adopted emancipation as a war policy. They did so again in 1864. Some at least of Sherman's soldiers must have been aware of that. But, with conflicting signals coming from the commanding general in Georgia, many more of them must have felt confused as to what the official 'politically correct' policy actually was.

The one belief Sherman held on to was the absolute necessity of preserving the Union. 'Man,' he said, 'must submit to an arbiter. He must not throw off allegiance to his government or his God without just reason or cause. The South had no cause – not even a pretext . . . .' To 'Uncle Cump', whatever else might stay in flux, the nation was bound together in an indivisible whole: let slavery come – or go.

Of course, Sherman was an eccentric – and he looked it. One historian has said he resembled a 'scrofulous vulture'; and the famous Civil Wartime photograph portrait by Matthew Brady makes him look just like that. His hair stands on end; his eyes have the 'half-wild expression', of which one contemporary reporter wrote, putting it down to 'the result of excessive smoking . . . . Sherman was never without a cigar'. Indeed, he scattered ash in all directions as he waved his arms and strode up and down, compulsively talking. He was tall 'and lank' someone said, 'built narrow and almost effeminate' with hair 'like thatch which he rubs up with his hands'. Everyone spoke of his incessant talking and laughing; and of what looked like his 'terrible cerebral excitement'. Some said he was the most American man they could imagine – 'the concentrated quintessence of Yankeedom'. Putting together the impression of numerous observers of Sherman, one gets an overwhelming impression of 'an explosive nervous energy and an almost manic elation'.

There were certainly people who at one time or another thought him literally crazy. It was an idea that stemmed from his odd behaviour in an episode in Sherman's military life shortly after the first Battle of Bull Run, when he was ordered to replace the general commanding in Kentucky. In this unsought-for position he began hysterically demanding from Washington thousands of reinforcements. At one point he shouted for 200,000 more men, an impossible number the government at that time could no more have provided than fly to the moon. Newspaper stories began appearing that Sherman had gone insane. He begged to be relieved and was sent home to rest. His wife was tortured by fears of his madness, for she knew that there was insanity in the family.

Yet after that break Sherman was able to pull himself together, and returned to the war. But even then, one brutally expressed obsession remained to him. 'To secure the safety of the Mississippi River,' he said, 'I would slay millions. On that point I am not only insane but mad.' The last sentence could have been written by S. J. Perelman and spoken by Groucho Marx.

Later, in one of his few references to this depressing time, 'Uncle Cump' expressed in these jocular, double-edged words his deep respect for his superior officer and sometimes tipsy mentor,

'General Grant is a great general. I know him well. He stood by me when I was crazy and I stood by him when he was drunk; and now, sir, we stand by each other always.'

Given his views on black civil rights, Sherman would not be very happy in Atlanta today. He might be tempted to let his soldiers get busy with their matches once more.

I found the city depressing in more ways than one. In the first place the centre of the city seems to be quite dead; for much of the time it was virtually empty except for the shambling presence of some possibly homeless, and evidently workless, blacks who may or may not have been on drugs. Their lurking, sinister presence, their apparent drug-addiction, their general air of destitution, matches inner ghettoes in other cities of America – Detroit, for example, and parts of New York. It is none the less gloomy for that.

Just as depressing was the sight, at the time I was there, of middle-class black students from the University of Georgia strolling about the city in T-shirts and baseball caps marked with the letter 'X'. This, of course, was a sign that they had seen a new movie biography of Malcolm X. Clearly they had decided to idolise Malcolm. Yet the 'X's were appearing in the city which produced Martin Luther King, Jnr, the city which honoured him with a Centre and a highway or two named after him. As well it might, I thought.

As one who had lived through the Civil Rights era of the early Sixties, I was puzzled. I asked Colin Campbell to put me in touch with a black reporter on the *Atlanta Constitution*. He did so, and I invited the reporter – a young black from Baltimore, whom I shall call John – to have lunch with me. 'Any place you like, John,' I told him, after explaining that I was an ageing British writer who had once marched with Martin Luther King.

'But I had better warn you. In exchange, I would like to ask you some questions. Some you might find stupid and others, I suppose, offensive. Will you take the risk?'

'Ask what you like,' he replied, cheerfully. 'I am impervious, if that is the word, to insult.'

When we met in a pleasant restaurant he chose near his office on Marietta Street, I explained that I was writing this book. Then I started with the questions.

'John, I see many black students here wearing "X" shirts. I realise they've seen the Malcolm movie and that for some reason they identify with Malcolm more, perhaps, than Martin. Okay, he's dynamic and streetwise and all that. But do these young men and women realise that Martin achieved a thousand times more for blacks than Malcolm? That before Martin began marching in Birmingham – and from Selma to Montgomery, Alabama, and elsewhere – no blacks at all in the South had a vote? And there were certainly no black sheriffs, or black mayors, or black police chiefs or black governors. Martin Luther King made all that possible. Do you find the young blacks of today are aware of that achievement? After all, it was a pretty colossal one.'

'Well, I think perhaps for the moment they've forgotten. It's a long time ago, you know.'

'I know thirty years goes back probably before you and they were born. But surely their parents were around then and they could tell them. And don't they themselves read history? John, it's thirty years ago, not three hundred.'

To me, as it happened, it seemed just the other day. I was a journalist for the *Observer* of London then, and as such I had accompanied the huge crowd of blacks and white liberals when they crossed the bridge on the road to Montgomery at Selma in 1965. Martin Luther King led the march from Brown's Chapel in Selma, and it took four days and nights. It was like a patrol through Vietcong-held country in Vietnam. Around us was a screen of federal marshals with the federalised National Guard of Alabama; the Army was with us, too; army helicopters buzzed overhead. White roughneck racists followed us, shaking fists and shouting obscenities, and a clever guy had put on a record of 'Bye-Bye, Blackbird' – well amplified – outside a music shop by the bridge. So we left Selma to catcalls, jeers and 'Bye-Bye, Blackbird': charming. Rednecks had been hanging about every evening under the shadows of trees that darkened the street leading to Brown's Chapel where the marchers were gathering.

'Hey, nigger-lover!' they shouted, 'Come here! Hey, come over here, nigger-lover.' Nobody went: murder lurked there under those trees, in those shadows. Before the march was over I forget how many people had been shot; one of them was a Northern woman, driving her car on the highway.

I didn't go into all those details with John. It wasn't necessary. He either knew them already, or wasn't interested.

True: it was thirty years ago. But how enormous Martin Luther King's achievement had been.

'What's the students' attitude to America now, John?'

'Well, they've turned their backs on Whitey's America. At least that's what they like to say.'

'John, you're not going to like this.'

'No, Gavin, I don't mind. Say anything. I can take it,' John was smiling.

'Well, you know, there is only *one* America. It's too bad maybe, but there is only *one*. And that one's Whitey's America; there is no other. A pity, but it's true. So if they're turning their beautiful black asses to Whitey's America, where are they turning their beautiful black faces?'

'To Africa, Gavin,' said John promptly. 'They say they're looking to Africa.'

Had all hard-won lessons of the last thirty years been ignored or just gone unheeded?

'John, look. Years ago, James Baldwin – you know Jimmy Baldwin – told the world that to his surprise, people in the Middle East and Africa considered a black American as American as any white. In fact, people said they regarded blacks as American as the whitest redneck racist from Mississippi or Texas. Don't these kids read books? You see, there's nowhere for them to *go* in Africa. Tell them that the only hope is for them to take a job with Save the Children or Oxfam – in Somalia or Rwanda or somewhere – and get to know Africa and the Africans that way.' I was making quite a speech. 'Tell your student friends that Africans take black Americans for just that – black Americans. *Not* Afro-Americans.'

I spread some butter on a piece of bread, and said, 'Sorry, John. Now I'm going to shut up.'

'Don't say sorry. This is interesting. You've been about the world, right?'

'Do you think I should give a lecture at Georgia University on these lines?' Naturally I wasn't serious. I couldn't imagine that anyone there would want to listen to this Ancient Briton whatever I had seen of the world.

John grinned: 'Not unless you want to start a riot.'

Depressed as I was, the thought that crusty old General 'Cump' Sherman would have been proud of me did nothing to cheer me up; Sherman had not marched through Georgia to free the negroes. Still, I thought of Martin Luther King and how in thirty years he had been half-forgotten by black students in his own home town.

I consulted Colin again.

I had remembered that by King's side as the demonstration crossed the bridge at Selma there had been a young black named Andy Young. Young, I know, had later served as President Jimmy Carter's Ambassador at the United Nations, had been American Ambassador in Nigeria, Mayor of Atlanta, and heaven knows what else besides. He was now in private practice in Atlanta working, Colin told me, with a prestigious engineering firm. That's where I went to see him. And in his office, I asked him what he thought of the depressing revelations provided for me by John.

He smiled and nodded. He'd heard it all before.

'You know,' he said, 'when I spoke out against the violence in Los Angeles that followed the Rodney King trial, I was condemned by many blacks here as an Uncle Tom. Well, it didn't worry me too much. They really can't make that one stick.'

Well, what, I said, *about* the obsession with Malcolm X? Who could compare Malcolm's with Martin's achievements for black people in America? In fact, had Malcolm done anything for them at all?

Young seemed unworried by those student attitudes.

'When one is young,' he said, 'one gets impatient with non-violent protests. They seem tame. One wants more action. Sometimes even with Martin, I, too, as a younger man wanted to go further and faster than he did. But he was right – and I was impatient and wrong.'

He sat forward in his leather armchair.

'Let me put it this way. It's rather like Britain between the wars. You know – Oxford and Cambridge. Students there voting not to defend king and country, whatever it was. And Auden and Isherwood and other middle-class kids becoming near-communists. Until, of course, eventually they reverted to basics: their middle-class anti-communism.'

He spread his hands.

'It's a bit like that. I think we'll find that in time these University of Georgia students will become good lawyers, engineers and doctors, and will join the mainstream of life in America. In due course, that is.'

In 1864, in the space of seventeen weeks, Sherman had moved his Union armies 100 miles south from Tennessee to Georgia's capital, Atlanta. Atlanta was impregnably defended by a series of twenty redoubts at prominent points around the city; they were connected by high breastworks and rifle pits revetted with heavy timber. These breastworks, in turn, were guarded by criss-crossed sharpened palings known as *chevaux de frise*, while in front of *these* were deep trenches. Although Sherman's troops outnumbered the Confederates by more than two to one, Sherman was not insane enough to tackle these defences head-on.

In fact, the battle for Atlanta was fought some distance from the city, which Sherman's army enveloped from three sides. The battle of Atlanta proper can fairly be said to have begun at the junction of Memorial Drive and Clay Street. And just as it did, the President of the Confederacy, Jefferson Davis, committed an error – which proved perhaps to be a fatal one for the South. He fired the

Confederate commander, General 'Old Joe' Johnston, the darling of the Confederate army in Georgia, and replaced him with a man far less well liked and admired, 'Fighting' General John Hood, despite threats by Johnston's staff to resign in a body.

Sherman's memoirs had this to say:

> At about 10 a.m., one of General Thomas's staff officers brought me a citizen, one of our spies, who had just come out of Atlanta, and had brought a newspaper of the same day containing Johnston's order relinquishing the command of the Confederate forces in Atlanta, and Hood's order assuming the command. I immediately inquired of General Schofield, who was his class mate at West Point, about Hood, as to his general character, etc., and learned that he was bold even to rashness and courageous in the extreme; I inferred that the change of commanders meant 'fight'.

As for Johnston, Sherman recorded his view on him that he was 'prudent' and 'cautious'. But on the next page of his memoirs, he was obliged to record something much closer to home: the death in action of one of his close friends, Major-General James McPherson, commanding officer of the Army of the Tennessee.

> McPherson was then in his prime [he wrote] about 34 years old, over six feet high, and a very handsome man in every way, was universally liked, and had many noble qualities . . . . The sound of musketry was heard, and McPherson's horse came back, bleeding, wounded, and riderless . . . . Within an hour an ambulance came in bearing McPherson's body. I had it carried inside and laid on a door wrenched from its hinges.

Sherman wept over the body of McPherson, and now there is a monument in Atlanta to the dead general. I arranged for a taxi to take me to see where it had been erected on the spot where McPherson was killed. The Sikh driver seemed determined to help me. But although for a longish time we drove up and down the tree-lined area of narrow back streets and single-storey houses in the appropriate suburb, we failed to find the memorial.

'We can try again tomorrow, sir,' said the driver, wagging his turbaned head sorrowfully. I thanked him and told him I wouldn't have time for that. I had to head east to Savannah – following Sherman again.

By the end of the first week of August 1864, 'Uncle Billy' had decided he must 'blitz' Atlanta – to shell it, make it uninhabitable, in fact to demolish it thus forcing the evacuation of its Confederate defenders.

When the blitz began the civilians of Atlanta were obliged to take refuge in bomb-proof cellars, much as the citizens of London did during the German aerial bombardment of the Second World War. One bombardment is as terrible as another to those compelled to endure one. There is not much variation. An eyewitness wrote this description of Atlanta under fire. He might have been describing London (or, I suppose, Sarajevo):

> All the fire of hell, and all the thunders of the universe seemed to be blazing and roaring over Atlanta. Shot and shell rained in every direction . . . . A shell crashed into a house on the corner of Elliott and Rhodes Streets, killing the superintendent of the Gas Company and his six-year-old daughter. Their bodies were frightfully mangled and they died instantly. A woman who was ironing some clothes in a house on Pryor Street was struck by a shell and killed. Solomon Luckie, a well-known Negro barber, was standing on the James Bank corner at Whitehall and Alabama, when a shell struck a lamp post, ricocheted and exploded. A fragment hit Luckie, fatally wounding him.
>
> A young lady, who was on her way to the car shed was struck in the back and fatally wounded. On Forsyth Street, a Confederate officer was standing in the front yard, taking leave of the lady of the house, when a bursting shell mortally wounded him and the lady's little boy . . . .

The bombardment continued despite furious protests to Sherman from General Hood. When the shelling finally stopped, it only did so because Sherman had decided to move south towards Macon. The Confederate defeat at Jonesboro was one result of this southward advance; the cutting of the Atlanta and West Point and the Macon and Western railroads was another, but the major one was that Hood now prepared to evacuate Atlanta. As a start, his soldiers blew up Confederate ammunition trains on the Georgia Railroad, and soon Marietta Street, as Franklin Garrett, a president of the Atlanta Historical Society, described it, was 'blue with Union soldiers, the Stars and Stripes flew over the city, and Sherman was ensconced in the handsome house of John Neal, on the present site of Atlanta's City Hall. From here he ordered the expulsion of the civilian population of Atlanta.'

Shortly before Sherman left Atlanta he ordered the final demolition of the city.

> Colonel Poe, United States Engineer, had been busy . . . . He . . . had levelled the great depot, roundhouse, and the machine shops of the Georgia Railroad, and had applied fire to the wreck. One of these machine shops had been used by the rebels as an arsenal, and in it were stored piles of shot and shell, some of which proved to be loaded, and that night was made hideous by the bursting of shells, whose fragments came uncomfortably near the house in which I was

quartered. The fire also reached the block of stores near the depot, and the heart of the city was in flames all night, but the fire did not reach the parts of Atlanta where the court house was or the great mass of dwelling houses.

Strangely enough, it didn't take some devoted Atlantans long to go straggling back through the ruins.

'. . . how silly of them to come back if there aren't any houses!' said Scarlett O'Hara in *Gone With The Wind*, watching them creep back.

> 'Miss Scarlett [she was told], they're living in tents and shacks and log cabins and doubling up six and seven families in the few houses still standing . . . . Now, Miss Scarlett, don't say they are silly. You know Atlanta folks as well as I do, stubborn as mules about Atlanta.'
>
> Scarlett nodded, a grim pleasure and pride in her adopted town filling her. It was a pushy, impudent place and that was why she liked it. It wasn't hidebound and stick-in-the-muddish like the older towns and it had a brash exuberance that matched her own. 'I'm like Atlanta,' she thought. 'It takes more than Yankees or a burning to keep me down.'

Early on the morning of 16 November 1864 Sherman left what remained of Atlanta and its population to start his march to the sea. The march was well planned, and, as before, the idea was to live entirely off the land. So his soldiers spread out to a front of 40 miles and proceeded, as they had become expert in doing, to tear up every inch of railroad track and burn every railroad station they went through. Uncle Billy's 'bummers' – Scarlett had shot one dead at Tara – looted farms, as usual, and pillaged private houses, destroying magnificent tapestries, pictures, pianos and furniture; stealing and shooting cattle, pigs, sheep and poultry as if they were Visigoths on the way to sack Rome. This presumably is what Sherman meant when he said he would 'smash things to the sea'. After all, he was a man who meant what he said.

Moving east on the Decatur road, he wrote,

> We naturally paused to look back on the scenes of our last battles . . . . Behind us lay Atlanta, smouldering and in ruins, the black smoke rising high in the air, and hanging like a pall over the ruined city. Away off in the distance, on the McDonough road, was the rear of General Howard's column, the gun barrels glistening in the sun, the white-topped waggons stretching away to the south; and right before us the Fourteenth Corps, marching steadily and rapidly, with a cheery look and swinging pace, that made light of the thousand miles that lay between us and Richmond [Virginia]. Some band, by accident, struck up the anthem of 'John Brown's soul goes marching

on'; the men caught up the strain, and never before or since have I heard the chorus of 'Glory, glory, hallelujah!' done with more spirit, or in better harmony of time and place . . . .

Atlanta was soon lost behind the screen of trees, and became a thing of the past. Around it clings many a thought of desperate battle, of hope and fear, that now seem like the memory of a dream; and I have never seen the place since.

Of the march to Savannah, Sherman wrote next:

Even the common soldiers caught the inspiration, and many a group called out to me as I worked my way past them, 'Uncle Billy, I guess Grant is waiting for us at Richmond!' Indeed the general sentiment was that we were marching for Richmond, and that there we should end the war; nor did they measure the distance, or count the cost in life, or bother their brains about the great rivers to be crossed, and the food required for man and beast, that had to be gathered by the way . . . . [But] I had no purpose to march direct for Richmond by way of Augusta and Charlotte, but always designed to reach the sea-coast first at Savannah.

Unlike those glorious ones of Sherman, the memories of the people of Atlanta who had clung to their smouldering city were simply a nightmare of shelling and burning. It is estimated that only about 400 out of 5,000 dwellings were left by the time Sherman had finished with it. The scene in *Gone With The Wind* in which Clark Gable drives Vivien Leigh in a carriage against a background of flaming buildings was not far from the truth. To the Mayor of Atlanta and his city council Sherman left a long message, in which was embedded the following warning: 'You might as well appeal against the thunderstorm as against the terrible hardships of war. They are inevitable.' He went on to say that the people of Atlanta could only hope to live in peace and quiet at home once more if they stopped the war and admitted that it had been begun 'in error' and was being perpetuated 'in pride'.

The Sherman credo was then set out: 'We don't want your negroes, or your horses, or your houses, or your lands, or anything you have, but we do want and will have a just obedience to the laws of the United States.' And leaving those words to frizzle the councilmen's ears, Sherman turned his back on them.

With one aspect of his troops' prowess Sherman was particularly delighted: this was their lightning ability to repair railroads damaged by the rebels.

He wrote proudly:

The rebels had struck our railroad a heavy blow [on the long march to Atlanta from Chattanooga] burning every tie, bending the rails for eight miles from Big Shanty above Acworth, so that the estimate for repairs called for thirty-five thousand new ties and six miles of iron. A thousand men were distributed along the break to replace the ties . . . and in about seven days the road was all right again . . . . So [the enemy] supposed that we had men and money without limit, and that we always kept on hand, distributed along the road, duplicates of every bridge and culvert of any importance.

Sherman went on,

A good story is told of one who was on Kenesaw Mountain during our advance of the previous June. A group of rebels lay in the shade of a tree, one hot day, overlooking our camps about Big Shanty. One soldier remarked to his fellows:

'Well, the Yanks have to git up and git now, for I heard General Johnston himself say that General Wheeler had blown up *the tunnel* near Dalton, and that the Yanks would have to retreat, because they could get no more rations.'

'Oh, hell!' said a listener, 'don't you know that ol' Sherman carries a *duplicate* tunnel along?'

Sherman rode a horse to Savannah. I took a bus. The second day out, he passed through

the handsome town of Covington, the soldiers closing up their ranks, the colour-bearers unfurling their flags. The white people came out of their houses to behold the sight, in spite of their deep hatred of the invaders, and the negroes were simply frantic with joy. Whenever they heard my name, they clustered about my horse, shouted and prayed in their peculiar style, which had a natural eloquence that would have moved a stone.

There was another, far less joyful side to Sherman's progress. The 'bummers' were active. On a plantation nearby,

a soldier passed me with a ham on his musket, a jug of sorghum-molasses under his arm, and a big piece of honey in his hand, from which he was eating and, catching my eye, he remarked *sotto voce* and carelessly to a comrade, 'Forage liberally on the country', quoting from my general orders. On this occasion, as on many others that fell under my personal observation, I reproved the man, explained that foraging must be limited to the regular parties properly detailed, and that all provisions thus obtained must be delivered to the regular commissaries to be fairly distributed to the men who kept their ranks.

Sherman must have known that many things – much worse things – were occurring that did not 'fall under his personal observation'. As a Union officer noticed, such 'things had occurred without number

84

already, and would continue to occur until the end of his march. So that, in a phrase which he himself liked to use, he could tell that segment of his memoirs to the marines.'

Indeed, Sherman half admits to his soldiers' misdemeanours:

> Often I was amused at the strange collections – mules, horses, even cattle, packed with old saddles and loaded with hams, bacon, bags of cornmeal, and poultry of every character and description . . . . No doubt, many acts of pillage, robbery, and violence were committed by the 'bummers'; for I have since heard of jewelry taken from women . . . . But [he adds] I never heard of any cases of murder or rape.

In Covington, from the windows of my bus I had more peaceful views and experiences. All I saw was a Chevrolet sales yard, a shopping mall, fast food outlets. And an ad in a window for pumpkin pies for $2.50.

The bus missed Milledgeville altogether, the town where Sherman had halted on a cold, raw afternoon, to take a gulp of whiskey from a flask brought by his orderly, and to light a cigar. Near the town, after supper, something rather touching occurred. He was sitting astride a chair, with his back to a fire, when he became aware that an old negro was scanning his face, holding a tallow candle close to it.

> I inquired [he recalled], 'What do you want, old man?' The old negro answered, 'Dey say you is Massa Sherman.' I answered that such was the case, and again inquired what he wanted. He said he only wanted to look at me, and kept muttering, 'Dis nigger can't sleep dis night.' I asked him why he trembled so, and he said that he wanted to be sure that we were in fact 'Yankees'.

Travelling in our bus by a more northern route, we passed a large expanse of flowering cotton. The fields were snow-white with the cotton which was being picked by towering machines. Cotton in Georgia, I had heard, had slumped towards the turn of the century; only now was it making a comeback. But there was a difference now in the method of gathering it and bagging it. Now, I saw that most of the men on the machines were black; and the people working manually in the fields were Latinos – Mexicans, I suppose – legal or illegal, who knew? As for the whites – were they wearing white collars and keeping the books in a cool office in Augusta? Again, who knew?

Near Savannah, Sherman came across a young Union officer who had been blown off his horse by a torpedo planted in the road. The horse had been killed instantly, and a surgeon was preparing to amputate the officer's leg. 'This was not war, but murder,' wrote Sherman later, 'and it made me very angry.' So angry that he immediately ordered a lot of rebel prisoners to be brought up, and made them march in close order along the road so as to explode their own torpedoes or to dig them up. 'I could hardly help laughing at their stepping so gingerly along the road,' he said, 'where it was supposed sunken torpedoes might explode.' This, to him, evidently was *not* murder, this was war.

Soon, however, he himself was under fire.

> I saw a white puff of smoke and caught sight of a [cannon] ball as it rose in its flight, and finding it coming straight, I stepped a short distance to one side, but noticed a negro very near to me in the act of crossing the track at right angles. Someone called to him to look out; but, before the poor fellow understood his danger, the ball (a 32-lb. roundshot) struck the ground, and rose in its first ricochet, caught the negro under the right jaw, and literally carried away his head, scattering blood and brains about.

The Confederate garrison of Savannah, under a 'competent soldier' (according to Sherman) called General William J. Hardee, decided not to defend the beautiful town and withdrew his troops from it. And so Savannah was spared the dreadful fate of Atlanta.

Entering the city, Sherman himself rode at once to the Pulaski Hotel, expecting to make his headquarters there. Instead he met a wealthy English cotton broker, Charles Green, who offered him his house. 'If you don't take it,' he said, 'some other general will. I much prefer you.' So Sherman moved into a comfortable suite on the second floor of the Green house, with a bedroom and a magnificent bathroom, and it was from there that he sent his famous present to Abraham Lincoln.

'I beg to present to you,' said his message to the President, 'as a Christmas gift, the city of Savannah, with one hundred and fifty heavy guns and plenty of ammunition, also about 25,000 bales of cotton.'

On Christmas Day, Sherman entertained to dinner a party of twelve people, including Charles Green. Three or four 'lovely turkeys' had been foraged for the victorious general, and hampers of wine were provided by merchants thankful that Sherman had saved their stocks from marauding soldiers and looters. The General was clearly in a good mood. It was even rumoured that in the midst of the jollifications a bold local bishop had dared to ask Sherman's permission to pray for the rebel cause at Christmas. 'Hell, yes,' Sherman was said to have replied, laughing. 'Jeff Davis and the Confederate government need all the prayer they can get.'

While Sherman ate turkey, most of the victorious Unionist soldiers made do with more commonplace fare. Breakfast: rice and beef. Dinner: rice. Supper: beef and rice. 'Rice is our favourite dish now,' a melancholy soldier of the 101st Illinois wrote home. One can't help thinking that those Illinois soldiers must have been singularly lacking in imagination. Other units sensibly drove their wagons to the river and loaded them with oysters; and then ate them fried, roast, in soup and on the half shell. 'A little top-heavy on oysters,' their colonel laughed. 'But we're not complaining.'

I moved at evening into a smart bed-and-breakfast place: a modernised mansion in old Savannah. At the earliest opportunity – that very evening of my arrival – I walked up through the beautiful, shadowy, tree-lined squares of Savannah towards the river. On the way I stopped among the trees to gaze at Sherman's old headquarters, the Charles Green house. The house looked as stately as ever, and stood next to a church. Quite reasonably at this hour, it was closed and dark. If I wanted to see it I was going to have to call again in the morning.

In the riverside part of the city I came across a place that no one had told me of, but which I was delighted to find so soon. This was 'Hard-Hearted Hannah's Bar', and when I had bought myself a drink in it, I found that it had a fine pianist called Emma Kelly who, although no longer young, evidently had what they used to call a 'golden heart'. Immediately I asked for it, she sang the song after which the bar was named. I knew it of old. I had heard it many times in New York, and had even met at Sag Harbor a well-known journalist called Shana Alexander, who is the daughter of the man who admittedly wrote it sometime in the 1920s. This was not Johnnie Mercer, who came from Savannah and is honoured by the city fathers who have named one or two streets after him – but quite a different man called Milton Ager.

The song – preferably accompanied by a jazzy lilt on a piano – goes:

> In old Savannah, I said, Savannah,
> The weather there is nice and warm;
> The climate's of the southern brand,
> But here's what I don't understand:
> They've got a gal there, a pretty gal there,
> Who's colder than an arctic storm;
> Got a heart just like a stone;
> Even ice-men leave her alone:
>
> They call her
> Hard-Hearted Hannah, the Vamp of Savannah,
> The meanest gal in town;

> Leather is tough but Hannah's heart is tougher;
> She's a gal who loves to see men suffer!
>   To tease 'em and thrill 'em
>   To torture and kill 'em
>   Is her delight they say, –
> An ev'ning spent with Hannah sitting in the easy chair
> Is like trav'lin' through Alaska in your underwear;
> She's Hard-Hearted Hannah, the Vamp of Savannah,
>   the Vamp of Savannah,
>   GA.

That was the version I knew. Emma Kelly added a couple of lines of her own:

> Talk about your refrigerated mammas
> Brother! She's the polar bear's pyjamas!

I liked those extra lines so much that I wrote them down.

I was still humming the tune to myself when next day I went to call on the Green house, although needless to say the song had nothing on earth to do with General Sherman.

The Green house was a grand place, all right. Sherman's second-floor suite was so spacious and comfortable, he must have left it with reluctance to resume his long, hazardous march northwards through the Carolinas and then into Virginia to witness the defeat of Robert E. Lee's forces there. Shown over the Green mansion by one or two elderly ladies of Savannah who made it their business to look after tourists like me, I asked one of them if General Sherman had used the next-door church when he was here – particularly over Christmas.

'Perhaps there's a plaque – ?'

'Ah don't imagine, Mr Young,' she answered sharply, 'that *Mister* Sherman was much of a church-goin' man.'

I noticed the emphasis on the '*Mister* Sherman' and the frost in her Southern voice. But she quickly smiled – she wasn't going to allow a moment's irritation to let her spoil a welcome for a British tourist in Georgia.

As a matter of fact, Sherman's two months' occupation of Savannah was quite different from his brutal treatment of Atlanta. Here he posted guards on civilian property, and looting was minimal; there was a curfew, too; and soldiers sleeping in camps outside town were allowed to enter Savannah only on a pass. Sherman himself said, 'No city was ever occupied with less disorder. Women and children walk in the streets with as much security as they do in Philadelphia.' And the Confederate city mayor helped maintain law and order by warning his co-citizens, 'Where resistance is hopeless it is criminal to make it'.

After two months, Sherman finally marched out of an intact and peaceful city to wreak havoc further north – rampaging to the victory that finally ended the war.

I took the bus back to Atlanta.

It might seem hard to be attracted to a man like Sherman – to such a dour soldier – yet even a discriminating man like Edmund Wilson in his fine study of the Civil War, *Patriotic Gore*, called him 'likeable' if 'harsh'.

There was a gentler side to Sherman, after all. He was an amateur painter in watercolours; he knew *Hamlet* by heart and *Coriolanus*, too. And he read and re-read Dickens.

Of course, Sherman obviously had a ruthless side – and his contradictions. He loathed the disloyalty of the rebels, and a demon possessed him to lay waste the disloyal, rebellious Confederacy, and to say to Grant, 'I can make the march, and make Georgia howl!' As Wilson said, Sherman was indifferent to God, and felt the 'ecstasy' of the lust to dominate 'which makes people see themselves as instruments of history'. He could laugh when a Union general deliberately spoke of a place called Barnwell as 'Burnwell'. At the same time he believed that 'slave labour is of great value and cannot be dispensed with'.

This strange and gifted man retired from the army in 1884, a year before Grant died of cancer. From then on, Sherman was regularly propositioned by both Republicans and Democrats to run for the presidency himself. He refused to entertain any such idea with all the ferocity he had shown in the conduct of the war. 'I will not accept if nominated and will not serve if elected,' he said in a famous phrase. And went on:

> I would count myself a fool, a madman, an ass, to embark anew at 65 years of age, in a career that may, at any moment, become tempest-tossed by the perfidy, the defalcation, the dishonesty or neglect of any one of a hundred thousand subordinates utterly unknown to the President of the United States.

And he added that to become President 'would kill any man of sensibility in a year'. From which one can see that Uncle Cump had no respect whatsoever for politicians or bureaucrats.

Instead, he attended numerous parades of veterans and gave old soldiers liberal handouts out of his own pocket. In speeches to veterans' groups his message was always the same: 'War is hell!' And he could be a wit, saying: 'I think we understand what military fame is. To be killed on the field of battle, and have our names spelled wrong in the newspapers.'

He criss-crossed the country, making a name for himself as a brilliant after-dinner speaker rivalled only by Mark Twain. From time to time, too, in some provincial theatre, he would spring up in the front row of the stalls, stop the performance and, with his knowledge of *Hamlet*, redirect, as it were, an entire scene – to the embarrassment of all concerned.

Towards the end, Sherman chose to live in New York, often attending the theatre, and he rapidly became known as a regular first-nighter. In 1886 he and his friend Edwin Booth, the actor, founded the Players' Club in Gramercy Park. It didn't matter that Edwin Booth was the brother of John Wilkes Booth, who earlier had assassinated Sherman's commander-in-chief, Abraham Lincoln. ('We try not to mention *his* name too often,' murmured the club's secretary when I went to see him.) Inspired by the Garrick Club in London, the idea of the Players' Club was to enable actors – members of a somewhat despised profession in those days – to meet businessmen and people well connected in better-respected spheres of activity. Sherman, himself widely lionised – by the theatrical set as well as by leaders of New York society – made it his mission to bring all of them together. He lived in a large house at 75 West 71st Street where he frequently went to ground, hermit-like, in order to be able to read in peace his beloved Shakespeare, Dickens and Robert Burns.

It is said that Sherman became more youthful as time went on; that women continually chased after him. At least he lost his 'scrofulous vulture' look, and later photographs of him show a plumper, less wrinkled and more benign face. The Sherman mouth retains its tight, wide, intimidating line, but the whole demeanour of the old general has become much more genial.

Did that mean that deep down he would have echoed the noble phrase of a later, victorious American general, Dwight D. Eisenhower, that 'humility must always be the portion of any man who receives acclaim earned in the blood of his followers and the sacrifices of his friends'? One wonders, too, if, in old age, 'Uncle Cump' was still 'talking up a storm', gesticulating and striding up and down, scattering cigar ash over the ladies and gentlemen he now consorted with as he had done over his officers in camp. Did he talk much of his experiences on the road to Atlanta, of the days when he was slim and making Georgia howl, and on his way to eternal fame?

What thoughts he had to distract him in later life.

Sitting in the studio for his head to be modelled by the sculptor

Augustus Saint-Gaudens for the equestrian statue that was erected in 1903 on the corner of 5th Avenue and 59th Street, did Uncle Billy's mind wander back to the day he had turned aside in the nick of time on the road to Savannah to avoid the cannonball he had seen coming straight at him – the one that blew the head off the poor negro almost within touching distance? Did he think of the victory parade in a Washington still draped and with its grog shops closed in mourning for the murdered Lincoln? Did he remember himself there – 'Uncle Billy' in the spanking new uniform – a phenomenon which had astonished soldiers accustomed to seeing him in old shabby campaign clothes at Dalton, Marietta, Atlanta or Madison? Surely he was proud to recall the victory march-past of 'Sherman's wolves', as his veterans were now nicknamed because they had looked so lean and hungry? Surely he must have remembered the bursts of wild cheering rising from the ranks of his beloved regiment of 'bummers' and looters, the survivors of Resaca, Pickett's Mill, and Kenesaw Mountain, as they snaked round the Capitol beneath banners proclaiming, 'Welcome to the heroes of the Republic. Honor to the Brave!'?

Sherman died aged seventy-one on 14 February 1891, at home in his rocking-chair rereading Dickens's *Great Expectations* for the hundredth time.

It is not recorded what page he had reached before the book slipped from his lap and joined the unfinished cigar on the carpet. It is a pity. I would like to know if he was still with Joe Gargery and Mr Pumblechook, or whether he had reached the point in the book when Magwitch had begun to turn Pip into a gentleman. Perhaps it doesn't matter. The march through Georgia lives in Sherman's own lively memoirs, and in a thousand other books about the Civil War. The statue stands there – over-gilded, it is true, but proud – with the general, uncharacteristically sashed and upright, hat clutched in his gauntleted hand.

Uncle Billy (or Uncle Cump) died of what might have been asthma or pneumonia, and the drama of his existence did not end with his death.

At his funeral Sherman's old Confederate opponent in Georgia, General Joe Johnston, stood bareheaded in the crowd as an honorary pallbearer. Urged by friends to wear a hat on such a cold day, the eighty-two-year-old soldier answered, 'If I were in his place, and he were standing here in mine, he would not put on his hat'. Ten days later the old Confederate general was himself dead of pneumonia.

William Tecumseh Sherman became commanding general of the Army in 1869, having declined two offers to become Secretary of War. He thus became the boss of the commander of the Division of the Missouri, General 'Little Phil' Sheridan, which is why I was to run into echoes of Sherman a good many months later when I came to visit Montana and the Little Bighorn battlefield where Sheridan's subordinate, Lieutenant-Colonel George Armstrong Custer, and his men were massacred by Crazy Horse.

Of course, I was to actually see Sherman on his favourite horse, Ontario, many times before and after that, at the corner where Central Park meets 5th Avenue. That Sherman – the one outside the Plaza Hotel – is a noble representation. Immaculate in a cloak that flows off his shoulders like the cloak of a victorious Roman general, he rides there on the edge of the trees, as proud as a golden peacock among the buggies, the pigeons, the sparrows and the horse droppings.

When I stand there and think of his strange career and even stranger personality, of his vainglorious boast that he could 'whip the creation', I find it hard to take my eyes off him. Was this glittering figure the scruffy, wide-eyed general his officers at Atlanta had described – the gesticulating neurotic who paced up and down puffing furiously at his cigar, shooting smoke from his mouth like pistol fire, drumming his fingers on the window-sill, and restlessly rubbing his hair upwards with both nervous hands? It was; but it was hard to believe.

Part Three

'Remember the Alamo!'

'Who will come with Old Ben Milam into San Antonio?'

BENJAMIN RUSK MILAM, 1830

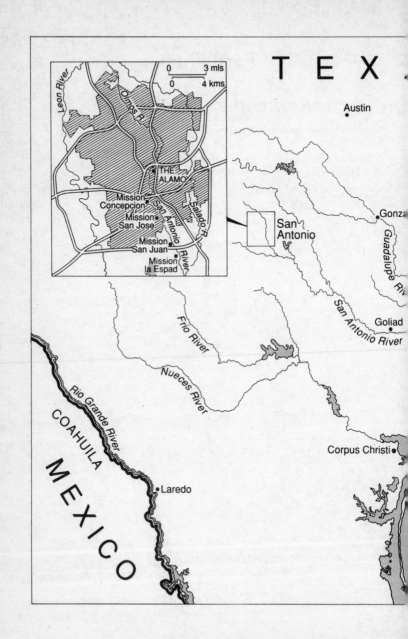

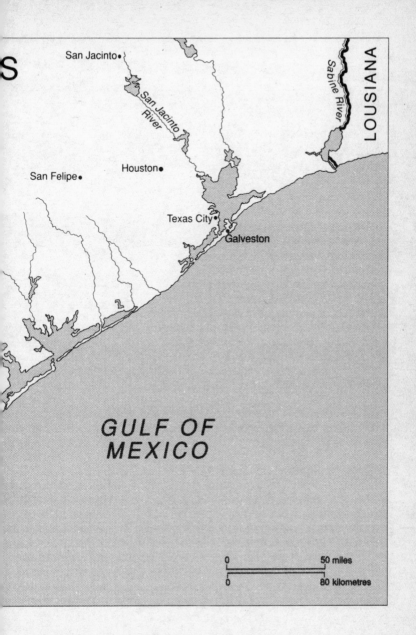

Chapter 8

'Who will come with old Ben Milam into San Antonio?'

The cry has a romantic ring to it; like something from Macaulay or Byron. I think even I would have responded, 'I will!' to old Ben Milam's call, and ridden off with him to the Alamo, waving a battered sombrero and yelling 'Yippee!' and 'Yahoo!'. It was a time, after all, of inspired patriotism.

When I actually did reach the Alamo one recent Christmastime, I surprised myself by being immensely impressed. It was almost like arriving at Christmas in somewhere very old and heavy with mystique, like Bethlehem. Subtly lit by concealed lights, the mission building itself looked distinctly otherworldly – at any rate much, much older than it really is.

Hung about with fairy lights, a 20-foot tree stood outside the Alamo's chapel, and the chapel's white barley-sugar pillars and delicately decorated doorway were themselves softly illuminated. One had the impression one was contemplating the façade of some ancient church in the Holy Land or some old church in Spain. A sign by the tree said 'Feliz Natividad', and the nearby shops were crowded. There were only ten more shopping days to Christmas.

I sat on a bench in the Plaza and tried to relive what I had learned of the battle. Because of the holiday crush, it was not easy.

Jostled by tourists and their flashing cameras, I found it hard to imagine the thunder of the Mexican and Texan cannon that nearly 157 years ago had turned this once remote and placid Catholic mission into a bloody inferno. Or to think one heard the shouts of the Mexican troops as they swarmed ('like sheep', an eyewitness had said) up their scaling ladders and poured through breaches their cannonballs had made in the walls of the Alamo compound, while a Texan defender shouted to his wife, 'Great God, Sue, the Mexicans are inside our walls!'

As I say, with the Christmas crowds around me, it was barely possible to imagine these pitiful scenes. Or to visualise the mutilated corpse of Davy Crockett huddled – just over *there* – by the Alamo chapel, where a Mrs Dickinson, one of the few survivors of the massacre, claimed to have seen him. His buckskin vest was slashed to shreds by Mexican bayonets, she said, and his peculiar coonskin cap had fallen to the ground by his side.

At the same moment to my left, in a small room in the Long Barracks, James Bowie had lain miserably shivering in his cot, with pneumonia in his lungs and whiskey on his breath. His pistol and his famous knife lay close at hand as he waited for the Mexican infantrymen to burst through the door and end it all. And what an end. He would shoot and stab one or two. Then they would impale him on their bayonets and toss him up and catch him on their points again 'like a farmer does a bundle of fodder with a pitchfork'. And so they played with him until he died.

I had shamefully confessed to Maury Maverick over drinks – grapefruit juice for him, whiskey for me – on my first evening in San Antonio, that when my Delta flight touched down there coming from New York and Fort Worth I was still under the impression that the Alamo was a *river*.

I saw the scene quite clearly in my mind's eye: a dusty plain dotted here and there with dried-up trees and occasional thrusting fingers of cactus; Mexican peasants in hats with wide brims slumped in the shade of a huddle of flat-roofed adobe buildings like clusters of somnolent mushrooms; and, standing unsteadily in a cantina, other sombreroed, mustachioed men with pistols on their hips and bandoliers across their chests, shouting impatiently in Spanish for mescal. Above all, I imagined the river – the Alamo, surely – a snake of muddy water, sluggishly carving a narrow ravine through San Antonio and the wastes of southern Texas towards the Gulf of Mexico.

Well, I had never been to Texas.

Once in the dim past I had seen a film about the famous battle. Called simply *The Alamo*, the movie had starred John Wayne, but I hadn't the faintest idea who else was in it. Nor could I recall what happened, except that there was a lot of noise and shouting and a lot of oddly dressed people dying in heaps.

That was a film, I suppose, of the Fifties or early Sixties. No doubt if I could have remembered Wayne himself in a racoon-skin cap I would have guessed that Davy Crockett – 'King of the Wild Frontier' in the words of a popular 1950s song – was somehow involved in the bloody affair; an episode which – this much, for some reason, I *did* know – led to the separation of Texas from

Mexico and its eventual incorporation into the United States of America.

But after all this time I had no recollection whatever of what Wayne wore on his head. For all I knew, it might have been a cowboy's felt stetson or a cocked hat covered with osprey plumes. Was he commanding a troop of the United States cavalry? If so, surely he had *won* the battle. After all, he was John Wayne.

Maury Maverick listened to my shameless confession of ignorance quite calmly, looking a bit like a gnarled version of Spencer Tracy. He sipped his grapefruit juice ('I haven't had a drink in fifteen years,' he told me) and smiled forgiveness, screwing an eyeglass into his left eye.

'I can assure you this eyeglass is not an affectation,' he said. 'I can see very little without it. Nevertheless, even without it, I can see I shall have to set you straight on the Alamo.'

Maury Maverick was now the best-known newspaper columnist in southern Texas. It was appropriate that he should be. The Mavericks were part of the place; they had, as it were, grown up with Texas.

'Sam Maverick, my great-grandfather,' Maury said, 'was the only Yale graduate in the Texan Revolution. He was one of three men who took the surrender of all the Union forces in Texas in the Civil War.'

More than that, he had contributed his name to the English language. Surely most people know what a 'maverick' is.

'See, properly speaking, old Sam Maverick was a real-estate man. He made money and apart from that was also probably well rewarded in kind for his services to the state of Texas. So he ended up with a hell of a lot of land and a hell of a lot of cattle. So many cattle in fact that he didn't give a damn about branding 'em. Just let them roam about at will. Maybe some of them roamed clean away. He wouldn't have known. And I dare say he wouldn't have cared.'

'So at first, a maverick was an animal; a steer wandering about at will? Unbranded. Unlabelled.'

'You've got it.'

It had been a short step, he said, from that to applying the term to any independent-minded human being who abhorred a label of any kind, someone who preferred to meander about in life as the passing whim took him.

Maury went on, 'And it went round the globe, that term "maverick". Texan cattle were being exported just about everywhere, and the ships' captains who transported them and the cattlemen who handled them all over the Western world generally took to talking about "mavericks" when in the way of business they mentioned my great-grandfather's animals. So it caught on. Now, of course, you find the word in every dictionary.'

Maury is a bit of a 'maverick' himself. Having fought the Japanese as a Marine in the exceptionally bloody battle of Guadalcanal in the Solomons, he later became a more than competent lawyer – a liberal and a particularly bold one at that. During the Vietnam War, for example, of which, perhaps surprisingly for an ex-Marine, he strongly disapproved, he had taken it upon himself to defend in court a number of young Texan conscientious objectors – and had won some notable successes.

It must have taken considerable courage for a Democrat Texan lawyer to defend young Texans, no doubt contemptuously categorised by many in that state as 'draft dodgers'. Particularly during a war being waged by the administration of a Democrat Texan President, Lyndon Johnson.

'I was not the most popular man in the state at the time,' Maverick admits, adding ruefully, 'L.B.J. was disappointed in me.'

I wondered if, in that time of passionate national disagreement, this evident 'dove' might have been physically threatened by Vietnam 'hawks' or even beaten up on his way from court. No, he said, that hadn't happened. And it says something for the tolerance of newspaper publishers and readers of Texas that in the 1992 Bush–Clinton presidential campaign, Maury had been free to continue writing his weekly liberal, pro-Democrat column in a newspaper that on the whole favoured President Bush's re-election.

'I tell you what,' Maury said now. 'I suggest you go and get a good look at the Alamo. Not the river, mind. San Antonio stands on the San Antonio River. Go to the oldest hotel in town, the Menger Hotel. It stands by the side of the Alamo on Alamo Plaza.' He grinned. 'You should be able to tell 'em apart.'

Straightening his Texan string tie, he clambered to his feet. 'See the curator of the museum there, Charles Long. I'll fix it up. He'll take you round the buildings; he knows them like the palm of his hand. Loves 'em, too.'

He held out his hand. 'Then when you have seen them give me a call and we'll talk some more. Okay?'

Alamo Plaza is a large, more or less rectangular open space full of trees, bounded on two sides by shops and on the other two by large hotels. One of these is the fine old Menger Hotel, an attractive place with green and white striped awnings overhanging balconies with delicate wrought iron railings. It looked something like 150 years old – ancient by Texan standards.

I walked past it that evening, crossing Crockett Street with the Crockett Hotel at the far end of it, and at last I found myself standing face to face with the Alamo mission. It was something to see.

The old chapel building is not large. At that moment it stood wonderfully lit by soft indirect lighting, its façade a fine arrangement of limestone that the illumination had turned the colour of pale honey. Its arched doorway, decorated in Spanish style, was flanked by two pillars twisted like barley sugar that enclosed two slender niches that must surely once have contained religious statues. Two other niches and a window rose above the level of the door, and then the roof of the building soared against the sky in a curiously graceful curve.

The chapel and the barracks of the Alamo, the stone wall and colonnades, particularly when seen from the Plaza, form a complex of buildings which, although only dating from the mid-1700s, gives the impression of something far older – perhaps even something constructed in the time of the Moghuls, or the Romans.

Even in the midst of the Christmas hubbub it exudes a strange and powerful aura of tranquillity, and as long as I was in San Antonio I found I wanted to visit it two or three times a day.

True to his word, Maury Maverick had arranged for me to meet Charles Long, the Alamo's curator, the next day. Before I did so I went to see the hour-long movie which recreated the Alamo battle and which was playing in a small hall at the back of Menger Hotel. I went as a precaution, as well as out of interest. I didn't want to face Mr Long, as I had Maury, with only the meagrest notion of what the Alamo incident had been all about.

The movie was shown on a special screen 30- or 40-foot high; and, from what could have been the world's most powerful speakers, the sound of roaring cannon and exploding shells came at you from all sides. The effect of this blitzkrieg on eyes and ears was to make one feel caught up in an extremely lively and gory battle: a battle between a small number of Americans defending the Alamo complex – evidently considerably bigger in 1836 than it was now – against a Mexican army of thousands of men dressed like extras in a film of Waterloo or Austerlitz.

A darkly handsome actor in tight breeches and a cocked hat on a nobly prancing horse played the part of the Mexican commander, the dictator, General Antonio Lopez de Santa Anna, and he looked – the General, who in real life was a devotee of the French emperor, would have approved the casting – a good deal like the young Napoleon.

By this Mexican Bonaparte the motley handful of Americans was doomed to be wiped out to a man. In their catastrophic end, as was the case with the slaughtered Spartans at Thermopylae, lay their fame.

For there were incidents at the Alamo that raised the disaster into American legend. At the height of the Mexican bombardment, for example, surrounded by an overwhelming enemy force, with no hope of rescue, Colonel William Travis, commanding the rag-tag Alamo garrison, is said to have drawn a line on the ground with the tip of his sword and to have made a heroic and dramatic appeal: 'Those prepared to give their lives in freedom's cause, come over to me.'

Every American schoolboy knows the response: for every man there, save one, crossed the line to Travis's side, even Colonel James Bowie – the notorious knife-fighter, who was confined to bed and immobilised by pneumonia, ordered his cot to be carried over it. Naturally David Crockett from Tennessee, wearing his familiar buckskins and coonskin cap and carrying his long hunting musket 'Old Betsey', was already there.

The short, tumultuous and ear-splitting movie spared its audience nothing of the ultimate bloody tragedy of 6 March 1836.

Maury had thoughtfully given me a pamphlet to read. It told the end of the story in these words:

> With bugles sounding the dreaded 'Deguello' (no quarter to the defender) columns of Mexican soldiers attacked from the north, the east, the south, and the west. Twice repulsed by withering musket fire and cannon shot, they concentrated their third attack at the battered north wall.
>
> Travis, with a single shot through his forehead, fell across his cannon. The Mexicans swarmed through the breach and into the plaza . . . . Crockett, using his rifle as a club, fell as the attackers, now joined by reinforcements who stormed the south wall, turned to the chapel. The Texans inside soon suffered the fate of their comrades. Bowie, his pistols emptied, his famous knife bloodied, and his body riddled, died in his cot.

One hundred and eighty-three Americans died at the Alamo trying in vain to defend this far-flung Texan outpost against the Mexican 'tyrant', General Santa Anna. The shooting over, Santa Anna ordered his soldiers to lay the dead defenders on a communal pyre – one layer of wood, a layer of bodies, a layer of wood, another layer of bodies, and so on – and to burn them.

That was after he had personally made sure the corpses of Travis, Crockett and Bowie had been identified.

I left the film a good deal better informed than I had been when I bought my ticket. I could face Charles Long with some confidence now that I knew that the Alamo was neither an American river nor an American victory.

In a souvenir shop where I went to buy a guidebook to the Alamo, I saw a fading poster on a wall advertising the old John Wayne *Alamo* film. From his buckskins and his fur cap, it was evident that Wayne himself had played Davy Crockett, and by the shop's door was a shelf of racoon-skin caps; real skins for $19.95, false ones for $9.95. I hoped racoons were not an endangered species; but anyway I didn't buy one. Maybe Wayne could get away with it. With that fluffy ringed tail hanging down my neck I would have looked merely idiotic.

The guidebook gave me the outlines of the dispute between Texans and Mexicans that led to the massacre.

The starting point was that Mexico had won its independence from Spain as recently as 1821, and that Texas was part of it. Mexico's shaky independence was made shakier by the intrigue and ruthless corruption of rival Mexican politicians and generals. But despite this a remarkably unxenophobic Mexican Constitution drawn up in 1824 permitted Americans to come and settle in the vast and empty wastes of Texas – provided only that they took an oath of loyalty to the host government. In return for security of land tenure and a minimum of central government interference, the Americans were perfectly willing to do this.

So far so good. But soon the obvious cultural and religious differences between American Texans and the Mexicans began to make themselves felt. When the Mexican government began to draw new lines on the map, Texas was joined to the state of Coahuila and its capital was moved from San Antonio to the town of Saltillo, which is a long way south of the Rio Grande. Furthermore, Texas was henceforth only to be allowed a single representative in a state legislature of twelve. Worse was to follow: in 1830 the Mexican government passed a law prohibiting any further immigration from the United States.

That was probably the moment when a parting of the ways became inevitable.

The Mexicans had a point or two on their side. For example, by 1830, 75 per cent of the population of the Mexican state of Texas was American. American companies had taken high-handed control of immense slices of 'Texan' (really Mexican) land. Furthermore, American settlers avoided paying Mexican taxes, engaged in widespread smuggling, and some were suspected of disregarding the government of Mexico's antipathy to slavery.

The American government had actually offered to buy Texas, but the Mexican government felt with increasing unease that it was in danger of losing the territory by default. A year after a new and overdue law was passed to redress these abuses, Mexican garrisons were sent to Texas to enforce Mexican laws that Americans were – or pretended to be – unaware of.

When this happened, Texans felt hard done by. As they saw it, it wasn't *their* fault that Mexican governments had been so absurdly easy-going. The new rules about irksome duties, paying taxes, ending smuggling and curbing the extension of slavery led to protests against 'tyranny' and to calls from American settlers in Texas for the Mexican government to return to the amiable 1824 Constitution; or even for Texas to break free from Mexico once and for all. William Travis, who later commanded the ill-fated Alamo garrison and died with it, called for Texan independence louder than most.

In November 1830 angry Texans, their patience exhausted, met in convention at San Felipe de Austin and issued what they called a 'Declaration of Causes'. This amounted to a simple declaration of revolt against Santa Anna's government.

> Whereas [it said] General Antonio Lopez de Santa Anna, and other military chieftains, have by force of arms overthrown the federal constitution of Mexico ... now the good people of Texas, availing themselves of their natural rights, Solemnly Declare:
>
> That they have taken up arms in defence of their rights and liberties, which were threatened by the encroachments of military despots, and in defence of the republican principle of the federal constitution of Mexico, 1824. That Texas is no longer morally or civilly bound by the compact of union ....

Before long a volunteer Texan–American army was facing San Antonio while its officers debated whether they should drive out the 1,200 Mexican soldiers who occupied the town and were commanded by General Martin Perfecto de Cos, a brother-in-law of the 'despotic' Antonio Santa Anna.

Those who favoured an immediate attack on the town were given an invaluable boost by Sam Maverick and a friend of his who had managed to escape from San Antonio. They now reported that the Mexican troops were hungry, if not starving, and generally in an appallingly low state of morale. At this point, too, came a dramatic intervention by the tough old plainsman called Benjamin Rusk Milam. Losing patience with the shillyshallying, he rushed out of his

tent, like some bewhiskered and sun-tanned Byronic hero, bellowing
to one and all, 'Boys, who will come with old Ben Milam into San
Antonio?'

'Yippee!' That challenge did the trick. 'With a roar of approval'
(according to various reports) 240 Americans sprang up to join him
in an attack on Cos's garrison.

It took four days of street fighting to take San Antonio. Poor
Ben Milam was not there to witness Cos's surrender. For on the
third day old Ben, whose fighting words had inspired the whole
adventure, was shot by a sniper hidden in a cypress tree and fell
back dead into Sam Maverick's arms.

Shortly after that, General Cos, hoisting a white flag, wrote
out and signed his own surrender in both Castilian and English,
agreeing to withdraw his troops below the Rio Grande. In doing
so, he abandoned the last Mexican post in Texas – not a retreat
of which Santa Anna, his brother-in-law, would approve.

Unconsciously, Cos had made it a certainty that the final fight
would take place at and around the Alamo. During his own battle he moved his headquarters to an old abandoned mission, the
chapel of which had stone walls 4-foot thick. The chapel's religious
significance had long since evaporated – there were five missions all
told on the San Antonio River and all of them had been secularised
about forty years before. From time to time since then this one had
been used as a barracks, and was eventually occupied by a garrison
of Spanish troops from the Pueblo de San José y Santiago del Alamo
in Mexico. Thus the old mission, now transformed into a half-ruined
fortress, became known simply as the Alamo.

' "Alamo", did you know, means a cottonwood tree?' said Charles
Long when I met him in the library of the Alamo complex.

There was only one cottonwood tree to be seen here now. I had
spotted it behind the chapel – a tall, graceful tree with ridged bark
and pale leaves on branches set noticeably high up on its slender
trunk.

Mr Long was an elderly, cheerful gentleman who had retired
as curator some time before, but who, because of his deep affection for the Alamo buildings, found it difficult to stay away from
them. He at once gave me a list of books on the battle, particularly
recommending Walter Lord's *A Time to Stand*, written some thirty
years before.

'It's a lively account,' he said.

I mentioned that the short film I had recently seen of the battle
gave the impression of a considerably larger Alamo complex than

the one I could see now. Was this moviemakers' artistic licence?

Long at once said with enthusiasm, 'Oh, no. That was true. It *was* much larger. Just about three acres. Come along. I'll show you what it actually did look like.' And we strode out into the Plaza, dodging traffic and the groups of tourists who stood gazing at the Christmas tree.

There were no walls here; most of the outlying ones, Mr Long explained, were no longer standing. Near the long line of shops that runs along the other side of the Plaza, Mr Long, casting about like an enthusiastic beagle tracking a pungent hare, excitedly pointed out tiny markers, sunk almost invisibly into the sidewalks to show where the outer walls had originally been.

'You may remember,' Mr Long said, hurrying along, muzzle figuratively to the ground, 'that in the movie you saw Davy Crockett run across the Plaza from near the chapel, swing round a small cannon and fire away at the northwest corner of the wall where the Mexicans were crowded and beginning to pour in. This was very near the end – the final slaughter, if you like.'

I did remember, I said.

'Well, perhaps it will help you to envisage the scene,' he stopped and pointed abruptly, 'if I tell you that Crockett's cannon was situated just about in this doorway here.'

'You mean in the doorway of "Wendy's Old Fashioned Hamburgers"?'

'Just about. Crockett must have done a lot of damage from here,' said Charles Long. He gave an unexpected little chuckle. 'Didn't stop the Mexicans, of course.'

We proceeded northwards, passing Woolworths (the main body of Mexican assault troops had broken into the Plaza about here), crossing a street to the Gibb Building, next to which there was another discreet marker in the sidewalk to show the northwestern limit of the old Plaza walls.

The unremarkable façade of the modern Gibb Building displayed a prominent plaque. It announced that from 1850 to 1870 this had been the site of the house of Samuel Augustus Maverick – who 'came to San Antonio in 1835; was guide for Ben Milam and other leaders in the first attack on San Antonio in December 1835'.

Maury's great-grandfather, it went on, had twice been Mayor of San Antonio, and then Chief Justice of Bexar County during the Civil War. The plaque confirmed that 'his famous practice of letting his cattle roam about unbranded gave the English language the word "Maverick", meaning an independent person as well as an unbranded animal'.

Following Mr Long at a brisk trot, I soon arrived at the door of the chapel itself. It basked contentedly in the pale winter sun and the state flag – white, red and blue with the white Lone Star of Texas in it – flew straight out from a pole above its northern wall.

'Davy Crockett was in charge of the outer wall just here,' announced Mr Long confidently, as if the battle had happened last week and he himself had taken a leading part in it.

He led the way into the chapel itself, stopping beside a glass-topped case in which a beaded buckskin vest with onyx buttons was on display.

'That's Crockett's vest,' he said, pointing to it with a certain awe, patting his stomach and adding a little wistfully, 'I've always wanted to try it on, but I might burst the buttons.' In another case lay a long awkward-looking musket – but whether it was really Crockett's 'Old Betsey' or simply a good replica I can't now recall. In any case it was very similar to the weapon Alamo paintings show him swinging round his head like a skull-cracking club in the final stages of the Mexican break-in.

Not surprisingly, the Bowie knife, gleaming in the glass case next door to Crockett's musket, attracted most tourists. It was a formidable weapon, single-edged, thick-bladed, heavy, about ten inches long, and curved upward at the tip – the better, I suppose, to penetrate an enemy's ribs.

'Maker-Searles-Baton Rouge', was all that was engraved on it. Was this the actual knife Jim Bowie died defending himself with? Mr Long shrugged and reflected. 'Well, Bowie had a good many knives,' he said evasively. He went on, 'You know, Bowie is probably my favourite Alamo hero. But I suppose, for most modern Americans, the pre-eminent Alamo hero is Davy Crockett.'

What a rum lot they were, the men who defended the Alamo. And none rummer than Crockett with his racoon-skin cap, long musket and beaded buckskin vest. Cap, musket and vest were for him all part of a sort of fancy dress. People reported that when playing the politician in Washington he wore a frock coat and a frilly shirt like everybody else. Wayne as Crockett in the Alamo film played another part, racoon-skin cap and all. For some reason, for all his toughness, Wayne seems as out of place defending a chapel in Texas as the unmistakably British actor Laurence Harvey, who played Travis.

A group of tourists had stopped and stared at Long, as he burst out with the Crockett song. Then, recognising it, they grinned and went on their way.

I said goodbye to Charles Long outside the library next to

a small fountain that tinkled prettily in the shade of a live oak tree.

He smiled when I thanked him. 'Oh, I always enjoy showing people around.'

The names Travis, Bowie and Crockett were engraved on the sides of the basin of the fountain, and a reddish-grey squirrel, perched unafraid on its rim, cast a greedy eye at the glittering objects on the bottom. Visitors had thrown a small fortune in one-cent pieces, nickels and dimes into the water. Presumably they thought it would bring them luck.

Chapter 9

I lost no time in finding – and buying – the book Charles Long had recommended: *A Time to Stand* by Walter Lord. I took it into the bar of the Menger Hotel on Crockett Street. As Maury Maverick had said, the hotel itself was a piece of San Antonio's history. So the bar had to be examined first: the book could wait a moment or two. Carrie Nation, the fiery old campaigner for prohibition, had once taken a piece out of the bar's wooden top with her axe; you could see the axe-cut.

'It's not as old as the Tower of London,' Maury had said of the place. 'But old for Texas.'

As bars go, it was pretty old for anywhere; it was said to be – and looked it – a replica of an old pub in London, full of booths, mirrors, glass cabinets; with a cherrywood ceiling and a kind of minstrels' gallery from which one could sit and watch the antics of the customers below.

The hotel had a history. In 1905, it was said, the Menger gave a ball to honour the Misses Eda Kampmann and Katherine Yoakum, two of San Antonio's most beautiful debutantes. Actually the ball was hosted by a Miss Clara Driscoll, who had been responsible for saving the Alamo from demolition. Why the famous Alamo should have been demolished, goodness knows; but at any rate Miss Driscoll was credited with saving it.

By that time the railroad had long ago reached San Antonio. A number of famous people came visiting – Oscar Wilde, for one, gave a lecture on decorative art. He said that the old Spanish missions gave him 'a strange thrill of pleasure'. No doubt – who knows? – he gave the Texans quite different feelings 'in his knee-length trousers, scarlet stockings, and silver-buckled slippers, as he strolled about the Menger sipping spiked lemonade and smoking long, foreign cigarettes'.

Somewhere behind what is now the Menger's Motor Entrance in Crockett Street there was once a famous garden with a small pool where alligators lived, drawing viewers from far and wide. I asked the hotel receptionist what had happened to the alligators.

'I guess they got old and died, sir,' he said, keeping a po-face.

A couple of old brass spittoons stood conveniently by the old wooden bar; less to do, surely, with that London pub than with Teddy Roosevelt, who had recruited many of his Rough Riders here to go to Cuba to fight in the Spanish–American war. A picture of the fiery future President on a charger, boldly gauntleted and spurred, bristled bellicosely on a wall. Throwing out the virile challenge of a recruiting poster, T.R. looked ready there and then to take up the White Man's Burden of empire from Havana to Corregidor.

'What are you waiting for?' he seemed to be saying. 'Sign up here, boys, for a whiff of gunsmoke and imperialism. Adventure, if you prefer to call it that. (The spittoon's over there.)'

A waiter came round the side of the wooden bar, and when I asked him what beer they had, he said, 'Lone Star is popular. That's Texas beer. There's also a good German beer, made locally, called Shriner.'

'Shriner'll do,' I said, thinking perhaps Germans made good beer even in America. They did: the beer was darkish, not too light, and above all not quite as full of gas as most American beer.

With the Shriner Bock beer on the table, I opened Lord's book. It was easy to read, as Charles Long had said. It told in an easy-going, chatty style an extraordinary story of bravery. Of stupidity, too, and much bloodshed – and an ultimate Texan triumph that came about largely through sheer good luck. It told me much of the Alamo affair I still didn't know.

For example, I didn't know that three months before the battle Jim Bowie had arrived at the Alamo with thirty men bearing a letter from Sam Houston, the Texan commander-in-chief. That letter quite plainly ordered Colonel Neil, the Alamo garrison commander, to withdraw from the old mission, and having first evacuated the artillery, to blow the place up. Houston had decided that the Alamo, isolated way out in the sticks, was more of a political liability than a military asset. It must go.

Unfortunately – or was it fortunately? – Houston, who knew James Bowie well and greatly respected him, added a personal, verbal message, 'Jim, much is referred to your judgment.'

Those casual, do-as-you-like words would change the history – and even the sheer size – of the United States.

Bowie at first found many things wrong with the Alamo's defences. There were no horses for scouting; no medical supplies; no rifle powder; no cannonballs for the 18-pounder. As for the men's morale, it was so low that they refused to drill or go out on patrol, and those who had settled into the chapel lived hand to mouth amid the rubble and the rubbish that General Cos's men had left behind them.

Yet, Lord's book tells one, Bowie, being Bowie, couldn't bring himself to carry out Houston's order to abandon the Alamo – despite urgent warnings from his many reliable local Mexican contacts that General Santa Anna was marching on Texas, intent on two things: revenging Cos's defeat; and giving the Texan rebels a lesson they would never forget.

The Mexican president was indeed heading straight for San Antonio with an overwhelming force of 4,600 men. It was time, as any Texan would say, to get the hell out. Yet day after day Bowie hesitated, and one wonders, as Walter Lord did, what inspired him to stand fast?

> Was it the place – this dramatic outpost, standing alone between the colonists and the Mexicans? Was it the Alamo's twenty guns, probably the strongest collection between Mexico City and New Orleans? Was it the 'frontier' in him – the pioneer's refusal to be shoved around? Bowie had plenty of that.

Whatever it was, Bowie suddenly determined not to leave the Alamo, but to pull it together, got to work. He rounded up corn supplies and ammunition for the 18-pounder; he repaired the walls of the fort; he built palisades to fill the gaps in them. He began to prepare, in short, to defend the Alamo against Santa Anna.

An excited mass meeting of the San Antonio garrison affirmed that the Alamo should be held. A bold resolution was passed which said 'We cannot be driven from the post of honor', and Bowie was the first to sign it. As the Mexican army reached the Rio Grande, Bowie – although plainly ill and clearly sickening for something serious – wrote, 'We will rather die in these ditches than give [the Alamo] up to the enemy.'

At about that time Lieutenant-Colonel William Barret Travis arrived with thirty reinforcements, and Neil, pleading a variety of reasons (some plausible, some less so) took himself off on leave. In retrospect who can blame him?

When Bowie collapsed completely with what was described as 'typhoid pneumonia' Travis willingly took command like a man who had been expecting a call from Destiny for some time. He, too, had arrived ready to evacuate the fort, and had been seduced into believing it defensible.

Meanwhile, the famous Tennessean Congressman and hunter, Davy Crockett, joined the doomed garrison with twelve devotees – the self-styled 'Tennessee Mounted Volunteers'. And his arrival created an immense stir. People poured into the Plaza to welcome him, and Crockett clambered dutifully on to a packing-case to address them, declaring heroically, 'All the honour I desire is that of defending the liberties of our common country.' Cheers filled the Plaza. Morale soared.

By this time Bowie had been carried off, shaking and sweating with fever, to a room in the barracks near the Alamo's main gate, and it was left to the romantic Travis to set the final – and fatal – ball rolling. Travis's reply to His Excellency General Santa Anna's ultimatum, itself a response to a final offer of negotiations by Bowie before his collapse (written in perfect Spanish, it is worth noting), was unmistakably insolent.

For his part, Santa Anna, his men ensconced by this time in siege positions around the little mission, could hardly have failed to notice that Bowie, too, stubborn and belligerent to the end, had crossed out the formal words 'God and the Mexican Federation' (*Dios y Federación*) at the end of his message and substituted 'God and Texas' (*Dios y Texas*). Santa Anna was thus virtually obliged to reply as he did, that 'the Mexican army cannot come to terms under any conditions with rebellious foreigners'. He demanded unconditional surrender, in return for which he promised to spare the garrison.

In the light of the appalling fate a little later under similar circumstances of the Texan garrison at Goliad, 95 miles further east, Travis was probably right to answer this ultimatum as he did – by aiming a cannonball from his heavy 18-pounder in the general direction of the Mexican dictator's tent. It missed him by a fraction. But Travis made his point.

He made an even bigger point – one that has echoed, as they say, down the corridors of history – when, on the brink of catastrophe, he penned his message 'To the People of Texas and all Americans in the World'. This appeal for moral support, written in a darkening room of the Alamo by a little-known man in a little-heard-of part of Mexican Texas, and emanating from what is now the doorway of 'Wendy's Old Fashioned Hamburgers', ran like a charge of electricity through the truncated United States of 1836. It caused a national furore. As Walter Lord says, virtually the whole country – if not precisely 'all the Americans in the world' – was shaken by it. It is certainly an impassioned document, even without its over-dramatic underlinings.

Fellow citizens and compatriots – I am besieged, by a thousand or more Mexicans under Santa Anna – I have sustained a continual bombardment and cannonade for 24 hours and have not lost a man – The enemy has demanded a surrender at discretion, otherwise, the garrison are to be put to the sword, if the fort is taken – I have answered the demand with a cannon shot, & our flag still waves proudly from the walls – *I shall never surrender or retreat.* Then, I call on you in the name of Liberty, or patriotism & everything dear to the American character, to come to our aid, with all despatch – The enemy is receiving reinforcements daily & will no doubt increase to three or four thousand in four or five days. If this call is neglected, I am determined to sustain myself as long as possible and die like a soldier who never forgets what is due to his own honour & that of his country – *Victory or Death.*

The last three words were underlined three times. And the signature is that of 'William Barret Travis, Lt.Col. commdt.'.

In order not to delay its transmission to the outside world, this message was entrusted to a Captain Albert Martin, who galloped away through astonished Mexican soldiers lolling idly on the Gonzales road. Next evening Martin, after an exhausting ride, handed the message on to another courier, Launcelot Smithers. Smithers would carry it from Gonzales to the next stop, San Felipe, the tiny business and political centre of Texas, 90 miles to the east.

There, before handing it over in his turn, Launcelot just had time to add his own urgent scrawl to the back of Travis's message: 'I hope that Everyone will Randeves at Gonzales as soon as possible as the Brave Soldiers are suffering. Do not neglect the powder is very scarce and should not be delad one moment.'

From San Felipe, both messages sped on their way by the hand of numerous other hard-riding couriers: to New Orleans – up the Mississippi – to the Atlantic ports by steamer. To New York. And finally it arrived in Washington, DC.

But by that time Travis and his companions had been dead more than three weeks.

The Americans who died at the Alamo are considered authentic heroes. But just who were these American heroes? Who was Davy Crockett? And Bowie? Who was Travis? Who, for that matter, was Santa Anna, the man who did for the lot of them: the deep-dyed despot from down Mexico way.

To take Santa Anna first. He had achieved a sort of glory while serving in the Royal Spanish Army; he had played a fair part in putting down an earlier Mexican uprising against the Spaniards at the Battle of Medina in 1813. Shortly after having gratefully accepted promotion by the Spanish from captain to lieutenant-colonel, he changed sides and joined the Mexican leader Augustin Iturbi.

It was typical of the eel-like Santa Anna that having sworn

undying allegiance to the 'Emperor Augustin I' – as Iturbi chose to call himself – he immediately launched a successful rebellion that turned Mexico into a republic. He it was, a professed liberal, who, in cahoots with conservatives, scrapped the liberal Constitution of 1824 which guaranteed states' rights (including those of Texas). Naturally, he preferred to run his own centralised government from Mexico City.

One bizarre aspect of Santa Anna's character – and perhaps an endearing one – was his self-identification with Napoleon Bonaparte. Others, similarly afflicted but judged certifiably insane, are notoriously allowed to stand about under discreet surveillance in barred cells practising noble poses with one hand in their shirt-fronts. Santa Anna was actually allowed to lead armies into the field.

Here he fulfilled a whim or two. For example, he dressed his dragoons in shiny breastplates; and his infantry, even his Yucatan battalion of warm-blooded Mayan Indians shivering in the cold mountains of Northern Mexico, were made to wear tall Napoleonic black shakos with pompoms and tiny visors.

Santa Anna himself, as Lord says, was 'a mountain of vanity'. His epaulets were heavy with silver; he carried a gold snuffbox; he collected expensive Napoleonic bric-à-brac. And he affected to despise the strangely garbed, rebellious American frontiersmen who faced his troops.

A spokesman perfectly expressed Santa Anna's views for him:

> The superiority of the Mexican soldier over the mountaineers of Kentucky and the hunters of Missouri is well known. Veterans seasoned by twenty years of wars can't be intimidated by the presence of an army ignorant of the art of war, incapable of discipline, and renowned for insubordination.

Walter Lord's description of Santa Anna leading his large but hopelessly mismanaged and unpaid army north towards the Rio Grande to avenge General Cos's defeat at the Alamo reads like extracts from Evelyn Waugh's *Scoop*.

> Santa Anna himself galloped far in the lead. Around him were his dragoons, splendid in their shining helmets and breastplates. Just behind, his ornate carriage rattled and swayed along the rocky road. Behind it lumbered his baggage train, loaded with the things he felt he needed – the striped marquee, the tea caddy and cream pitcher ... the monogrammed china ... the decanters with their little stoppers ... the silver chamber pot.

As for the Americans, in a way Santa Anna's contempt for them was understandable.

Charles Long himself had described the Texan 'army' to me: 'Farmers, plainsmen, mostly. No discipline. Illiterate. Even Davy Crockett didn't have any schooling.' So Davy Crockett was a hick? Long made a joke of it: 'Of course. That's why he was elected to Congress,' he smiled.

'I didn't know he had been.'

'Oh yes. "The Coonskin Congressman". Myself, I think I've told you, I've always had a soft spot for Bowie.'

'Yes, so you said. The drunken knife-fighter.'

'Well, it was a rough life where he came from in New Orleans. People liked him, though; he was real popular, really respected. And then the pneumonia, or whatever it was, got to him. Just before the Mexican soldiers, of course.'

The Texan–American force was indeed, as Santa Anna had sneered, a sort of rabble: it had appalling problems of insubordination, a terrible lack of discipline. The Bowie faction was little more than a brawling, drunken mob, refusing to obey anyone's orders in the earlier days at the Alamo, certainly not Travis's. Bowie himself was no teetotaller and he was no admirer of Travis either. To that extent, Bowie's collapse with the fever was a godsend; the two men – temperamentally quite different – had been at loggerheads over who should take command. Bowie's collapse settled things once and for all.

Naturally, few of the Americans stranded in the Alamo had come to Texas actually seeking martyrdom in a massacre. Far from it. Most of them, pushing west on new-fangled railroads and river boats, were in search of their ultimate land of opportunity. Something people called 'Texas fever' had swept America, South and North, and those inspired by the 'bug' simply put up a sign 'G.T.T.' (Gone To Texas) over their doors, packed up the furniture and headed westwards. In the familiar children's story the Yellow Brick Road led to Oz; and for these would-be pioneers of the nineteenth century the wonderful land of Oz lay just across the Sabine River (the western border of Louisiana), in the Mexican province of Texas.

It seemed worth any effort to get there. At that time Texas, says Lord, 'proved to be an eye-opening, breathtaking sight .... The sheer abundance of everything staggered the imagination .... Game was everywhere – bear, deer, rabbits, prairie chickens. Mustangs and buffalo roamed at will – there for the taking'.

He goes on:

It was enough to give birth to a Texas penchant for superlatives that was destined to endure. Travellers described sugar cane that grew twenty-five feet in a single season ... pumpkins as large as a

115

man could lift . . . a sweet potato so big that a whole family dined on it, and there was enough over to feed the pigs.

. . . Exaggerated or not, the reaction was immensely significant. It meant that at last these restless people had found what they wanted. Old sorrows were forgotten in the discovery of this great new land, and from the beginning, they were determined never to lose it again.

There was one threat to this new-found paradise; and, as barriers to greater happiness tend to, it went unheeded.

This threat was based on a growing Mexican fear – and who's to say it was not justified? – of Anglo-American expansion into Texas. Even in the United States itself, Northern abolitionists accused settlers, as American as themselves, of seeking to extend slavery into the Mexican hinterland south and west of the Sabine. It seems more reasonable today to say that the defenders of the Alamo did fight for freedom – meaning their own freedom – their freedom to prosper economically without bureaucratic interference from the Mexican government, which they saw as tyrannical.

In the year of the Alamo – not much more than fifty years after the American Revolution and only twenty-four since the War of 1812 against England – 'freedom' and 'liberty' were still simple, emotive words to fight and die for. For Americans the romance of liberalism was still in the air.

Take, for example, William Travis. Travis was a blatantly born-again romantic: he saw himself as Byron in Greece; he read avidly the novels of Sir Walter Scott; he dreamed of chivalrous knights valiant for truth, independence and 'liberty'. He equated the Texans with the Greeks, who had recently risen against the Turks. For Americans like him, however, there was a very significant difference – Texans had a distinct advantage over the Greeks: Texans were *here*; Texans were '*ours*'.

The men and women across the Sabine were friends and relatives. They came from no hallowed plain of Marathon – they were from Boston, Charleston, Natchez, the farm down the road . . . . The Texans were 'bone of our bone and flesh of our flesh'.

It was hard to resist such a call – especially when seasoned with the promise of land.

As Sam Houston, the brilliant former Governor of Tennessee, the man with the shrewd businessman's eyes and the boxer's jaw, himself infected by the 'Texan fever' – who stayed to become famous as one of the creators of the modern Texan state – put it most seductively: 'If volunteers from the US will join their brothers in this section [Texas], they will receive liberal bounties of land. We have millions of acres of our best land unchosen and unappropriated.'

The message, put fair and square, said: 'Come and get it!' And if that land-grabbing message did not entirely square with Travis's image of himself as a selfless Byron or Quentin Durward, it did not concern anyone but Travis.

As for Colonel David Crockett, the semi-literate former Congressman from Tennessee, 'in his coonskin cap, Indian moccasins and buckskin shirt, he made a virtue of backwoods ignorance,' wrote Walter Lord. 'He was the man who shot forty-seven bears in one month . . . who killed six bucks in one day . . . who rode alligators for exercise . . . who grinned a bear into retreat . . . who once aimed up a tree, only to have the coon come down and surrender.'

Crockett, by the time of the Alamo, was an established national figure: he deserved to be played by another national hero, John Wayne. There were some people who chose to portray him as a drunken country bumpkin. Others saw him as a backwoods philosopher, even though he could barely string the right words together.

Davy Crockett seems to have been a genuinely kindly soul, full of blarney, as warm and naïve as they come. Old portraits of him show a sensitive face with long black hair, and – this is the most distinctive feature about him – a rather fine, elongated nose, almost Roman. He had a good face, oddly resembling that of the actor Fess Parker, who, having played Crockett in a number of films based on his exploits, seems to have totally disappeared from public view.

If Crockett was a tiresome practical joker, he was also a natural frontiersman: in his time an honest magistrate in western Tennessee and an elected colonel of the local militia. Elevated to Congress in 1827, he pursued the solitary goal of seeing that the frontier peoples should be allowed to keep the land they occupied. Nothing else interested him, and he judged friends and enemies on that issue and no other.

As a Congressman, Crockett did now and again wear dark clothes like everybody else, although he often added a flamboyant Byronic collar and a white hat. Nevertheless in the end people became fed up with this frontier jokester with the one-track mind, and in the congressional election of 1835 Crockett lost his seat by 230 votes.

He had prepared for his own defeat in advance. 'If you don't elect me,' he warned his constituents, 'you can go to hell. I shall go to Texas.' And so Crockett joined the southwestward trend, and his progress towards Texas was an uproarious junket. He was fifty years old by now, slightly overweight, and, probably aware that his best days were over, he was determined to have one last fling. With

'Betsey', his old musket, by his side, and with a growing band of 'good ole boys', he sailed gaily down the Mississippi; raised hell in the Union Hotel bar in Memphis; contrived to be found skinning a deer in the backyard of the City Hotel in Little Rock; and raised hell once more while a fife and drum entertained the company with 'Hail the Conquering Hero'. In Texas at last, a cannon banged out a personal welcome, and then there were still more banquets to celebrate Crockett's well-advertised arrival.

It was a wildly improbable train of events that ended in the famous massacre and Crockett's death.

The last vision of Crockett alive and fighting was that given after the Alamo battle by a Mexican officer – Captain Rafael Soldana of the Tampico battalion.

> A tall man, with flowing hair, was seen firing from the same place on the parapet during the entire siege. He wore a buckskin suit and a cap all of a pattern entirely different from those worn by his comrades. This man would kneel or lie down behind the low parapet, rest his long gun and fire, and we all learned to keep a good distance when he was seen to make ready to shoot. He rarely missed his mark, and when he fired he always rose to his feet and calmly reloaded his gun seemingly indifferent to the shots fired at him by our men. He had a strong resonant voice and often railed at us, but as we did not understand English we could not comprehend the import of his words further than that they were defiant. This man I later learned was known as 'Kwockey'.

I have an idea that if Davy Crockett could have read that little vignette of himself under fire, he would have been extremely pleased. 'You can go to hell!' that strong resonant voice might have been shouting to Santa Anna's Mexicans, just as it had shouted to his own reluctant constituents, 'You can go to hell! I shall go to Texas.'

The 183 'Texans' who died at the Alamo had little in common, except the fact that most of them had arrived there fairly recently. Very few of them were the frontier type. They came from many parts of the American northeast and south; ten of them were from England; twelve from Ireland; three from Scotland; and one each from Wales, Denmark and Germany.

Some were fleeing the wrath of fathers of girls they had thoughtlessly seduced; others were fleeing creditors; others were escaping from boredom or trying to forget failure; still others were getting away from the overcrowded cities and too few jobs. There was one famous exception. James Bowie, the forty-year-old bear hunter,

Indian fighter, adventurer-turned-Mexican-citizen, had lost the wife he adored – she was an aristocrat of pure Spanish blood – in a cholera epidemic, and then in his grief had taken to liquor. But most of these men, Bowie and Crockett included, had at least one thing in common: they had all wanted a new start.

Some, naturally, are more memorable than others. One John McGregor was so Scottish he even carried his bagpipes to the Alamo, and he kept up the garrison's morale by playing raucous duets with Crockett (who had discovered an old violin). McGregor died there with all the rest. So did an Englishman, Anthony Wolfe, and two of his sons, whose youth – they looked under twelve years old – did not save them. Robert Evans from Ireland was in charge of the powder-magazine, and already wounded when he saw the Mexicans had broken into the Plaza. He limped towards it with a lighted torch, intending to blow it up. Before he reached it, one of Santa Anna's men shot him dead.

The Alamo story is full of chilling details.

One of the most sinister is that the doomed garrison had been obliged to listen to their own death knell. This came in the form of the signal for the final Mexican attack, followed by the dreadful bugle notes of the '*deguello*', which signified that those attacked were to receive 'no quarter'. It recalled the savagery of the Spanish wars against the Moors, and was sometimes known as the 'fire and death call'. To the ears of the men in the Alamo it conveyed one inexorable message: 'death without mercy' was to be their lot. Santa Anna evidently wanted to make his intentions brutally clear to the rebels who defied him.

Today the names of those 183 rebels are carved on a great monument whose inappropriately massive marble block, thrusting up 40 feet or more, fills – overfills rather – the north end of the Alamo Plaza. It is a pity, that monument. It is far too big and grossly pretentious in a rather Mussolini-fascist way.

The monument displays life-sized statues of a good many of the Alamo's heroes. Romantic Travis is there, in tall boots and a short military jacket. So is Bowie, recovered evidently from 'typhoid pneumonia', stonily robust in a thigh-length coat with big buttons over an open-necked shirt, a waistcoat and a sword-belt. Davy Crockett, of course, is there too: a slim, long-haired and youthful portrait in stone, wearing his fringed buckskin jacket, with 'Betsey's' long barrel held close to his side with one hand, his coonskin cap grasped in the other. Others, bearded veterans or impossibly innocent-faced youths, stand, sit, squat, or simply look defiant. An inscription says:

In memory of the heroes who sacrificed their lives at the Alamo, March 6 1836, in the defence of Texas. They chose never to surrender nor retreat; these brave hearts, flag still proudly waving, perished in the flames of immortality that their high sacrifice might lead to the founding of this Texas.

The Alamo story is a mass of myth and hearsay. The far greater tragedy of Vietnam – full of myths and false reports of its own that are infinitely more sinister and destructive – had not the happy outcome of the sacrifice of the 183 doomed men of San Antonio. If only, one is left to think, the Alamo's memorial was as moving in its simplicity as the Vietnam Memorial Wall in Washington, DC. That, in fact, the Alamo's dead had no memorial other than the Alamo chapel itself.

Chapter 10

'They make a good margarita here,' said Maury Maverick when we next met in the Menger Hotel, referring to the heady cocktail the Mexicans make of tequila, lemon juice and salt. 'Famous for it. Don't drink 'em myself any more, though.'

He looked carefully round him as if casing the joint. He sounded almost embarrassed. 'My family didn't only contribute the one word "maverick" to the English language. We added another word as well, you may be interested to know. Would you like to hear it?'

'Yes please.'

'Gobbledy-gook,' he said with a serious expression.

'Gobbledy-gook?'

'That's right. Gobbledy-gook. Meaning over-formal, complex and pompous. As in the English language. You can look it up in H. L. Mencken's book.'

When later on I did look it up in Mencken, I found that on 30 March 1944, Maury's father, then wartime chairman of the Smaller War Plants Corporation, had 'boiled over' and formally prohibited any of his staff to go on using what he called 'gobbledy-gook language'. 'People ask me,' he explained later in a newspaper interview, 'where I got "gobbledy-gook". I don't know. Perhaps I was thinking of the old bearded turkey gobbler back in Texas, who was always gobbledy-gooking and strutting around with ludicrous pomposity. At the end of the "gobble" there was a sort of "gook".'

Maury Junior said, 'My father – Congressman and later Mayor of San Antonio, by the way – was always in favour of simple language and plain talk. A good example of what he hated would have been this version of Nelson's signal at Trafalgar. You know the "England this day expects every man to do his duty" signal. Which in gobbledy-gook becomes "England anticipates that, as regards the current emergency, personnel will face up to the issues and exercise appropriately the functions allocated to their respective occupation groups". You know the sort of official rubbish. He hated that. He leant forward and jabbed a finger at me. 'And so do I.'

Then he went on: 'As for the Alamo, there's all sorts of controversy about what happened there. Some details, I guess, will remain controversial for ever. Walter Lord sets out some of them.'

Indeed Lord had set aside a whole chapter listing the vexed questions over which historians and Alamo 'experts' like to haggle. Among them were the following:

Did Houston *really* order the Alamo to be blown up?

Did Travis *really* draw that dramatic line on the ground with his sword, challenging all who were prepared to stay and await death with him to cross it?

Was it *really* true that only one man – named Louis Rose – hung back from the line and thus escaped the ensuing holocaust?

Where was Bowie *actually* killed?

Did Davy Crockett *really* surrender, only to be executed on Santa Anna's orders?

How many Mexican casualties were there?

The answers – there are several – to that last question seem to vary between 65 Mexicans killed and 223 wounded and 2,000 Mexicans killed and 300 wounded: a big variation. The most plausible estimate, I think, turns out to be 600 Mexicans killed and wounded. If, as it seems, 1,800 Mexicans took part in the final assault on the Alamo, that figure represents 33 per cent of the attacking force: quite a high casualty rate, but a perfectly possible one.

'I suppose,' said Maury, 'that to work out the truth or untruth of all those other things would hardly be worthwhile except to a deep-dyed *aficionado* of such matters. You see, some details – of Bowie's death for instance – were based on so-called eyewitness accounts. And there were not likely to be any really reliable eyewitnesses left after a massacre. Those who did survive it were almost certainly shell-shocked, were probably illiterate to begin with, or would want to make a sensation by claiming to have seen things they hadn't. Human nature, isn't it?'

Again, Maury looked the hotel lobby over as if expecting to see the past lurking there.

'I'll tell you something. Those guys then, they took Texas as the British took India. Slicker than owl-shit.'

'Slicker than what?'

'Owl-shit. You must have the same expression in England.'

'We may have. I never heard it, though.'

'Never mind. Look at it this way, if Santa Anna hadn't been such a son-of-a-bitch, this hotel we're sitting in would have been called the Gonzales Hotel or something.'

That seemed to be a surprisingly valid and historically interesting point, and in a little while Maury went on, 'San Antonio is a good town. A good mix – quite a lot of Poles, a good many Germans, Irish and English. No race problems to speak of. Good relations with the Mexicans, too. Pretty good, at least. Of course, the Alamo – well, it's practically a shrine to brave Americans who were wiped out by an overwhelming Mexican army but who won Texan independence anyway. So it's still a source of some – er – resentment among American Mexicans. It's a touchy thing. Luckily, in the last ten years or so, historians have at last begun praising the Mexicans who fought *with* the Americans at the Alamo. There were quite a few of 'em.'

He considered some more. 'Yes, it's a touchy thing. Bound to be. Emotional. You get to see people weeping as they come out of the Alamo.'

It was growing dark when we left the hotel and walked out into the Plaza. The evening crowds wandered past us towards the giant Christmas tree, and approached the chapel's illuminated porch with something like reverence. From a shop in the Paso del Alamo floated a recorded voice singing a sweet and vaguely Country and Western song that rang out into the street –

> There may not be snow in San Antonio,
> But Christmas means Texas to me-ee.

Maury stopped abruptly on the sidewalk outside the hotel. 'There's something I must warn you about,' he said, deeply serious. 'That question: did Davy Crockett surrender? Never air it in Texas even in jest. Not if you value your life. "Davy Crockett *surrender*? Are you crazy?" That's the *nicest* thing people would say.'

Maury gave me a craggy smile. 'I just thought I should warn you,' he said.

Santa Anna's invasion of Texas did not end with the fall of the Alamo. 'It was but a small affair,' was the view of the Mexican Napoleon. After all, he had many more troops still in the field, even if he had lost 10 per cent of their total number in San Antonio. And to finish the job – to put down the rebellion once and for all – there was a 'Texan government' to deal with, and a Texan 'army' under Sam Houston to destroy.

Even so, it remains a plausible theory that if Santa Anna had not been, as Maury said, such a son-of-a-bitch, Texas might still be one of the Federated States of Mexico. The trouble is, though, that to have killed everyone's hero, Davy Crockett, was enough in itself to have damned Santa Anna for ever in the opinion of thousands of Americans who up to then hadn't given a damn about Texan affairs. From then on, the name and person of Santa Anna were poison. It was as simple as that; people adored Davy Crockett, the martyr, even people who, while he was alive, would not necessarily have given him the time of day.

The Natchez *Courier* was one newspaper which expressed this adoration in a typical and tearful paragraph:

> *Poor Davy Crockett!* – We lament the fate of the sick Bowie – we feel sad and angry, by turns, when we think of the butchery of the gallant Travis – but there is something in the untimely end of the poor Tennessean that almost wrings a tear from us. It is too bad – by all that is good, it is too bad. The quaint, the laughter-moving, the fearless upright Crockett, to be butchered by such a wretch as Santa Anna – it is not to be borne!

Something even worse than a massacre at the Alamo was about to occur. Santa Anna, Maury's s.o.b., was about to go one step even further into infamy. One of his cleverer lieutenants managed to trap the Texan garrison of the town of Goliad, 95 miles down the San Antonio River, in an open place where it had no business to be.

Outnumbered and out of food and water, the garrison's error-prone Texan commander, James Fannin, had to surrender and his men were marched back to Goliad as prisoners. The terms of Fannin's surrender implied they would be repatriated. But Santa Anna contemptuously revised those terms, and instead of release, the entire Texan contingent was led into the woods and shot.

The reverse at Goliad – and its brutal aftermath – spread fear and rage across the rest of Texas. The advance of Santa Anna's large force obliged the remaining Texan troops, such as they were, to burn Gonzales, the next garrison town on his route, and run for their lives. There seemed no alternative to Sam Houston, the Texan commander-in-chief, but to scuttle back across the Colorado River; Santa Anna's armies only had to catch Houston's much smaller army once on his own chosen ground, and the Texan Revolution was over. Among the deep forests of east Texas, Houston thought, he might have a chance of taking on Santa Anna with some hope of success. So he ran east: *reculer pour mieux sauter*.

We can see now how great Houston's achievement was. He faced an almost impossible task. The Texan 'army', for a start, was an absurd misnomer. In reality this so-called 'army' was little more than an undisciplined, sickly and insubordinate mob: untrained, undrilled, permanently on the verge of mutiny. Two hundred men deserted during Houston's retreat to San Felipe; mindlessly impatient to fight the Mexicans, all they could think about was to avenge the victims of the Alamo and Goliad. They couldn't see the hideous danger they faced or grasp the vital importance of further retreat, and they accused Houston of cowardice.

When a few of his officers, too, bridled at retreating any further and threatened to cause a full-scale mutiny, Houston needed all his diplomatic skills to bring these firebrands to heel. He even threatened court martials and shootings for insubordination. What, he demanded to know, could he *do* with untrained troops and no artillery against the much larger and relatively disciplined force of Santa Anna, who now drove after Houston's miserable band of insubordinate Texans in a pincer movement and with some of the verve, a generous American historian has said, 'shown by Napoleon at Marengo and Jena'. The Mexicans were coming on in three columns, any one of which was larger than Houston's little band. 'If one of them caught him, the other two would move in like wolves circling a cornered stag.'

It is a good thing for present-day Texans that Houston was strong-minded enough not to give way to insubordinate officers. If he had, there probably would be no state of Texas today. For, presently, as Santa Anna moved even further eastwards from the ashes of San Felipe on the Brazos River, he heard that the terrified government of Texas was fleeing southeast of him to Harrisburg. And in his glee, at that point the Mexican generalissimo made a most un-Napoleonic error.

Over-confident and thinking he could shorten the whole Texan campaign by entirely ignoring Houston's army and by putting the entire Texan government in the bag at Harrisburg instead, he himself led 800 of his men at a most casual and leisurely pace in that direction. But, on the wings of its fear, the government of Texas had fled to safety ahead of him.

On the other hand, Houston, hearing Santa Anna was at Lynch's Ferry on the Jacinto River, couldn't believe his luck. After an agonising forced march in mud, rain and bitter cold, he caught up with the Mexicans. Now the Americans were no longer outnumbered; the Mexicans were unaware of their approach, and there was the prospect of capturing the Mexican President himself.

The two armies faced each other – although Santa Anna, in his fatal over-confidence, only learned too late of the American presence – at the mouth of the San Jacinto River. Here Houston made precisely the speech his impatient, almost rebellious men needed to hear. 'The army will cross and will meet the enemy. Some of us may be killed and must be killed; but, soldiers – remember the Alamo! The Alamo! The Alamo!'

'Remember the Alamo! Remember Goliad!' – those were the battle-cries of the Texans at San Jacinto. Houston's men had tried to sleep in soggy clothes and had gone without supper the night before – an especially cold one – but at least there was no more talk of cowardice or mutiny. Despite the rigours of the forced march, Houston had no difficulty rousing them on the morning of the battle. They were going to fight – and no one could have stopped them.

Luckily, Santa Anna, so complacent, had neglected to post any sentries; there was no one to tell him that the Texans were in line of battle a mere thousand yards away. When the Texans moved forward, many of the Mexican soldiers were still lounging idly in the sun, and were only roused by a strange sound of foreign military music played on three fifes and a drum, and the sudden alarmed shouting of their officers.

Sam Houston, ahead of his ragged line on a white stallion, had little control over his advancing men, and in pure excitement a number of Texans began discharging their weapons indiscriminately. But by this time a general mêlée was taking place.

Houston himself, racing ahead, had two horses shot from under him and took a wound in the leg that made him limp for the rest of his life. Overrunning Santa Anna's positions, the Texans, shouting 'Remember the Alamo!' and 'Remember Goliad!', were soon slaughtering as many Mexicans as they could lay hands on; and terrified Mexicans, attempting to escape, began shrieking desperately in broken English 'Me no Alamo!' and 'Me no Goliad!' Many died none the less. In the noise and the shouting, Houston had virtually no chance of halting the slaughter.

The Mexican Army was routed in eighteen minutes.

Santa Anna himself was found next day. His was an absurd and ignominious end. The Napoleon of the West had stumbled away into some nearby marshes, sloshed trembling through the mud, and spent a miserable night huddled in the reeds. The next day, dressed in shabby clothing he'd borrowed from a slave, and covered in mud and bits of reed (but vainly retaining the diamond studs in his shirt) he was discovered by the Texans who led them to their camp. There to his annoyance he was immediately recognised by the astonished Mexican prisoners, who gaped and shouted '*El Presidente*!' at him. Although he did his best to silence them, it was too late; he was hauled before Sam Houston, who was lying in pain from his leg wound under a large tree.

Many of the furious Texans witnessing this final confrontation wanted to string Santa Anna up there and then from a branch of that very tree, but Houston calmed them. He saw that a Mexican president, defeated and alive, could be more use to Texas than a dangling corpse.

Witnesses said Santa Anna was trembling in fear of instant retribution, but evidently defeat had not subdued him very much. He was able to give Houston an arrogant harangue, saying that the man (Houston) who had been lucky enough to capture the Napoleon of the West (himself) should be generous to the vanquished. Houston calmly and reasonably replied that Santa Anna should have remembered that at the Alamo and at Goliad.

Those things, answered Santa Anna coolly, were done under the orders of his government.

'You yourself,' Houston shot back, 'are the government of Mexico.'

Houston won that brief debate, but a more positive encounter took place later between Santa Anna and President Burnet of Texas. The result was a treaty signed by the two presidents, which declared that hostilities were now at an end and that all Mexican troops would leave Texan soil. Henceforth the Rio Grande would be the boundary between the Republic of Texas and Mexico.

So after all the emotion and the deaths – not to mention the creation of an enduring legend – Sam Houston had created the state of Texas. His monumental patience with his wild Texans had paid off. So in a roundabout way had the bloodletting at the Alamo and at Goliad.

And Houston's victory was to mean much more even than the end of hostilities and the defeat of a posturing tyrant. On the monument that marks the site of the Battle of Jacinto, there is the following inscription:

> Measured by its results, San Jacinto was one of the decisive battles of the world. The freedom of Texas from Mexico won here led to annexation and to the Mexican War, resulting in the acquisition by the United States of the states of Texas, New Mexico, Arizona, Nevada, California, Utah, and parts of Colorado, Wyoming, Kansas, and Oklahoma. Almost one-third of the present area of the American nation, nearly a million square miles, changed sovereignty.

It was certainly just as well for Americans that His Excellency General Antonio Lopez de Santa Anna *was*, in Maury Maverick's words, 'such an s.o.b.'. But he was, and so, in the end, Travis, Bowie and Davy Crockett did not die for nothing.

A million square miles of territory cannot be said to be 'nothing'.

If you think it is, try and imagine the United States without those states today.

I stayed on a little longer near the Alamo. I knew now it wasn't a river, but a beautiful haunted building; and one I found difficult to hurry away from.

I have mentioned its beauty – have I talked of its tranquillity? The little patio outside the library, shaded by live oaks, is an oasis of peace. And the Low Barracks, where once the Spanish infantrymen were housed, with its dark colonnade and open well, and its splendid outlook on to 'Wendy's Old Fashioned Hamburger' emporium, is another quiet place.

I spent part of my final day visiting the other four missions established on the San Antonio River between 1731 and 1740: Concepcion, San José, San Juan and Espada. They are dotted along the narrow, meandering waterway, among golf courses, tawdry 'mobile homes' and dismal auto-tube repair sheds. None the less, despite their dreary surroundings, the old missions, described as the most beautiful examples of Spanish Colonial architecture in the United States, somehow manage to retain their dignity and even a certain mystery.

Emerging from a cloister in the Mission Concepcion, I found myself confronted by an elderly lady with a camera and extremely thick glasses.

'Mah God, ah thought John Wayne was day-id,' she quavered, blinking up at me nervously.

I was not put out to be taken for a dead actor. I don't look like Wayne, but I *am* 6-foot-3, my eyes tend to narrow in sunlight and I *do* have a good many creases on my face.

Flattered to be mistaken for the great man, even by an old lady who could barely see her hand in front of her own nose, there was nothing I could adequately say in protest or in thanks for a compliment.

Should I have told her she had the wrong mission, and that John Wayne, Richard Widmark and Laurence Harvey were alive and well, in spirit at least, only a few miles downriver at the Alamo?

Part Four

Los Angeles: Chandler and Marlowe

It's what we fellows are up against in police work. We get all the homicide and doubtful death reports from outlying districts. We're supposed to read them the same day . . . . That's a rule like you shouldn't search without a warrant or frisk a guy for a gun without reasonable grounds. But we break rules. We have to.

RAYMOND CHANDLER: Farewell, My Lovely

Chapter 11

To me – to a great many people, I suppose – Los Angeles means Raymond Chandler and his private eye hero, Philip Marlowe, one of the first and toughest of that breed.

When I arrived there from San Antonio, Texas, the verdict in the second trial of the white Los Angeles police officers involved in the videoed beating of a black man called Rodney King was eagerly and daily expected. An earlier trial had dismissed the case against the officers, thus sparking off riots and a national wave of outrage, particularly among the black community of Central South Los Angeles. If there should be a second dismissal, and if the police officers should be freed, even more violent riots were anticipated.

In their time, Marlowe and Chandler had had some pungent and none too complimentary things to say about the Los Angeles Police Department – although Chandler said nice things about any good officer he happened to meet. These days, the police were regularly being hauled over red-hot coals. So I felt in the mood to try to trace Marlowe's footsteps round the mean streets of this huge and increasingly dangerous city.

I started by closing with relief the endless newspaper accounts of the Rodney King affair, and by opening a book by a writer who had been a fervent admirer of Chandler. Here is an extract from it, which will also (to vary the pace of *this* book) serve as a brief test for Chandler fans.

Only one guess – who wrote this, and where does it come from?

> She fed me a kiss that throbbed all the way down my fallen arches. Then, suddenly from the doorway a roscoe said 'Katchow!' and a slug creased the side of my noggin. Neon lights exploded inside my think-tank . . . . She was as dead as a stuffed mongoose.

Or again, this:

> And then, from an open window beyond the bed, a roscoe coughed 'Kat-chow!'. . . . I said, 'What the hell –! and hit the floor with my smeller . . . . A brunette jane was lying there, half out of the mussed covers. She was as dead as vaudeville.

Early stuff by the great Raymond Chandler, you would almost certainly say. And you would be very close. But as a matter of fact the two imaginary extracts above come from the neon-lit think tank of the much-lamented S. J. Perelman, since whose demise in 1979 many would say American humour has been as dead as a stuffed mongoose and vaudeville put together. Chandler himself referred to these extracts as 'Perelman's wonderful parody' of his work. And who does not instantly recognise the style and the pace?

Raymond Chandler, of course, died ages ago: at La Jolla, California, on 26 March 1959, aged seventy. It's painful to believe he's not still around. As painful as realising that Philip Marlowe, his magnificent (fictional) private eye, is coming up to be eighty years old.

Not too long ago, to ease the pain and assuage a great curiosity to see (this was before the riots of 1992) if many things had changed recently in Chandlerland – in the mean streets of Los Angeles and Bay City, the settings for *The Big Sleep*, *Farewell, My Lovely*, and *The Lady in the Lake* – I went back there. My friend, the photographer Nik Wheeler, who lives up a canyon above Marlowe's old home, came with me. For my protection. His big lens is often mistaken for a Frontier Colt with an eight-inch barrel.

We know quite a bit about Philip Marlowe. He was born, Chandler told us, in a small town in Northern California called Santa Rosa, though even his creator confessed that his date of birth is 'uncertain'. He had a couple of years at college (University of Oregon, probably), and then seems to have had some useful experience as an investigator for the DA of LA County. He lost that job, and Chandler wouldn't be very specific about how he did so. 'Let's say he got a little too efficient at a time and in a place where efficiency was the last thing desired by the persons in charge.'

Marlowe is slightly over six feet tall and weighs about 13-stone-8. When he was younger he had dark brown hair, his eyes are brown and he is 'passably good-looking'. According to Chandler, 'I don't think he looks tough, but he can be.' When Hollywood fell under the spell of Chandler he never saw Robert Mitchum as Marlowe. He thought Bogart in *The Big Sleep* was the best tough-guy actor around – 'he could be tough without a gun'. One Hollywood Marlowe, Alan Ladd, was merely 'a small boy's idea of a tough guy'. If he himself had ever had the opportunity of selecting an actor to play Marlowe, Chandler said he would have chosen Cary Grant. Personally, I think he would have been pleased with Mitchum.

Los Angeles, it has been said, is a conglomeration of villages and small cities. Westwood, Pasadena, Beverly Hills for the rich; Watts for the poor blacks; East LA for Mexican Americans; and characterless streets from West Hollywood to the Pacific Ocean beaches. It has no real centre, no real identity, even now. 'A big hard-boiled city with no more personality than a paper cup,' wrote Chandler, who went to live there in 1912. 'I used to like this town. A big, dry sunny place with ugly homes and no style, but good-hearted and peaceful. It had the climate they yap about now. Intellectuals used to call it the Athens of America. It wasn't that, but it wasn't a neon-lighted slum either.' It became 'a world gone wrong', and some very tough people checked in. That was the penalty of growth. The penalty has not diminished in recent years.

My 'search' for Marlowe started when Nik drove me to Marlowe's office building, and parked his white Cherokee Chief near the corner of Cahuenga and Hollywood Boulevard. Maybe instead of a Cherokee it should have been a 1928 Nile-green Buick sedan, with a spotlight and little egg-shaped fender-lights on rods, but 1928 Buicks don't exist outside a museum.

The sidewalk on this block of Hollywood Boulevard is paved with stars in some pinkish, mottled stone like anaemic salami outlined in bronze and set in black terrazzo squares. The names of Hollywood 'greats' are inscribed in the stars. I stood between 'Marlene Dietrich' and 'Joseph von Sternberg' outside the Tick Tock Restaurant and craned my neck at Marlowe's office building. It was solid and tall, 1920s, Hollywood Classical Revival, part Athenian, part Byzantine in style. A large sign across its face announcing 'Security Pacific Bank' seemed like a warning.

Were we invading its privacy? I would have been happier wearing white pigskin gloves, a cane, a snap-brimmed hat set too far back on my head and a cream-coloured overcoat hiding a long .38 with a six-inch barrel. I would have turned the collar up around a lot of white silk scarf like Lou Hargen, the doomed gambler in *Finger Man*. As it was I felt vulnerably exposed – in olive-green Hong Kong-made slacks, a blue Ralph Lauren short-sleeved shirt, blood-red Marks & Spencer Oxford Street socks and unshined Florsheim Hush Puppies – to any galoot as big as Mike Tyson, who might wander up, sneer, 'What is your wish, amigo?' and not go for my pitch. Even the possibility of finding Marlowe wasn't worth a smack in the puss on the corner of Cahuenga.

While Nik snapped the building I shoved through the stream of passers-by on to a star saying 'Claude Rains' and peered up again at the high double windows with their handsome barley sugar stone frame. The sixth floor had a notice that said, 'Office space for

Lease'. That was the floor Marlowe operated out of. It was tempting to go to the drugstore advertising a condom sale ('Old stock. Must go.') and try telephoning Glenview 7537, Marlowe's number, for an appointment.

I could visualise the office. A dusty reception room with nothing there but an old red davenport, two odd chairs, a bit of carpet, and a library table with a few old magazines on it. No secretary. Through a locked door – lettered 'Philip Marlowe . . . Investigations' – is the private office, a swivel chair, back to the window, behind a desk where the office bottle is stashed in the special drawer (once standard in American desks), the depth of two ordinary drawers and intended to contain file holders. There is an ashtray on the desk with a bulldog pipe resting on it and a wooden chair opposite the desk. And there's a wardrobe where Marlowe keeps a change of bourbon.

But I didn't go up. I knew a modernised period building when I saw one. There'd be an open-plan office up there with a glass elevator opening into it, piped air, and lots of strip lighting. And ten to one there'd be no stiff on the floor.

Instead, we drove east down Hollywood and Sunset where drugstores become *Farmacias*, the film ads are in Spanish and the United Artists cinema promises us *Niñas gratis Lunes a Sabato*. Then across Spring Street south on Alameda, admiring the magnificent Spanish arches of Union Station.

'Okay, bo,' I said, 'snap it up.'

Nik said, '*Farewell, My Lovely?*' He made it a question.

Luckily I knew what he meant. 'Yeah, Florian's.' And we headed for the fly-blown no-man's-land of Central Avenue, above Watts. What's left of it after the Rodney King riots, that is.

If you want to see a good many washed-out acres of flops, clip joints, old car bodies and Skid Row human beings, come to Central Avenue around 54th Street. But empty your pockets first, and stick close to the curb.

Nik said, 'Surely, Marlowe wouldn't have come down streets quite so mean as these.' But it was here outside Florian's that Marlowe had first met Moose Malloy.

It was difficult – impossible – to identify Florian's 'the second floor dine and dice emporium' where Moose, fresh from the slammer, had come looking for his Velma. 'A big man but not more than six feet five inches tall and not wider than a beer truck. On Central Avenue, he looked about as inconspicuous as a tarantula on a slice of angel food.' Well, Nik Wheeler, ankle-deep in garbage, in designer corduroys and what looked like a $500 okapi-skin jacket by Calvin Klein, with his lens pointing at a dive called Venus Bar, was about as unobtrusive, as Chandler said of Betty Mayfield in *Playback*, as a kangaroo in a dinner jacket.

Central is a mainly black neighbourhood now. 'Smokes, dinges, shades' were Moose Malloy's terms for blacks in Marlowe's day, but we didn't care to test those terms for longevity on passers-by. It seemed unlikely the Heritage Society had preserved the widow Florian's house at 1644 West 54th Place, though there were plenty of places that matched Chandler's description of it:

> A dried-out brown house with a dried-out brown lawn . . . . A large bare patch round a tough-looking palm tree and unpruned shoots of last year's poinsettias tap-tapped against the cracked stucco wall. A line of stiff, yellowish half-washed clothes jittered on a rusty wire in the side yard . . . .

Most of the houses left here were still like that. It would take a brave man to rap on one of those ramshackle doors – even if there had been a better than million-to-one chance of being rewarded by the sound of old Jessie Florian's voice 'dragging itself out of her throat like a sick man getting out of bed'.

We slid away from there, after an hour or two, vowing we'd come back to case the local nightlife in depth – and knowing we wouldn't. Then we cut across town to the Polo Lounge in the Beverly Hills Hotel (before its owner, the Sultan of Brunei, could close it down), to nibble a reviving cocktail. I can't imagine that we were followed.

For grandeur Marlowe's office building has nothing on the Bryson Apartment building in Wilshire, where in Room 716 the beautiful and intelligent Adrienne Fromsett lived in *The Lady in the Lake*. Tall, lean, light-haired, she worked for Derace Kingsley, whose wife Marlowe was trying to trace, holding the fort in his office by day and his hand after hours.

When Marlowe saw the Bryson building it was 'a white stucco place with fretted lanterns in the forecourt and tall date palms. The entrance was in an L, up marble steps, through a Moorish archway.' It hasn't changed. We parked behind a Rolls-Royce painted in rainbow colours with a sticker on it that said, 'If you don't think money can buy happiness, you don't know where to shop', and climbed the steps.

The lobby was too large and smelled of old carpet. It had seen far better days. It contained silence and a concierge's desk in the far left corner. When Marlowe and the brutal Bay City police lieutenant, Al Degarmo, had called, the clerk asked, 'Whom do you wish to see?' and Degarmo had looked at Marlowe wonderingly.

'Did he say "whom"?'

'Yeah, but don't hit him. There is such a word.'

Degarmo licked his lips. 'I knew there was. I often wondered where they kept it.'

This concierge was a tall, courteous young man in glasses, happy to tell me the building, put up in 1912, once belonged to an Englishwoman, a Lady Bryson. It had been grand then all right, the lobby had elaborate mouldings and was lit by ornate brass lamps. 'It was a very prestigious hotel,' the clerk said.

The Fromsett frail, with her large, cool dark eyes, would be in Room 716. She would always be – wearing a quilted blue robe over her pyjamas and tufted slippers with high heels. The room would be narrow, with several handsome oval mirrors, and furniture upholstered in blue damask. Next door would be her bedroom, decorated in ivory and ashes of roses. There would be a heavy miasma of Derace Kingsley's product Gillerlain Regal, the Champagne of Perfumes, a kind of sandalwood chypre, and no give-away, for those days, at $100 an ounce.

The friendly clerk said these days all the rooms were real cheap – $675 a month; full of students and senior citizens. 'The marble-floored ballroom on the top floor was famous, I believe.' He shook his head. 'Now it's nothing but a pigeon-loft.'

We went outside and looked up. The clerk was right. The whole top floor was wide open to the air and pigeons flew in and out as if they owned it.

From that crumbling wedding cake of a building it was a long drive up into the mountains of 'Puma Lake' (actually Arrowhead Lake) where Derace Kingsley's wife so gruesomely reappeared under Marlowe's eyes. To get there we drove over Mulholland and down into the San Fernando Valley and followed the smog eastwards towards Pasadena and all those other suburbs that are as much a part of LA as Queens is of New York.

As Chandler had promised, after a couple of hours the road twisted out of the valley and climbed 5,000 feet in 15 miles. Tall oaks gave way to taller pines. Past Horsethief Canyon, a hilltop village called Crestline sat astride a long ridge, appropriately named the Rim of the World, from which hundreds of feet below you can see the great expanse of smog-ridden townships, distant tarmacked streets, narrow and straight on the valley floor, glittering like steel rails, and now and again a silver plane descending through the clear blue sky.

High on the ridge smart clapboard chalets crouch among the conifers; you imagine interiors of knotted pine, beautifully polished; Indian rugs; mountain mahogany driftwood fires spitting on stone hearths. Running Springs (Bubbling Springs, in the book) has a population now of 2,000, and past the Squirrel Café, and Johnnie's Restaurant, innumerable signs announce 'Car Wash' and 'Home Cooking'. The place was packed with tourists; no longer the placid retreat Chandler and his wife Cissie had loved. Everyone seemed to be there but the Pope's tomcat – and it looked like he was expected.

At Blue Jay we ate lunch in a diner – nothing could be finer – then took the winding road to Big Bear Lake and Arrowhead Dam to see where the army sentry had blasted the murderous Lieutenant Degarmo to hellangone. (*The Lady in the Lake* appeared in wartime when the dam was well guarded, in case the Japanese Army stormed ashore at Malibu.)

The dam is larger than my little finger, though a good deal smaller than Boulder Dam, and it took some recognising. It held back barely enough water to satisfy a thirsty Pekinese. Maybe we got the wrong dam.

I peered hopefully into the still green water. Nothing that 'looked too much like a human arm' waved languidly at us from the depths. No 'swollen, pulpy, grey-white mass floated up to us; without features, without eyes, without mouth, but with a necklace of green stone half-embedded in what had been a woman's neck'. Nor was Kingsley's disabled, hard-drinking caretaker, Bill Chess, beside me, croaking, 'Muriel! Sweet Christ, it's Muriel!'

That had been nearly fifty years ago, and I felt suddenly old and sad. All that came to me now through the thick, silent growth of trees was the roaring of pleasure-boat engines on the little lake and the laughter of Dick Francis readers from the yacht marina . . . .

Bay City (really Santa Monica) was the epitome of Chandler's crooked American town. 'Sure it's a nice town,' he wrote. 'It's probably no crookeder than Los Angeles. But you can only buy a piece of a big city. You can buy a town like this all complete, with the original box and tissue paper.' For Chandler Bay City epitomised civic hypocrisy. It was where he was given the runaround by the Chief of Police and his henchman, Hemingway, a dumb and corrupt officer so nicknamed, Marlowe sneered, 'because he keeps saying the same thing over and over again until you begin to believe it must be good'.

Hemingway (the cop) said: 'A guy can't stay honest if he wants to. He gets chiselled out of his pants if he does . . . . You know what I think? Take Moral Disarmament. There you got something, baby.'

'If Bay City is a sample of how it works,' snapped Marlowe, 'I'll take aspirin.' If he had had to watch the famous video of the Rodney King beating of 1992 that was to spark off the burning and looting of a good deal of Los Angeles, he'd have reached for something stronger than aspirin.

We parked the Cherokee Chief off Ocean Avenue, Santa Monica's Promenade des Anglais, which runs along a bluff fringed with trees falling away to a very wide beach. Under the trees sprawl the bums; scores of them, shaven heads, dreadlocks, passing joints in a sweet aura of hash. A couple of mounted policemen were questioning a fragrant old geezer under a palm. But their smiles that day were well pinned on.

A moth-eaten pier ran out across the beach to the Pacific Ocean where Catalina Island lay in the distant haze. Marlowe would have seen the old gambling ship out there, too; in *Farewell, My Lovely* it was owned by Laird Brunette, a svelte killer in dinner jacket and cummerbund, who might have had his hooks into Moose Malloy's old flame, Velma.

The 100-year-old pier was badly damaged recently by storms, but there's a move to restore it. Just in time. Men were fishing from its barnacled underpinnings. A sad, dropsical building, like an old bath-house, had 'Sinbad's. Cocktails. Dinner' painted on it, and outside it a black man stood playing on a sax a mournful dirge that might have been 'Bay City Blues', and which sounded like a tune played in a dirty bathtub.

Still, Santa Monica, no Côte d'Azur certainly, has improved since Chandler's day. There's a small Sheraton and a Shangri-la Hotel, a French restaurant, even a pub, Ye Olde King's Head, where Nik and I ate shepherd's pie and fishcakes under photographs of beer-gutted English visitors with waterfall moustaches. My spirit preferred to stay with simple, golden-hearted Marlowe, the tough-guy invention of a hard intellectual out of Dulwich College. And if that was snobbism, nerts to it.

Idaho Street was where – in *The Little Sister* – Orfamay Quest's erring brother, Orrin, had shacked up – and nearby was Dr Sonderborg's so-called Convalescent Home to which, in *Farewell, My Lovely*, Hemingway, having sapped him, had admitted the unconscious Marlowe so that the unscrupulous doctor could turn him into an instant junkie.

'You could know Bay City without knowing Idaho,' Marlowe said of that street. 'You could know a lot of Idaho without knowing No. 449.' That's doubly true now. Idaho runs a short way, then stops, and No. 449 is buried under a modern development as Orrin is buried, no doubt, back in Manhattan, Kansas. But spotting something very like Dr Sonderborg's looney-bin a block or so away, we sidled along to have a squint. The result was unexpected.

An elderly crone with a face like Tug Boat Annie, dressed in a poinsettia-red nightie, roared out: 'Hey, mister, $50 to take a picture of this historic home.' She leered furiously at me, showing numerous teeth which, as Marlowe would have said, certainly hadn't grown in her mouth. Fifty rugs a snap? I thought of giving her a shove on the beezer, pushing past and catching Sonderborg syringing dope into Philip Marlowe. But what the hell. Telling her to go take a powder, we left Marie Dressler scowling from her porch.

Then on to Police Headquarters, home in the 1920s and 1930s of the Third Degree and the length of rubberhose that leaves no visible wound, where I had made a date with the present Chief of Police. It was a handsome complex of 1950s' vintage. What did I expect? Marlowe had described the undecorated office; a linoleumed floor, a brass spittoon, a desk and two hard chairs: and a cop with a harder face flinging cigar-butts on to the linoleum to smoulder in the corner.

It was quite different now. The Chief of Police, a genial man in civilian clothes ('I hate uniforms,' he said), shook hands, then sat relaxed in a comfortable modern room, with deep comfortable chairs, prints of Remington paintings of the Old West on the walls, lots of books, and a London bobby's helmet like an incongruous toy on a shelf. There was no spittoon. No cigar-butts, either.

The Chief had moved here from Boston thirty years before and was happy to have done so. 'I've watched the place prosper. Main Street used to be just poor thrift shops, small diners. Now you can't buy property, it costs so much. Look, I bought a house here years ago for $35,000. Now it's worth, I don't know, $750,000.' He had barely heard of Chandler or Marlowe. 'Private eyes are really into hi-tech stuff nowadays. I can't think of anyone who goes about beating the bushes like the old days.'

Was the Mob – Bugsy Siegel and Co. – still in those bushes?

'No,' the Chief said. 'Let me tell you something. If the Siegels of this day and age can't buy the police, the mobsters can't flourish.' I was interested. He'd raised the corruption issue, I hadn't. 'The Law is where you buy it in Bay City,' Marlowe had said. The Chief, I thought, was being frank. Since the big clean-up in the LA Police Department in the 1950s by Chief Parker, the mobsters, the grifters, the chisellers had mostly retreated back to Las Vegas. Now a police officer could earn at least $30–40,000 a year after three years' duty. As Chandler drily noted: 'It's always nice to know the police no longer have bad dreams when they see themselves trying to live on their pay.' This Chief of Police looked like he slept pretty well. Santa Monica once flaunted some prize mobsters, like Siegel and Meyer Lansky. Now the problem was a familiar one: drugs and the homeless.

'Homeless from all over the country,' the Chief said. 'They reach here and stop – well, they can't swim the ocean. You get drug-takers. And mentally retarded drunks. The crime rate's always been quite high. Seven, eight homicides a year.' That didn't seem high to me in a population of 96,000. In the days of white dinner jackets and the gambling 'wrecks', Laird Brunette's gunsels might have accounted for that number in one quiet weekend.

There remained a visit to a modern Private Eye. Philip Marlowe wasn't in the phone directory; and he was eighty years old and might be running in a new set of dentures. The first couple of LA gumshoes I phoned failed to answer and a recorded voice said their numbers had been discontinued. Unpaid bills? Were they on the lam? Finally – there he was: Milo Speriglio of the Nick Harris Detectives down in Van Nuys.

'A real private eye,' wrote Chandler in the 1950s, 'is a sleazy little drudge, a strong-arm guy with no more personality than a blackjack, and as much moral stature as a stop-and-go sign.' This certainly does not apply to Mr Speriglio, bright as a tack, director of the 'oldest investigative academy in the world' which celebrated its eightieth birthday in 1987.

Milo (Milo/Marlowe) is a sprightly fellow with a mobile face and a warm, easy smile. He dresses snappily in an expensive shirt and slacks with a lot of jewellery round wrists and fingers that the earthy Marlowe might sneer at. A former rock-and-roll disc jockey, he looks alert and reliable. His agency building is nothing like Marlowe's Cahuenga place: it's one-storeyed and modern, set in a sleek suburb with wide streets; its room decorated with framed testimonials, memorabilia, and signed pictures of recent Presidents of the USA.

Clearly Milo is A Top Gumshoe.

I ran a hawk's eye over his loose shirt, said, 'What, no rod?' He laughed.

'Know what we use today instead of guns? A phial of teargas.'

Deftly, he unclipped a black leather case from his waist that might have contained an unusually fat thermometer. 'This is small-bore: range 10 feet. A larger one'll reach 25 feet. You need a state licence.' Nick Harris, the founder of the firm, he said, used to carry a gun. Different times. Milo is high-profile, has written an exposé of the Marilyn Monroe murder 'cover-up' he believes in. Harris became famous on national radio recounting his case histories, and he certainly made more money than poor Marlowe with his pre-war $25 a day plus expenses, rising postwar to $40 a day and mileage. Milo's rate can go to $150 an hour. But Marlowe wasn't in it for money. And Marlowe's opinion of Big Money was succinct: 'To hell with the rich. They make me sick. They misuse power and are careless about other people.'

The Nick Harris operative's course is mostly surveillance, how to detect clandestine wiretaps, searching for concealed bank accounts, tracing missing persons (who often turn up after months of search, living practically next-door, hiding from creditors), heir-searching, drug investigation, and so on. 'Karate? We dropped our bodyguard school. No demand for it,' shrugged Milo, standing under a framed picture of Nick Harris arresting Clara Phillips, known as the 'Hammer murderess', in 1922.

Milo Speriglio hadn't read Marlowe or Sherlock Holmes. 'Mostly I read law books, reference books, criminology.' He didn't know the derivation of the word 'Shamus', meaning 'gumshoe' or private cop – but who does?

'Ever find a body in the lake?' I asked hopefully.

'Not very often. In thirty years I've never found one.'

He admits to several mafias in LA – Japanese, Chinese, Mex, even Jewish – but they don't tangle with him or vice versa. Still, just in case, he keeps a .38 Detective Special in his drawer and he *does* practise at the range once in a while with his .357 Magnum with a four-inch barrel ('Clint Eastwood's in *Dirty Harry* has a six-inch barrel.')

'See this girl.' A slim, leggy blonde slid into a seat by me; just the sort to make Marlowe's fallen arches throb riotously. 'She's a sharpshooter. Great,' said Milo proudly, 'with either hand.'

'I'll bet she is,' I said, appreciatively.

Nik Wheeler's Cherokee was due outside by now. Time to tear myself away. I thanked Milo Speriglio and shook his hand.

It had been a long day. Suddenly the independent spirit of Marlowe surged into my soul. I wanted to get out of this overpopulated high-techery. I thought wistfully of Marlowe's lonely apartment off Yucca Avenue with 'its honey smell of dust and tobacco, the smell of a world where men live, and keep on living'. He wouldn't be there any more, though. He might be in a home for senior citizens. That thought made me want to treat my tonsils to five fingers of firewater and set fire to a cigarette, but the pint flask on my hip was empty and I'd stopped smoking fifteen years ago.

On the way out, I'd have liked to drop a grand or two into the pretty receptionist's lap, murmuring, 'Here, sweetheart, buy yourself some stardust.' But I had only $5.35 in my pocket.

Nik Wheeler was toot-tooting impatiently at the curb. I walked across to his heap, made a roscoe out of my forefinger and thumb, snapped it through the window at him, and said, 'Kat-chow!' Then I got in beside him.

'Okay, pal, let's dangle,' I snarled. I adjusted the heater in the holster under my arm and pushed my fedora to the back of my head.

'Step on the gas, amigo!'

Nik ground the jalopy into gear and we tooled back to Hollywood through the smog.

Chapter 12

Does it seem strange that Raymond Chandler, more than any other writer, succeeded in making anyone who read his detective novels feel profoundly acquainted with that strange and timeless city, Los Angeles? Although Chandler was an American of mainly Irish descent and born in Chicago, he spent virtually all the years of his youth in Britain, was educated at an English public school, served in the First World War in the Canadian army and subsequently the Royal Air Force and, as a result of all that transatlantic experience, didn't get back to America until he was thirty-one.

Yet Chandler's father, Maurice, was as American as they come. An engineer who worked for a Western railroad company, while on an assignment in Laramie, Wyoming, he met his wife Florence, born in Waterford and wholly Irish. Maurice Chandler and Florence Thornton settled in Chicago, where Raymond was born in July 1888. Later Maurice took to the bottle in a big way, divorced Florence, and was never heard of again. Which is why Florence took Raymond, then aged seven, to England to live with her mother, first in the south London suburb of Norwood, then in another suburb, Dulwich.

Raymond went to Dulwich College Preparatory School, then on to the college proper, arriving as a pupil there a few years after a very different writer, P. G. Wodehouse, the creator of Jeeves and Bertie Wooster. That Chandler – like Wodehouse – loved the whole public school system and became a lifelong anglophile, shows in his writing, despite the pungent American vernacular style he painstakingly developed and which gives his novels such characteristic verve and humour.

For example, it is not difficult to detect the clear-cut moral standards of Dulwich College in the make-up of that tough 'private eye' and romantic, not to say sentimental, character Chandler called Philip Marlowe, who became a familiar hero to millions of admiring readers. Why should it be? Marlowe was as deeply American as Chandler himself, but the standards Chandler gave Marlowe were his own, and as Englishly 'decent' as would befit a very hard-boiled Robin Hood. If Marlowe had been a reading man (and had been born a few decades earlier) he might have found himself as enthralled by the historical romances of Sir Walter Scott and the poetry of Lord

Byron that called for fair play for Greece, as William Barret Travis, the defender of the Alamo, had been.

Back in America after the First World War, Chandler lost no time in seeing as much of California as possible. He married an already twice-married woman, Cissy Pascal, in Los Angeles and for the next several years shunted her round the city to a bewildering variety of houses, seemingly unable to settle.

At the time of their marriage, in February 1924, Cissy was fifty-three to Chandler's thirty-five – and not surprisingly some cruel people sneered that 'he had married his mother'. He had joined an oil syndicate and did so well that quite soon he was put in charge of the company's Los Angeles office.

So far so good. He was married and earning a good salary. But he was not, as he dreamed of being, a writer, even though now and again he could compose a rather sloppy romantic poem. The trouble was the oil company kept him too busy for serious writing, and he and Cissy were forever leap-frogging about LA looking for the ideal house to live in. Perhaps the one good thing about the frenetic house-hopping was that it coincidentally gave Chandler a knowledge of the city that would later prove useful when he *did* start writing.

Then all at once – it is difficult to tell why – he began to become his own worst enemy. He became rude and irritable and had begun to go off on long weekend binges – with or without girls – only returning to the office on the following Wednesday with a blinding headache. Obviously such erratic behaviour could not continue indefinitely and he was finally fired. In 1932, aged forty-four, Raymond Chandler was jobless, on the skids, apparently washed up.

That this was a terrible blow is to put it mildly. His income, of course, fell with a thump, and it was lucky that he had never liked flamboyant living. As Frank MacShane, his biographer, remarks, typical of Chandler's resilient nature was his attitude that being fired at least 'taught me not to take anything for granted'.

So at the ripe old age of forty-five Raymond Chandler at last began to try his hand at writing. Why he plumped for crime is not explained, but he started with the pulp magazines – so called because they were made from wood pulp and therefore cheap enough to chuck away when finished with – and of which the best at the time was *Black Mask*, founded in 1920 by H. L. Mencken and George Jean Nathan. One of *Black Mask*'s contributors was Dashiell Hammett, and Chandler immediately spotted Hammett's special talent for swift, no-time-to-waste dialogue. Casting about for a model on which to base his own style, he began assiduously to study Hammett's no-nonsense way of writing.

What fascinated Chandler was Hammett's easy use of authentic day-to-day American language to illustrate what were, after all, modern *American* crime stories. In the age of Al Capone, Hammett, he said, 'took murder out of the Venetian vase and dropped it in the alley . . . . He gave murder back to the people who committed it for reasons, not just to provide a corpse.' And his enthusiasm went further. Hammett's style, he thought, 'at its best', could say almost anything.

These days, I think, many people comparing Hammett's and Chandler's work would judge, while admitting that the two of them were the supreme inventors of the hard-boiled murder story, that Chandler was the more imaginative writer. Though, as he said, Hammett's style could say almost anything, Chandler found ways of saying things that Hammett did not even feel the need to say. The Hammett style, Chandler himself noticed, 'had no overtones, left no echo, evoked no image beyond a distant hill'.

That became Chandler's view over a period of time, but at first he was content to admire and to strive to emulate. 'I had to learn American like a foreign language,' he explained. And during the slow evolution of the Philip Marlowe character, he practised that American language, polishing and repolishing that smart repartee, in the many short stories he wrote for *Black Mask* and other pulps featuring early prototypes of Marlowe.

You see Marlowe evolving gradually, like a statue from a sculptor's block of granite: from early prototypes like John Delmas, Ted Carmady, Johnny Deruse, Peter Anglish and Sam Delaguerra, all of whom were, as Frank MacShane says, in the rough-hewn Robin Hood tradition; all of them tough, independent and living by their own strict moral standards. If they all shared one other trait it was that they all were disliked and resented by the police. And vice versa.

That police violence and corruption have long been more common in Los Angeles than most other American cities was demonstrated in a book written many years ago. The book, called *Our Lawless Police*, was written in 1931 by Ernest Hopkins, and it is easy to see why private detectives like Marlowe would put backs up among the regular police organisations. They would seem too good to be true, these Robin Hood characters in their fedoras and double-breasted suits, these men going down 'the mean streets', as Chandler described them in a famous passage, 'men who are not themselves mean, who are neither tarnished nor afraid'.

Perhaps the most attractive aspect of Raymond Chandler (apart from his humour) is his utter honesty – with himself and his writing. He struggled extremely hard to achieve a new realism in his hard-boiled novels and stories, but at the same time, as MacShane reveals, he knew perfectly well that a real person as sensitive and intelligent as Marlowe, bursting with muscles and morals though he might be, simply would not work as a private eye. 'The private detective of fiction,' he said, 'does not and could not exist. He is the personification of an attitude, the exaggeration of a possibility.'

In another famous burst of candour, Chandler explained:

> The whole point is that the detective exists complete and entire and unchanged by anything that happens, that he is, as detective, outside the story and above it, and always will be. That is why he never gets the girl, never marries, never really has any private life, except insofar as he must eat and sleep and have a place to keep his clothes. His moral and intellectual force is that he gets nothing but his fee, for which he will if he can protect the innocent, guard the helpless and destroy the wicked, and the fact that he must do this while earning a meagre living in a corrupt world is what makes him stand out.

He is, in fact, as imbued with the British public school spirit as was his creator. How far removed is a certain type of Dulwich schoolboy, from the description of Marlowe that Chandler gives us in his revealing essay, 'The Simple Art of Murder'? Surely not very far.

> He has a sense of character, or he would not know his job. He will take no man's money dishonestly and no man's insolence without a due and dispassionate revenge. He is a lonely man and his pride is that you will treat him as a proud man or be sorry you ever saw him. He talks as a man of his age talks – that is, with a rude wit, a lively sense of the grotesque, a disgust for sham, and a contempt for pettiness.

The Dulwich College prefect is not *very* far away, even when we remember that Marlowe was totally American, that Chandler began writing about him when he was fifty years old and that between Dulwich and *The Big Sleep* and *Farewell, My Lovely* were long years of residence in California.

At the time of my writing this, desperate things were going on in Los Angeles.

I had come back to California after some years to rediscover the writer who has best depicted the violence and corruption in the mean streets and high places of this tormented city. Chandler's novels, even though they were written in the 1940s and 1950s, are still relevant. It's just that things since he died have simply got much worse.

Coming back this time, from the window of my hotel on Sunset Boulevard near the corner of Laurel I could see at night the neon glare that hides the big city's latent rage behind coloured lights. This time the rage, real rage, could erupt again at any moment. It was nearly the first anniversary of the riots that had ravaged the South-Central part of Los Angeles – the poor, largely black-, Latino- and Korean-populated areas – in the wake of the beating of an Afro-American man called Rodney King by a handful of white policemen. As it happened, the incident achieved nationwide exposure on TV, since the fearful incident was recorded on video film for the world and posterity by George Holliday, an amateur cameraman and plumbing salesman, who happened to walk on to his balcony and get his camera rolling. The policemen were acquitted by the jury. And violent riots, burning and looting followed the acquittal.

There had been riots in Los Angeles before but not on this scale. This time the Police Department, under its Chief Darryl Gates, was accused of a tardy reaction to the violence; Gates was forced to resign; and the four police officers involved in the beating of Rodney King faced a second trial – a federal one, this time – on charges of violating King's civil rights. I arrived to investigate Chandler's ghost just before the second verdict on the King incident was due. Even more pregnant with violent potential, some people thought, was the trial due to start a little later of some black rioters charged with dragging a white truck driver from his cab during the King riots and severely beating him. Everyone was wondering what that verdict would be. Would 'those people' riot again?

'Kill cop' messages were spray-painted on walls. (I think that was just before 'rap' singers began chanting similar messages.) Military assault weapons had multiplied on the streets. Casual shooting of cops in those same streets increased to a hitherto unheard-of level. In brief, the feeling in Los Angeles was one, as Chandler wrote years ago, of a 'restless emptiness, indifference and ugliness'. The difference was that now you could toughen those words up to powerlessness, hopelessness and a deep vulnerability.

In this time of fear and uncertainty I read an interesting article in the *Los Angeles Times*. The writer suggested a plan of action for anyone who might genuinely want to do something about the city's plight.

Let him leaf through the telephone book for the name of his County Council representative [the article suggested]. Let him head down to City Hall. Let him demand to gripe with his councilman about the urban chaos that's pushing him to madness. Let him get shuffled off to a staff aide [a nice and realistic touch, that]. Let him storm out and demand his councilman's fund-raisers statement. Let him seethe at the tens of thousands of dollars contributed by real-estate developers and slum landlords, liquor industry lobbyists and other influence peddlers. Let him begin writing down the names. Let him begin visiting those guys.

Good idea, because one trouble is that some businesses and industries which a year ago, in the panicky aftermath of the riots, promised money to rebuild the riot-torn areas of downtown Los Angeles have largely failed to deliver. By now those downtown areas, seedy and forbidding refuges for the homeless and the haunt of crack dealers, are in urgent need of revival. Few people would want to walk there at night.

I looked out the writer of that article on downtown. We met for a rather sombre breakfast in the John O'Groats diner on Pico Boulevard. Over sausages and hash browns we discussed his experience with the gangs of South-Central Los Angeles, and he opened up a whole new area – no, continent – of gloom.

'The gangs are usually black or Latino – seldom mixed,' he began by saying. 'There's no work for them in sight. And of course it's difficult to get about such an enormous area to look for it.'

It had taken me a surprisingly long time even to get to this diner by taxi, so I understood what he meant by the vast distances one had to cover in this city. The really important thing he had to tell me about the youth gangs was this:

'Try to imagine the incredibly limited outlook on life these kids have. I know of a group of kids who were taken from Central to look at some studios in Hollywood just over the hill. When they got there, they looked about them and asked, "Hey, man, are we still in the same state – still in California? Where is this?" '

Leaving the diner and all the way back to my hotel in a cab I thought about that true story. Yes, I thought: try to imagine that youthful mentality; try to imagine you have no knowledge of geography – even the geography of your own city. Imagine never having read a book, never having had the intention or the means to open one. Imagine, on top of this, living surrounded by thugs and drug dealers, abject poverty, no work; sheer naked fear and thuggery, day and night. Imagine in these conditions watching the fat cats tooling by in their sharp limousines. Imagine the distant dream world of Beverly Hills; of palm trees and neat lawns and houses built like Spanish farmhouses; a world only a few miles away.

Imagine all these things, and see yourself inextricably stuck with the ghastly life you have inherited. Then tell me why you would not have a barely containable urge to burn something down.

I thought about all those things in the cab back to my hotel. As a matter of fact I am still thinking about them. I haven't yet come up with a good answer.

What would Philip Marlowe do about the present turmoil in Los Angeles? He would be baffled by much of what he would see today: by the ubiquitous use of hard drugs, for example. Poverty, of course, is not new – it was ever present even in the old days. And there were guns and hoodlums and gambling. Race, too, was a problem. The bad feeling among whites about blacks was as bad then as it is now, if not worse: one only has to remember Moose Malloy casually taking apart a 'dinge' joint in Central in the first few pages of *Farewell, My Lovely*.

As for the police, Chandler was famously harsh on their propensity for violence. He never spared them. If they were brutal he said so. If a couple of cops had watching and waiting eyes – the sort of eyes he disliked and mistrusted – patient and careful eyes, cool, disdainful eyes, he said they had cops' eyes. They got them, he explained, at the passing-out parade at the police school.

Chandler made Marlowe deeply concerned about the behaviour of the Los Angeles police. In *The High Window* he lectures them severely:

> Until you guys own your own souls you don't own mine. Until you guys can be trusted every time and always, in all times and conditions, to seek the truth and find it and let the chips fall where they may – until that time comes, I have a right to listen to my conscience, and protect my client the best way I can . . . .

But Chandler was not simply a cop hater. True, at least one of Chandler's cops, Big Willie Magoon, was a brute, but detective Bernie Ohls was a humane and reasonable man, though of course he could be tough as well. It was not simple toughness that worried Chandler. What in him went very deep was a pathological hatred of ruthless bullies – in any walk of life.

As a matter of fact he had sympathy for the cops – with their dirty and dangerous job, their skimpy pay and their poor working conditions. As MacShane noticed, Chandler visited the Los Angeles Police Department Homicide Bureau to jot down in a notebook what he saw for future reference. He noted that the Bureau occupied a mere two rooms on the Main Street level of City Hall; rooms roughly 15 feet square with brown linoleum on the floor.

The outer room contains a walnut table, a few wooden chairs, three

> or four telephones and about fourteen plainclothes dicks .... They
> stand around, smoke, talk, telephone and as the occasion requires,
> walk through the open door in a pebbled glass partition without any
> formality into the room of the Captain in charge of the Homicide
> Bureau. He has a flat-top business desk and two telephones on a
> shelf to his right. There is no other equipment of any kind on the
> table. He has a hard wooden swivel chair without even a cushion or
> a felt pad .... The remaining furnishings of this office consist of a
> couple of green metal filing cabinets and one straight wooden chair
> without arms. This is absolutely positively all.

Of course, these days the Captain's office would have more equip-
ment – a fax, for example, cushions and more comfortable chairs.
He might even prefer to keep the door closed. But the improvements
would be relative. A policeman's job today is much the same as it was
then, and probably even more dangerous. They have always seen a
different world from the one we do. For cops, explained Chandler,
civilisation had no meaning. 'All they saw of it was the failure, the
dirt, the dregs, the aberrations and the disgust.' And in *The Little
Sister* he has Christy French, the Homicide Bureau's chief, let off
steam to Marlowe:

> It's like this with us, baby. We're coppers and everybody hates
> our guts. And as if we didn't have enough trouble, we have to
> have you. As if we didn't get pushed around enough by the boys in
> the corner offices, the City Hall gang, the day chief, the night chief,
> the chamber of commerce, His Honour the Mayor in his panelled
> office four times as big as the three lousy rooms the whole homicide
> staff has to work out of .... We spend our lives turning over dirty
> underwear and sniffing rotten teeth. We go up dark stairways to get
> a gun punk with a skinful of hop and sometimes we don't come
> home anymore. And nights we do come home, we come home so
> goddam tired we can't eat or sleep or read the lies the papers print
> about us. So we lie awake in the dark in a cheap house on a cheap
> street and listen to the drunks down the block having fun. And just
> about the time we drop off the phone rings and we get up and start
> all over again. Nothing we do is right, not ever. Not once. If we get a
> confession, we beat it out of the guy, they say, and some shyster calls
> us Gestapo in court and sneers at us when we muddle our grammar.
> If we make a mistake they put us back in uniform on Skid Row and
> we spend the nice cool summer evenings picking drunks out of the
> gutter and being yelled at by whores and taking knives away from
> grease-balls in zoot suits. But that ain't enough to make us entirely
> happy. We got to have you.

You don't hear the term 'grease-ball' any more and 'zoot suits'
are out of fashion, but in that emotional speech Chandler was
doing his best to explain the psychology of policemen. I doubt

whether any cop could put the police point of view with more heartfelt passion.

It was not only the world of cops and hoodlums Chandler excelled in describing. His books are littered with telling phrases which bring Los Angeles as a whole to vivid life. Writing of the San Fernando Valley on a breathless day, Chandler says:

> The valley had a thick layer of smog nuzzling down on it. From above it looked like a ground mist and then we were in it and it jerked Spencer out of his silence.
> 'My God, I thought Southern California had a climate,' he said. 'What are they doing – burning old truck tyres?'

Even with all the anti-pollution efforts, that scene can recur.

And a short passage in *The Long Goodbye* brings to vivid life one small but basic aspect of America especially well.

Terry Lennox is speaking:

> I like bars just after they open for the evening. When the air inside is still cool and clean and everything is shiny and the barkeep is giving himself that last look in the mirror to see if his tie is straight and his hair is smooth. I like the neat bottles on the bar back and the lovely shining glasses and the anticipation. I like to watch the man mix the first one of the evening and put it down on a crisp mat and put the little folded napkin beside it. I like to taste it slowly. The first quiet drink of the evening in a quiet bar – that's wonderful.

Marlowe agrees with him. So do I. One doesn't have to be a drunk to agree with that description of a bar in America – the special degree of professional pride of American barmen, their smooth expertise, the spick and span neatness that American bars have that bars in other countries seem to lack. It is in such short interpolations that Chandler brings alive the California he loved to write about.

Here is another:

> At 11 o'clock I was sitting in the third booth on the right-hand side as you go in from the dining-room .... A girl in a white sharkskin suit and a luscious figure was climbing the ladder to the high board ....

The girl dives, then leaves the pool and enters the dining-room. Marlowe watches her:

> She wobbled her bottom over to a small white table and sat down beside a lumberjack in white drill pants and dark glasses and a tan so evenly dark that he couldn't have been anything but a hired man around the pool. He reached over and patted her thigh. She opened her mouth like a firebucket and laughed. That terminated my interest

in her. I couldn't hear the laugh but the hole in her face when she unzipped her teeth was all I needed.

Frank MacShane remarks that 'without saying anything about life in Beverly Hills, this says everything'. Not *everything*, I would say; but quite a lot.

Chandler's verdict on Los Angeles, it seems to me, can be summed up in the following passage from *The Long Goodbye*, his last novel and, I think, his finest:

> When I got home I mixed a stiff one and stood by the open window in the living room and listened to the groundswell of the traffic on Laurel Canyon and looked at the glare of the big angry city . . . . A city no worse than others, a city rich and vigorous and full of pride, a city lost and beaten and full of emptiness.

Yes, it all depends on where you sit.

After the Second World War, the Chandlers moved from Los Angeles to the pleasant seaside town of La Jolla. They had had enough of Los Angeles. They had begun to find the city too aggressive, and Chandler, after some success turning out screenplays – and enduring a good deal of the frustration most good writers found in Hollywood – was not averse to the change, if only for Cissy's sake.

In his life of Raymond Chandler, Frank MacShane describes La Jolla, Southern California, as one of those American towns from which the ugly aspects of life have been carefully excluded. Chandler himself described it as a 'reluctant suburb' of neighbouring San Diego.

It was a beautiful place – and still is – hugging the Pacific shore, but after his years in the big city further north Chandler's view of it was that it was too damned genteel; so genteel that his first impulse was to 'get out into the street and shout four-letter words'. He had become used to the hurly-burly of Los Angeles, a rough-and-tumble city where you could get out into the streets and few people would notice what you shouted.

Nevertheless, Chandler got accustomed to La Jolla pretty quickly. From the beginning, his wife, Cissy, seventy-six by the time they moved there in 1946, liked it more than he did; perhaps she talked him round to it. In any case, he went on living and working there, writing his best novel, *The Long Goodbye*, on those cliffs with sounds of the sea. And there he died – slightly more than four years after Cissy – in 1959.

I drove the two hours south from Los Angeles the other day to see that house which he moved into shortly after it was built. No. 6005 Camino de la Costa is a charming bungalow with a tiled roof near the sea. You drive down the beach, swing right into Prospect, then take a turn on to Camino de la Costa, which runs along a long ridge of cliffs. The house, half hidden on a corner under cascades of flowers, shrubs and small trees, was white and fresh-looking, not right on the sea but with a good view of it through a gap in the line of cliff-top houses opposite. It looks like the perfect place to write books in.

I strolled to a gap between two houses overlooking the sea, where there was a rail to lean on as one took in the view southwards and seawards. The headlands that thrust out separated La Jolla from the great bay of San Diego. It reminded me of the coast of Cornwall in southwestern England where I was brought up, although here in California there were more housing estates. The ocean here was more gentle: no high breakers pounded the low Californian cliffs; no high-flung waves sprinkled the neat gardens of La Jolla with salt spray. One could see the diminishing levels of rock as they shelved away into the deeper water, and brown, inscrutable, gull-like birds stood in the shallows, occasionally delving with their beaks under the surface for whatever sea-creatures the tide had abandoned there.

I can't remember that Chandler wrote much about the ocean near the home he shared with Cissy, or about the soft sound of its ebb and surge, which he could easily hear from his porch.

By coincidence another American writer took a keen interest at that time in the ocean-life of the same part of the Southern Californian coast. John Steinbeck, born in Salinas, further north, in 1902 – fourteen years after Chandler – was to write a good deal about the human inhabitants of the coastal townships of Monterey and Carmel that lie about halfway between Los Angeles and San Francisco. One of them – Steinbeck called him Doc – was a small, strongly built, bearded man, the owner and operator of the Western Biological Laboratory in Steinbeck's *Cannery Row*. One of the best-loved and respected of fellows who lived in Monterey, 'Doc' – in real life Ed Ricketts, marine biologist and Steinbeck's closest friend – thought of the sea rocks and beaches of the whole coast as his private stockpile.

Doc made a point of getting to the good tides along that coast in order to keep up his laboratory's collection of marine animals. All the articles of his trade were filed away on the coast: sea cradles here, octopi there; tube worms in another place, sea pansies in another. As Steinbeck put it, Nature locked up these items and only released them occasionally. Thus it was up to Doc to know the tides, and know when to be ready to pack his collecting tools in his car, and drive, at short notice, the 500 miles to the boulder-strewn coast at La Jolla. Doc knew that little octopi lurked in the caves and crevices on the sandy bottom of the sea where they could hide from predators and protect themselves from the waves. On the same flat there would be millions of sea cradles, and Doc would wade about in the shallows replenishing his stocks just below Raymond and Cissy Chandler's flowery bungalow.

One morning Doc stumbled on a tragedy. It was an unexplained something that seemed a good deal more in Raymond Chandler's line than Doc's or Steinbeck's. At any rate, it scared the daylights out of Doc.

Steinbeck described the scene.

> The tide goes out imperceptibly here. The boulders show and seem to rise up and the ocean recedes leaving little pools, leaving wet weed and moss and sponge, iridescent and brown and blue and China red. On the bottom lies the incredible refuse of the sea, shells broken and chipped and bits of skeleton, claws, the whole sea bottom a fantastic cemetery on which the living scamper and scramble.

The terrible thing was this. In preparation for wading, Doc had pulled on his rubber boots and his rain cap. He had his buckets and jars, his crowbar, his sandwiches and his thermos. He went down the cliff and over the flat as the tide moved out. He began pulling out little squirming octopi and filling his jar.

That day it was good hunting; Doc popped twenty-two little octopi into his wooden bucket. As the tide moved out he came at last to the outer barrier where long leathery brown algae hung down in to the water.

Then he saw this unbelievable thing. A girl's face looked up at him, a pretty, pale girl with dark hair.

> The eyes were open and clear and the face was firm and the hair washed gently about her head. The body was out of sight, caught in the crevice. The lips were slightly parted and the teeth showed and on the face was only comfort and rest. Just under the water it was and the clear water made it very beautiful.

Music sounded in Doc's ears, 'a high thin piercingly thin flute'.

Doc very slowly raised his hand and let the brown weed float back and cover the beautiful face. 'He sat there hearing the music while the sea crept in again over the bouldery flat.' Then he went slowly back towards the beach. And while the girl's face went ahead of him, Doc heard the strange flute playing that unbelievable melody.

In a little while a voice seemed to waken him. A man stood

over him. 'Say, aren't you feeling well?' the man said. 'You look sick.'

Doc shook off the music, shook off the face, shook the chill out of his body. 'Is there a police station near?'

'Up in town. Why what's wrong?'

'There's a body out on the reef. Will you report it? I'm not feeling well.'

Then Doc started towards his car, and by that time 'only the tiniest piping of the flute sounded in his head'.

In 1945 Steinbeck wrote about this tragedy of the shallows in *Cannery Row*. The next year Chandler came to live in Camino de la Costa, which overlooked the place in which Steinbeck said it had occurred.

As far as I know there's no way of finding out if Steinbeck's little bit of horror is fact or fiction. When I went up to Cannery Row at Monterey after leaving La Jolla, I couldn't find anyone even there who knew if there was more to it.

As it happened, Chandler made Philip Marlowe find a drowned woman in a novel called *The Lady in the Lake*. But she had been in the water for some time, and there was nothing of rest and comfort in *her* face. There wasn't enough of her face left to be anywhere near restful or beautiful. And Marlowe certainly heard no music. So I suppose it was coincidence that both novels involved drowned women. In any case Chandler's novel was published in 1943, two years before Steinbeck's.

Part Five

The Grapes of Wrath

Those families which had lived and died on forty acres, had eaten or starved on the produce of forty acres, had now the whole West to rove in. There in the Middle- and South-west had lived a simple agrarian folk who had not changed with industry, who had not farmed with machines or known the power and danger of machines in private hands.

And then suddenly the machines pushed them out and they swarmed on the highways .... They were migrants. And the hostility changed them, welded them, united them ....

And in the West there was panic. Men of property were terrified for their property. Men who had never been hungry saw the eyes of the hungry .... They reassured themselves that they were good and the invaders bad. They said, These goddamned Okies are dirty and ignorant. They're degenerate, sexual maniacs. These goddamned Okies are thieves. They'll steal anything. They've got no sense of property rights.

JOHN STEINBECK: *The Grapes of Wrath*

Chapter 13

In 1945 Steinbeck, famous as the author of *Of Mice and Men* and *The Grapes of Wrath*, had tried to retire and live in Monterey, which he loved. He tried in vain. Bitterly disappointed by the venom and jealousy he found there, he wrote, 'This isn't my country anymore. And it won't be until I am dead' – and this turned out to be an accurate prediction. So he returned to New York which he found 'a wonderful city', more tolerant of success than the rest of the country, because littleness and viciousness get swallowed up there.

Even as late as 1960 Steinbeck, after a last visit, felt his final departure with Charley from Monterey as a sort of flight. While there he had revisited one of his old friends, Johnny Garcia, in his bar. He found Johnny strangely changed – as, evidently, Garcia found Steinbeck changed. Their last reunion was sad and bitter – a reunion of strangers, of ghosts. 'Tom Wolfe was right,' John Steinbeck wrote sadly in *Travels with Charley*. 'You can't go home again because home has ceased to exist except in the mothballs of memory.'

Of course, Steinbeck and Garcia talked nostalgically of the past and also drank to it a good deal. They talked of and drank to dead friends like Ed Ricketts and Flora Woods, the only owner of the Bear Flag flophouse, the best known in Monterey County, until Johnny moaned, 'It's like we was in a bucket of ghosts.'

'No. They're not true ghosts. We're the ghosts,' said Steinbeck sadly.

And then, suddenly and mysteriously, things in the bar changed for the worse. Steinbeck felt a stir of bellicosity, of restlessness along the bar, shoulders hunched, legs were uncrossed, and he said to himself, there's going to be trouble.

Johnny delicately set yet another bottle on the bar between them; his eyes were wide and dreamy.

He shook his head. 'I guess you don't like us any more,' he said. 'I guess maybe you're too good for us.' It was sinister. Steinbeck noticed Garcia's fingertips playing slow chords on an invisible keyboard on the bar. And he thought: Hell, I'm too old for trouble like this, and in two steps he made it to the door.

'Okay,' he called. 'See you tomorrow, Johnny.'

And, all at once, he was on Alvarado Street – 'and around me it was nothing but strangers.'

> It was true [he wrote later in his account of this sad last meeting], what I had said to Johnny Garcia – I was the ghost. My town had grown and changed and my friend along with it. Now returning, as changed to my friend as my town was to me, I distorted his picture, muddied his memory. When I went away I had died, and so became fixed and unchangeable. My return caused only confusion and uneasiness. Although they could not say it, my old friends wanted me gone so that I could take my proper place in the pattern of remembrance – and I wanted to go for the same reason.

Yes, alas, Tom Wolfe was right. You can't go home again.

The last 'formal' and 'sentimental' thing Steinbeck did before he fled his past for ever was to drive Charley up to Fremont's Peak, the towering point in the hills nearby, a solitary stone peak that overlooks the Salinas Valley. In happier, more youthful days he had wanted to be buried on that peak where, as he said, he could see everything he had been brought up to know and love. There, now, about to leave never to return, his memory myth repaired itself and Charley, 'his nose moist with curiosity, sniffed the wind-borne pattern of a hundred miles'.

The afternoon of my own visit to that high point, it was so hazy that the glorious Bay of Monterey was fuzzy and barely visible in the distance. But, like John Steinbeck before he left it for ever, I felt and smelled and heard the wind blowing up from the long valley. Down the valley below me somewhere, Steinbeck's mother had shot a wildcat. And one long-ago day on one of those oaks his father had burnt his name with a hot iron together with the name of the girl he loved.

Steinbeck drove down from Fremont's Peak with Charley, leaving behind him Salinas and Carmel and Cannery Row for ever, and took the road followed by the Joad family in his own early masterpiece, *The Grapes of Wrath*, although in the opposite direction to them:

> I printed the view once more on my eyes, south, west, and north, and then we hurried away from the permanent and changeless past where my mother is always shooting a wildcat and my father is always burning his name with his love.

Then he bucketed his truck, Rocinante, out of California by the shortest possible route – one he knew well from the old days in the 1930s when he was preparing to write *The Grapes*. From Salinas to Los Banos, through Fresno and Bakersfield, then over the pass and into the Mojave Desert, a burned and burning desert, he found it, even that late in the year. The highway he would take is a famous one, Route 66, called the 'Mother Route', America's Main Street. When you travel on it you can see why.

I intended to join Steinbeck's and Charley's flight path at Barstowe, starting from Los Angeles to which I had returned from Carmel and Monterey. I was aiming to cross Southern California eastwards to the Colorado River, and from there continue through northern Arizona as far as the Painted Desert. On the way, as Steinbeck had done, I would cross the Mojave Desert after climbing over the 4,257-foot high pass of Cajon near San Bernardino. The Desert sounded exciting, but it was apparently nothing to what lay ahead – the guidebook promised what it called 'knuckle-whitening' adventures and 'alarming canyon-hugging' roads in the badlands of Arizona. It seemed to imply with a sneering smile that the route was not one for faint-hearted people like me.

Well, I would see about that.

Route 66 runs for 2,100 miles across eight states from Chicago to Santa Monica in California – or, if you prefer it, from Lake Michigan to the Pacific Ocean. America's Main Street. A good many Americans will end up travelling on one stretch of it or another sometime during their lifetime. Tragic to think – as I set out on it – that one American who will travel it no more is the one writer who seemed to personify such wild American roads and even the wilderness itself. This was Wallace Stegner, author of short stories and the novels *Angle of Repose* and *Crossing to Safety*; a writer, as the *New Yorker* magazine said when he died, who first provided people with a way of thinking about the American West that 'shows the importance of a true partnership between human beings and the land'.

Stegner once wrote, and I agree, that 'It may be the love of wilderness that finally teaches us civilised responsibilities'. The tragedy was that the day before I started out along Route 66 towards Arizona, Wallace Stegner was killed in a car accident near Santa Fé, aged eighty-two, a quarter of a century after the death of John Steinbeck.

After the guidebook's dire predictions of a dangerous ride, the initial hour or two between San Bernardino and Barstowe turned out to be mere child's play. All I had to do was to avoid bumping into formations of elderly 'hell's angels' who suddenly appeared on the road in menacing Nazi-type helmets and a good deal of tight black leather weaving high-powered Harley Davidson motorbikes erratically about the highway. With their rearing, arrogant handlebars and roaring exhausts, they had a threatening air.

From a distance, that is. Close to, one saw the zippered chaps that protected their middle-aged, and probably arthritic, knees from the cold and the corsets that supported their aching backs. One, the fiercest-looking of them, had a chestful of medals that would have turned the head of Hermann Goering. But none of them were tearaways; not even the scowling brute with a wicked-looking Bowie knife in his belt and silver spurs – *spurs* on a motorbike? – on his boots.

I caught up with him at the first gas station and saw his ponytail was grey with age and when he asked a garage-hand for a full tank, the scowl fell away and his voice had the nervous sound of an elderly bank clerk. He might have been a retired hairdresser heading for his Last Round-up. In any case, the whole posse of them branched off quite soon in a burping flash of chrome towards Las Vegas, leaving us to cross the Mojave Desert unmolested.

The Mojave is still a wide and potentially frightening wasteland. Ridges of clinker blacken an apparently endless sage-strewn and sun-lashed plain. A distant range of heat-bleached hills seems an infinite distance away. And when Route 66 veers off in a southern loop towards Amboy you are thankful to be in a jeep with not many miles on the clock, a full gas tank, and an icebox on the back seat stocked with beer, water and a packet of soggy sandwiches.

Even so, the memory cannot help, in this region of dead, defeated and waterless earth, slipping back to stories of earlier travellers here – travellers on foot, some of them – or to the land-deprived Okies of the Depression John Steinbeck wrote about in *The Grapes of Wrath*, his masterpiece. Desperate for work, they came rattling in old jalopies across the burning land with radiators steaming and loose connecting rods hammering through the black cindery hills.

'Look out for the desert,' they had warned one another. 'Take plenty of water, case you get hung up. The desert's a son-of-a-bitch. She'll cut the living Jesus outa you.'

A rattlesnake will die in an hour of full sun, Steinbeck said. Warm-blooded creatures survive as Nature has taught them: a rabbit taking moisture from a leaf, a coyote from the blood of a rabbit. There was a dead rabbit on the side of the road now.

Out here the Joad family of *The Grapes of Wrath* learned a lot about rabbits. 'Depression is over,' they joked. 'I seen a jackrabbit, and they wasn't nobody after him.' A mean, bitter joke; with a mean, bitter point to it in that terrible time of hunger and little hope.

Just before the tiny isolated dot of Buster Burris's Roy's Café at Amboy, I did pass a pick-up stalled at the roadside with two men peering under the raised bonnet.

'I seen pitchers once says they was bones ever'place,' the Okies told each other.

'Man bones?'

'Some, I guess, but mos'ly cow bones.'

Looking at the stalled pick-up I joked to myself, 'I'll see their bones on my way back.' But the men were in no danger. There was a fair amount of traffic on this highway; someone would be bound to give them a lift to Roy's Café.

There, at Roy's in the diner behind the roadside petrol pumps, two old geezers in shirt-sleeves were ordering something to eat from a tall blonde waitress.

'One ah-ced tea. One do-nut. Chocolate cay-ake.' A group of belated hell's angels roared by, and the waitress said, 'Buster's out there by the pumps,' and I went out for a word.

Buster Burris, pleased to answer questions from *aficionados* of Route 66, said he'd been here in Amboy, in the middle of the Mojave, since 1937. Yessir. Well, he was eighty-two now, he added, a little defensively, I thought. Oh, the Okies. He remembered the Okies well. 'A lotta them we had to help out,' he said. 'Free gas.' He waved a hand towards the pumps.

'Took a bit of getting used to being out here,' he went on. 'Gets real hot here. Forty degrees in winter, day and night. One hundred and thirty degrees in summer.' General Patton brought his troops out here in the Second World War, Buster said. 'To get 'em used to the desert heat before the North African campaign. Get used to the rattlesnakes, too.'

'Sure,' he added. 'We have plenty of rattlers here. I've got twenty cats busy keepin' 'em down.'

I bought a postcard later in his bar – a great big California rattler as thick as my forearm. For some reason the postcard was printed in Ireland.

Buster was a quiet old man with a white thatch of hair and sensible eyes. 'I'm Texan, really,' he said. 'From San Antonio. By the Alamo, know it?'

'Yeah, I know it.'

When I asked him if he was ever lonely in this god-forsaken desert, he showed a little extra animation.

'No, sir. No time for that. I'm busy fourteen hours a day.' And he began fiddling with the pumps to prove it.

Buster Burris had humour, too. Above a smelly trough a sign said, 'Please do not Throw Cigarette Butts in the Urinal. It Makes Them Harder to Light.'

I could see distant mountains as long lines of purple haze,

as the road presses on through the sage towards the town of Needles on the Colorado River dividing California from Arizona. After Amboy there are no townships, only small straggling oases consisting of a few shady trees and an ugly pile of mouldering car bodies. At intervals along Route 66 there are these dumps: scores of junked cars, simply left to rust away in unsightly heaps of scrap.

They do absolutely nothing to enhance the romance of the Mother Road. Although they do, alas, enhance the American-ness of it. Piles of rusting metal are one of the sad trademarks of the American landscape. It is an eyesore the nation's ecologists have yet to concern themselves with.

At Essex, a few scorching miles further east, one more pile of scrap at the roadside signalled the ample presence of Doug Smith, who lives in its depths. A genial figure, no longer young and now bulky with beer, he looms out from behind the stack of cars waving a plump hand with a bottle in it, inviting you into a bungalow as much like a depository of ill-assorted bric-à-brac as the junkyard that surrounds it.

'Have a beer,' he suggests at intervals, as he leads the way round the junked cars in the front rank of which stands the rust-red skeleton of a Model T Ford, circa 1923. That Model T could easily be a broken-down relic of the Depression, abandoned by the Okies in the early 1930s. But Doug Smith, it turned out, was born in 1930 and only began his old car collection on his discharge from the Navy after the Korean War.

'Sure you don't wanna beer?' he repeated hopefully, leaning his considerable bulk against the roof of an old Studebaker. He looked like he was a twenty-beer-a-day man, and I would have gladly joined him in his twenty-first. But I explained I had a long way to go and gave *him* a parting gift: a bottle of Irish ale from *my* icebox.

Across the Colorado River, sharp peaks called Needles rise out of the white rock walls of Arizona.

'This here's a murder country,' young Tom Joad had said in *The Grapes of Wrath*, looking back in awe at those rugged peaks. 'This here's the bones of a country.' And the weary Okies stripped off their clothes in the willows on the river bank and sat their exhausted bodies down on the sandy riverbed with only their heads stuck out of the water. 'Jesus,' Al Joad, Tom's brother, said. 'I needed this.'

These days this part of the Colorado has changed into something like a seaside resort. Motorboats tow surfers on the river and neat little bungalows come down to its edges. A plaque near the Needles bridge said:

The Colorado River links the Mojave Indian lands visited by Father Graces in 1776. Near this location the American explorer Jedediah Smith and his band of Rocky Mountain men crossed the river in 1826 and opened the pioneer trail to Southern California.

Just a little over a hundred years after Jedediah, Pa Joad, cooling off in the water, said 'Wait till we get to California. You'll see nice country then.' And Tom told him, 'Jesus Christ, Pa! This here *is* California.'

The Mojave Desert lay just ahead of them.

I had chosen to take the 'short cut' – a road that wiggles and ducks up the canyons and peaks that look across other greater peaks, high as heaven, through the Sitgreaves Pass, through the main street of Oatman, full of donkeys, and finally emerges at Kingman. A stretch that the guidebook had threatened would provide much 'white-knuckle' driving.

Oatman itself was a 'ghost town', that is, a place carefully (perhaps *too* carefully) preserved for tourists as an old gold-mining town – which it once was – with droves of semi-wild burros (donkeys) wandering about cadging snacks off passers-by, and once or twice a day elaborately staged gunfights.

But the glory of Oatman lies in the surrounding landscape.

The hills – the murderous rock-walls of Arizona – rise like waves in an angry ocean, black on blue, towards the skyline with now and again a sun-crowned peak showing between. The narrow road twists and turns higher and higher through gulches of red gravel scattered with giant boulders, joshua trees, and grey-green sage bushes that hide disused gold mine shafts.

After that the white road swoops straight as an arrow into the Sacramento Valley where occasional houses are dots of white on the wide green plain, and to the south a row of violet mountains steps down the misty horizon like the diminishing teeth of a saw.

No wonder that Pa Joad, in a transport of excitement, called out, 'We're there – we're in California!' When his family had rattled its way across these hills in their ancient Hudson Super-Six, he looked back across the river in something like disbelief, at the terrible ramparts of Arizona that he, and we, had just passed through, which were purpling now in the shadows of an April sunset.

Kingman sits astride this plain – a large, long sprawl of a town that was once a mining and business centre and a terminal for the Santa Fé railroad. On its main street – named after a once well-known comic cowboy film actor with a squeaky voice called Andy Devine, it also has an old hotel, the Beale, which may or may not be revived and reopened as a historic monument.

You come into Kingman past a roadside billboard that says, 'Get Your Kicks on Route 66' – which is a much-repeated motto hereabouts, and another sign that says, 'Old West Brothel' – the significance of which I am afraid I never grasped. (It is not, I assume, a working replica of a Wild West cathouse.)

'Is it the Bates Wing?' I asked the receptionist at the Quality Inn, referring to its cheapness. But those cheap rooms at the Inn were far from anything in Alfred Hitchcock's film *Psycho* – they were clean, large, and air-conditioned. My room had a name on the door: 'Ronald McDonald slept here', and it took the reception-ist to identify the name of the clown who advertises McDonald's hamburgers.

Kingman is a sizeable place for this desert-wrapped stretch of Route 66. It has a shop selling CDs and tapes; an Indian Jewelry Emporium (Mojave Indian): something called a 'Praise Chapel' announcing that 'Jesus Lives'; and a solid-looking Masonic chapel. It also contains a Ramblin' Rose Motel, and a shadowy Steak House, in which a Vietnamese in dark glasses played billiards – presumably, to him, in total darkness – under a notice saying, 'We will not serve anyone who appears to be intoxicated.'

The nights were not peaceful. The Santa Fé railroad freight trains shrieked and trumpeted through the town at intervals through the night, sounding like Andy Devine at his most squeakily manic and the denizens of the Old West Brothel out on the town together.

It was a relief to get back to the desert. At Hackberry you drove (why stop?) past a solitary general store that looked as if it had gone bankrupt at about the time the Joad family rattled past it without buying anything. 'Sorry we're closed', a notice on the door said to the empty plain, adding politely, 'Call again, Please'.

At Tuxton the Frontier Café, by contrast, dispensed steaks and eggs and bacon and considerable warmth. This, the guidebook said, was cattle country. On the lonely road from Kingman, what looked like Hereford cattle had blinked blankly at us from the edge of a wide grassy range that ran back to a reddish escarpment as big as a monstrous girder that rose massively against the northern horizon, and looked as if it held up the sky.

At the Frontier Café 86-year-old Alvin Byers, the owner's father, scratched his head and watched me drinking a mug of coffee.

'That's where all the cattle are,' he said, pointing vaguely north. 'Indian cattle.' He indicated the escarpment. 'See those mountains?

168

That thah's Indian reservations. The Hulapais. They live all the way to Peach Springs down the road.'

The coffee, I noticed, was a good deal better than usual. 'Farmer Brothers', the label said. When an old lady who could only have been Mrs Byers poured me more of it, I asked her, 'Where's this coffee from?' She looked blank, and said, 'Don't rightly know.' A pity; I would have bought some. Good coffee is certainly not easily come by on Route 66. So everyone be warned: kicks come from Route 66, but not good coffee.

Alvin Byers said, 'I'm from Oklahoma meself. Cherokee country. Born there in 1907. That was before Oklahoma became a state.' As he spoke my eyes wandered to the far end of the diner where a silent group of Indians sat intently drinking from steaming mugs. A sad little bunch, they said nothing at all to me; or for that matter to each other.

'You can see real cowboys in the Black Cat Bar at Seligman down the road,' said Alvin Byers. 'Actin' jest like Texans.' He grinned, and added, 'Some of 'em may even come from thah, too.'

I made a point of visiting the Black Cat Bar, and as it happened Seligman proved to be my perfect Arizona township. More than that, in Angel Delgadillo, the town's barber and probably the nation's Number One *aficionado* of Route 66, I found the man who, above all others, I would most like to see again.

Endlessly smiling, endlessly helpful, in a shop bursting with old photographs of himself and his family, and with business cards of scores of well-wishers who wanted to be remembered by him, Angel chatted away about the past as, with the gay abandon of a d'Artagnan, he gave the local customer sitting in his barber's chair an immensely short back-and-sides in record time, something he laughingly called 'a Kojak'.

He remembered very well, he said, between wild sweeps of his scissors, the processions of Okies in their broken-down cars through Seligman in the early 1930s. 'It was easy to tell the better-off Okies,' he said. 'They had two mattresses strapped to their automobiles. The others had only one.'

Okies, these miserable, uprooted American fugitives were generally called – but in fact they came from other places, too: from Kansas, Oklahoma, Texas, New Mexico; from Nevada and Arkansas. They came in carloads, caravans, all of them homeless and hungry; 'twenty thousand and fifty thousand and a hundred thousand and two hundred thousand'. An army, scurrying to find a home, work and food.

They passed through Seligman in Model Ts with wobbly wheels and worn fan belts. They cranked by in fifth-hand Buicks, Nashes, De

Sotos; in ancient Appersons, Chalmers and Chandlers (who remembers such cars today?); in La Salles and Pontiacs. The Joads had managed to lay their hands on a Hudson Super-Six sedan, had cut off the top in the middle, and put a truck bed in and high top rails. You could feel the motor fighting for life under the floorboards, Steinbeck said.

With a wild surmise the young Delgadillo had watched people like the Joads chugging by like bugs. Had seen the kids huddled and hungry. Seen them all heading west to California, scurrying for work, for food, and most of all for land. Who could forget a sight like that?

Big-hearted Patti Larimore, who owns the Black Cat Bar Alvin Byers had praised, was far too young to have seen those earlier Americans: those half-starved Okies. If she had been around then, I would bet my last dollar she would have invited them in and fed them ham hocks and Polish sausage for free. Those were the items advertised as available on the door of her fridge; with pickled pig's feet, too, for a mere $1.50.

Patti confirmed what Alvin Byers had said, that this was really cattle country. Apaches and Navajos were big cattle owners in these parts, she said – the Apaches surprisingly the richer and more industrious of the two, despite the fact that the Navajos made the turquoise jewellery that sells for such high prices in cities like New York.

Indians, Patti said sadly, often find it difficult to hold their liquor. On the whole she regretted that she couldn't encourage them to come into her bar (although she certainly didn't make a practice of turning them away).

There were no Indians in Seligman's other bar, the 'OK Saloon', either.

A jolly barmaid there poured me what she described as a Miller's Gen-u-ine Draft ale (how could it be *genuine* draft and come out of a bottle?) and referred me roguishly to an array of notices above the counter.

One said: 'Please be Extra Kind and Gentle to Our Female Employees. All are Virgins . . . Except *One*.'

Another one I particularly liked warned: 'Unattended Children Will be Sold as Slaves'. And there was a fine list of joke telephone charges:

Just left	.50
Haven't seen him	.75
Not here	$1.50
Never heard of him	$2.00
Misc. Lies	$3.00

It was a beautiful night when I left the OK Saloon. A full moon

170

was hanging over the mountain ridges behind Seligman's low roofs, silvering their topmost peaks. Part of a ditty that had caught my fancy in a story by Wallace Stegner popped into my head, and in my room in the Route 66 Motel I sang it under my breath:

> And I built the Rocky Mountains,
> And placed them where they are,
> Sold whiskey to the Ind-i-ans
> From behind a little bar . . . .

Then, turning out the light, I vowed I would return to this place at the first opportunity.

The Painted Desert – it lies between the heights of Flagstaff and the New Mexico border – gives one the impression that one is standing on the edge of a great bowl of layered ice cream.

In the hour just before sunset, the best time to see it, the muted colours in the strangely shaped ribs and spurs of rock come into their own. Then the mainly red tones mingle with the contrasting dark amber of the shadows.

It is odd. The levels of the land you look down on from a number of observation points are very oddly humped. Rivulets of white, resembling licks of salt, separate ridges shaped like cockscombs or escarpments creviced into steps, scooped out by centuries of desert winds.

Sometimes the escarpments are green and shadowed in purple. Now and then a flat plain runs away in a wash of pale green, powdered with dusty white like icing sugar. Knuckles and saddles of rock push up through occasional patches of grass. A massive outcrop called the Pilot Rock dominates the middle distance; and on the horizon a long high ledge like the towering deck of an enormous pink-tinted aircraft carrier marks the beginning of Navajo Indian territory.

A short distance south of the Painted Desert, heading towards the Petrified Forest, the road runs through hills that are wind-worn pyramids of layered rock, their tops capped with white like dollops of cream, and, below, alternate levels of pink, orange, dark red, violet, and white again. The effect is oddly appetising. You seem to be moving between huge scoops of Italian ice cream; all you need is a spoon.

There is a museum in the Petrified Forest, and horizontal on the ground at the back of it lie the hard segments of ancient trees that eons ago turned to stone and lie there for ever as heavy, pinkish chunks of severed rock. Dire penalties are threatened for anyone found taking pieces of this rock away in their cars. Numerous signs say: 'Removal of Petrified Wood is Prohibited'. So isn't it strange that numerous stalls and shops outside the park area advertise 'Petrified Wood' for sale?

We turned back towards California, through Holbrook with its ugly main street of 'Rock Shops', bars and giant plastic models of dinosaurs, and took once again the westward trail Steinbeck's Okies had followed.

Soon the mountains and the sage pressed in upon us from every side – a phrase I borrow from Wallace Stegner. And for the first time I noticed the tall red drooping flowers of the thorny Jacob's Staff cactus, and the dry bundles of tumbleweed that careened across the road in front of the jeep.

A strong cold wind swept down from the southwest and whipped up the dust on the undulating landscape, forcing me to take refuge at the 'Empty Pockets' bar to wash out my parched mouth with a Michelob draught for $1, and five pronghorn deer stood a little way down the road and calmly watched the jeep, pricking inquisitive ears in its direction.

As Steinbeck had noticed, the narrow concrete miles stretch and stretch ahead. On the way I began to notice hitherto unnoticed things. The roadside pull-ins, for example, were more or less as Steinbeck had described them – 'two gasoline pumps in front, a screen door, a long bar, stools, and a foot rail; salts, peppers, mustard pots, and paper napkins. Beer taps; coffee urns and pies in wire cages.' Signs then had said, 'Ladies May Smoke But Be Careful Where You Lay Your Butts.'

In Depression days, the customers had been truck drivers and tourists; truck drivers mainly. And the barmaids had been called 'Susie or Mae or Minnie, middle-aging behind the counter, rouge and powder on a sweating face, saying sweetly' (though now it was old, kind Mrs Byers at the Frontier Café):

'Well, what's it gonna be?'

'Oh, a cup of Java. What kinda pie ya got?' (Passing through Tuxton again, I asked Alvin Byers why people used to refer to coffee simply as 'Java'. He said he didn't know.)

'Apple pie.'

'Cut off a hunk, then,' the driver would say, adding 'Make it a big hunk . . . .'

'God Almighty, the road is full of them families goin' west,' one dumb truck driver said. 'Never seen so many. Gets worse all the time. Wonder where they all come from.' He spoke at the height of the Great Depression. 'Cut down cars full a stoves an' pans an' mattresses an' kids an' chickens.'

The cars of the migrant people (wrote Steinbeck) crawled out of the side roads on to the great cross-country highway, and, hungry and restless, they took the migrant way, 'the great plain rolling like a ground swell', to the westward. And the cars whizzed viciously by the gas pumps and hamburger stands on 66 to Holbrook, Joseph City and Winslow – as we did. And then there was Flagstaff in the high mountains, and the tall trees began – as I saw – and there the old jalopies had spouted steam and laboured up the slopes which our brand-new jeep soared over. The Okies, dispossessed and homeless, streamed through the stone desert and debris around Oatman; and when the daylight came they saw the Colorado River below them. Just as I did.

That's the historical, sociological and literary importance of Route 66, written down so unforgettably by John Steinbeck, who actually accompanied for some of their way these caravans of wretched American migrants.

And so the other day, I myself, following the way the Okies had taken, came at last to the summit of the Californian mountains, and descended, like them, precipitously across the Mojave Desert and, at last, into a plain as green as salad. Towards the warm acres of fruit trees. And finally to the shining blue Pacific Ocean.

Chapter 14

A great deal about the central Californian coastline on Highway 1 between Los Angeles and Big Sur, Carmel and Monterey – Steinbeck country – brings back vivid memories of the north Cornish coast on which I was brought up: the sheer cliffs, the raging sea on the rocks below, the great ocean disappearing to the distant horizon.

True, the Californian cliffs seem much higher than the Cornish ones once you drive north of Santa Barbara. And that may be partly because, past the turning to San Simeon – the vast pile built for his girlfriend, Marion Davis, by the newspaper mogul William Randolph Hearst, and made famous by the film *Citizen Kane* – the twisting road runs so perilously close to the high edge of the cliffs and the pounding sea beneath them.

The most spectacular single feature is the enormous knob of rock called Big Sur – originally El Sur Grande (or the Big South) – from which a great sweep of mountains, the Santa Lucias, rises to the eastern horizon like a giant cockscomb.

At any rate the resemblance to the Cornish Wreckers' Coast is so striking that I am pretty sure that, during the Second World War when German U-boats and air raids over England ruled out the use of the real West Country locations, Hollywood film directors simply filmed this Californian coastline. This might well have been true in the case of Hitchcock and his film *Rebecca*. Indeed, I have an idea that an old friend, Joan Fontaine, who starred in that picture and as it happens lives in Carmel today, told me that it was.

These days Carmel is a nice place, a safe place; almost too good to be true. Neatly laid out like a perfect tree-lined grid; a dozen art galleries to every street; four antique stores to every block. Genteel is the word that comes to mind: it is clean; there is no violence here; peaceful troops of middle-aged holiday-makers stay in cheap and friendly seaside pensions, and at the bottom of the parallel avenues there is the calm sweep of a sandy bay. Carmel permits no disfiguring billboards and no dazzling neon. Signs of all kinds are restricted, and so are streetlights at night. Shops selling expensive knick-knacks display names like 'Cabbages and Kings' and 'The Corner Cupboard Gift Shop'. The population of Carmel is roughly 4,000, and includes, I think I was told, four blacks, four Latinos and about twelve Asians, so there is no 'inner ghetto' problem here. Day or night, you can walk everywhere and no one will try to mug you.

Early on I made a mistake – a genuine and not a particularly funny one. Clint Eastwood, the film star, who had just achieved an Oscar for his film *Unforgiven*, of which he was principal actor and director, had been the Mayor of Carmel a few years back. He was also part owner of a saloon called the 'Hog's Breath' bar. Eager to see it, I asked a middle-aged woman in a car if she could kindly direct me to the – I had forgotten the name:

'– Horse's Ass Bar.'

It was an unintentional error and, as I have said, not meant to be funny. The woman's initial outrage seemed to me exaggerated; was she going to call a cop, claiming sexual harassment? Harassment of one sort or another was all the rage in America just then. But, this woman was a good sort; she soon began to giggle – 'My, my! The Horse's . . .' – and gasping, between splutters of laughter, she put me on the right track. As a matter of fact, Clint's bar – the customers looked eagerly up when I came in (had 'the Star' himself arrived?) – was a disappointment. I preferred one called the 'Jack London', which advertised a knockout drop called 'The Call of the Wild' – which I avoided. Yet another bar nearby offered an 'Unforgiven' cocktail in honour of Clint's film.

'I'll try one of those,' I told the barman. 'I'll try any drink once.'

Under the barman's interested gaze, I took a swig of what tasted horribly like sweet cider and curaçao.

The barman grinned. 'I know what you're going to say now. You are going to say, "It should be called an 'Unforgivable' cocktail." That's what you'll say. Right?'

I had no intention of saying anything. I was concentrating on getting into the fresh air without being sick on the carpet.

It is not easy to think of little Carmel as anything but a staid middle-class tourist haven. Certainly, not as the left-wing artists' colony it once was when Sinclair Lewis lived there and Lincoln Steffens had a house near the beach on San Antonio near Ocean Street, in which John Steinbeck met the various labour activists who pointed him in the direction of material for *In Dubious Battle* and his great book, *The Grapes of Wrath*.

Robert DeMott says of Steinbeck that he never became what dyed-in-the-wool activists would consider 'fully radicalised'. I have seen him described as 'a Jacksonian democrat', and once, years later, he strenuously denied ever having had the remotest links with hardcore Marxism. The Californian writer Jack London, a generation or two before him, had been a revolutionary socialist; not Steinbeck.

That he was regarded as little more than a left-wing agitator by some myopic conservatives – even people in his own bailiwick, so to speak, of Salinas and Monterey – was one tragic part of the success of *The Grapes of Wrath*. It drove Steinbeck to deep anger and humiliation. For example, he wrote to a friend what happened when, after the nationwide publicity for the book, he tried to rent a room in Monterey simply so that he could work in the neighbourhood he came from.

> In Monterey there is only one office building, owned by a man named Parsons. I tried to reach him for 3 days and this morning got him by phone. I said, 'I want to rent an office for a couple of months.'
> 'Very well,' he said, 'we have some vacancies. What is your name?'
> 'Steinbeck,' I said.
> 'And what is your business?'
> 'I am a writer,' I said.
> There was a long pause and then – 'Do you have a business license?'
> 'No,' I said, 'none is required in my business.' Another long pause, then
> 'I'm sorry – we don't want people like that. We want professional people like doctors and dentists and insurance.'

So, Steinbeck said, he cleared out a woodshed and set up a table, adding in the letter: 'I just thought you'd like to know that I can't get an office in my own home town and that the building owner never heard of me. *Sic transit* or perhaps it never existed.'

The Grapes of Wrath, as the world knows, had had a phenomenal success. *Of Mice and Men* – another nationwide best-selling triumph – had preceded it. Was it possible that a man in Monterey called Parsons had never heard of a local writer named Steinbeck? One wonders what Mr Parsons (or his offspring, if he had any), would think now about having spurned and insulted a future winner of the Nobel Prize.

One major result of that spurning was that Steinbeck moved from his beloved Monterey to New York to avoid any more examples of venom and ignorance. It was only much later, as we have seen, that he set out from Sag Harbor with his poodle, Charley, to say goodbye for ever to his birthplace, eight years before he died.

By the end of the Second World War, John Steinbeck had achieved an amazing fame. I suppose some people found it an ambiguous fame. In *Dubious Battle* and *The Grapes of Wrath* he produced two stunning populist and revolutionary novels. They were controversial and stirred things up – as they were meant to.

Steinbeck ends his Chapter 25 of *The Grapes of Wrath* with this tough and outspoken passage:

> There is a crime here that goes beyond denunciation. There is a sorrow here that weeping cannot symbolise. There is a failure here that topples all our success. The fertile earth, the straight tree rows, the sturdy trunks, and the ripe fruit. And children dying of pellagra must die because a profit cannot be taken from an orange. And coroners must fill in the certificates – died of malnutrition – because the food must rot, must be forced to rot.
>
> The people come with nets to fish for potatoes in the river, and the guards hold them back; they come in rattling cars to get the dumped oranges, but the kerosene is sprayed. And they stand still and watch the potatoes float by ... and in the eyes of the hungry there is a growing wrath. In the souls of the people the grapes of wrath are filling and growing heavy, growing heavy for the vintage.

Tough talk – and why not? After all, he himself had witnessed the death, the disease, the starvation – the whole appalling misery of the migrant condition, the *American* migrant condition. 'I must go over into the interior valleys', one of his letters of 1938 says. 'There are about five thousand families starving to death over there, not just hungry but actually starving. The government is trying to feed them', but the utilities and banks and rich farmers of America were sabotaging things all along the line.

In *The Grapes of Wrath* there is tough talk, all right, and some harsh descriptions of horrific scenes. Harsh they may have been, but true, too. Steinbeck himself had seen them, and worked in such scenes. He wrote: 'The local people whipped themselves into a mold of cruelty. Then they formed units, squads, and armed them – armed them with clubs, with gas, with guns. We own the country. We own the country. We can't let these Okies get out of hand.' He had seen for himself the ignorant vigilantes organised by the Fruit Growers' Association from the 'dupes' and 'suckers' of Salinas, and heard them rave and threaten. He had seen the strike of 1936 in Salinas smashed by organised terror, and the 'killings in the streets of that dear little town where I was born'. The lesson of history he bluntly set down in Chapter 19 of *Grapes* for Americans to read was not one some people would like:

> And the great owners, who must lose their land in an upheaval, the great owners with access to history, with eyes to read history and to know the great fact: when property accumulates in too few hands it is taken away. And that companion fact: when a majority of the people are hungry and cold they will take by force what they need. And the little screaming fact sounds through all history: repression works only to strengthen and knit the repressed.

How many Americans in 1938 – leave alone today – would believe what Steinbeck found in the sea of mud and debris – water a foot deep in the tents at Visalia (in Tulaila County, California) where thousands were starving to death, children up on the beds, no food, no fire, and people saying, 'Well, the problem is so great we can't do anything about it. So they do nothing.' Steinbeck described such a situation, not surprisingly, as 'devastating', and 'heartbreaking'. It must have resembled some cataclysmic scene in India after an earthquake or a flood. Yet this was in America – in California, where oranges grew on rows of trees, and David O. Selznick in Hollywood was prepared 'to spend millions of dollars making *Gone With The Wind*'.

Reading *In Dubious Battle* and *The Grapes of Wrath* today, one wonders how left-wing intellectuals in the rest of America could remain so obsessed with, say, communism in the Soviet Union or Italian or German fascism, when in great tracts of America itself American citizens were being thrust from their livelihood into penury and actual starvation by fellow Americans. Those fellow Americans were temperamentally not so very far removed from the black-and-brown-shirted foreigners goosestepping about on the other side of the Atlantic Ocean. That America recovered from the terrible, unprecedented trauma of the Depression says a lot for American democracy – or, at any rate, for the fact that the country had a President who could rise above the crisis of capitalism. One can thank God for the compassion and swiftness to act of that President: Franklin D. Roosevelt.

Of course, *The Grapes of Wrath*, though extravagantly and rightly much praised, was bound to be much vilified, too. Lauded, for example, by Eleanor Roosevelt in her syndicated newspaper column, it was taken as a sociological case study for Senator Robert M. La Follette's reform of California's tyrannical labour laws. On the other hand, to their everlasting disgrace, numerous school boards and libraries banned it. Right-wing ministers, corporate farmers and – naturally – conservative politicians denounced it. A Neanderthal Oklahoman Congressman, Lyle Borden, called the book 'a lie, a black infernal creation of a twisted, distorted mind' – which says some unpleasant things about Mr Borden and the Oklahomans of that time who elected him. He (and they) failed to see that the men and women whose children died in the mud and ankle-deep water at Visalia had made the migrants seem more real than politicians.

It was war, of all things, that ended the tragedy of the Okies – the desperation of the migrant workers of America.

It was to be the ironic aftermath to this unparalleled American drama. The Japanese had finally brought the Second World War to America's door, military service was created, and the inevitable recruitment of migrant families into defence plants and shipyards began in the wake of a booming war economy. Before long – hard though it is to believe – Californian fruit growers who had recruited and paid squads of toughs to club and gas other Americans – the Okies – simply to get them out of their way, were soon whining pathetically that there was an acute *shortage* of seasonal labour.

You come over the gentle slope between Carmel and Monterey, and the sudden sight of the wide sweep of bay all the way to Santa Cruz, sparkling in the early summer sun and apparently infinite, makes you brake the car, pull into the side and whistle with amazement.

This is the other Californian world of John Steinbeck, a world quite free from grim echoes of the Okie tragedy I associated with Route 66 and the valleys round Salinas and Visalia. Quite different even from the little touristy, art-gallery-ridden enclave of Carmel-by-the-Sea.

This new Steinbeck world had its own gritty landscape, that of *Tortilla Flat*, *Cannery Row* and *Sweet Thursday*; the down-to-earth world, in the old days, of sardine fishing; the world of 'Doc', and Dora Flood and her sister Flora (later known as 'Fauna'), successive madams of the 'stern and stately' Bear Flag 'house', the world, too, of Lee Chong, the courteous Chinese grocer, whose cheap Old Tennessee whiskey (guaranteed four months old) was much appreciated in the neighbourhood and known to one and all as 'Old Tennis Shoes'.

The Grapes of Wrath changed Steinbeck – the outrage, the emotional involvement, the exhausting on-the-ground research, the total commitment, the pity and the disgust. In the opinion of the editor of the journals he kept while writing *Grapes*, a less hardy writer might have become an anachronism after such success. But Steinbeck showed the capacity to survive through change; he avoided repeating himself.

His Monterey stories certainly dealt with a totally different kettle of circumstances from the miseries of homeless migrants and murderous vigilantes. In fact, they portrayed a joyous and uplifting world; and when he wrote of it Steinbeck revealed quite a different personal mood. He revealed a sense of fun and enjoyment of life.

I was going to need a guide to this strange new world, someone to lead me across the Monterey peninsula and introduce me into the departed milieu of Cannery Row. And I found John Thompson, who was just such a person, living in a tucked-away two-storey house, a house cluttered with books and bric-à-brac on the outskirts of Carmel. John Thompson was a friend of friends of mine in Los Angeles – an artist and a freelance writer, and his business card said he was President of the Concerned Citizens for Environmental Health which I imagined was some sort of 'Green' save-the-ecology organisation. As a writer John had been interested in the recent past of Carmel, Monterey and Salinas. So he was well up in the matter of John Steinbeck, and he personally knew people who had known Steinbeck in the old days. Some of them, he said, were still alive and visitable.

Chief among these survivors was an articulate and talented artist called Bruce Ariss, who in 1934 had moved to Pacific Grove on the Monterey Peninsula with his young bride Jean, a writer and poet, for their honeymoon. They had been so delighted with the place that they have never really left it. Luckily, too, Ariss decided early on that it would be well worth immortalising the vigorous – and, he rightly suspected, transitory – life on Cannery Row in a number of sketches of Monterey, and these brilliant drawings, preceding by about a decade Steinbeck's novel *Cannery Row*, are now preserved in bound volumes. The novel, published in 1945, is all about the doings of the extraordinary 'bums and saints': the eccentrics who inhabited Monterey's waterfront in what Ariss calls those 'really revolting' Depression days.

John Thompson and I parked the car near Cannery Row (or Ocean Avenue as it was called in Steinbeck's day when Monterey was known as the Sardine Capital of the World). Then we walked up the street to what had been Ed Ricketts's Lab. That is where Bruce Ariss had said he would be waiting for us. The man who had known Steinbeck was in a small upstairs room: a biggish, handsome man with thick curly white hair and a friendly manner. We stood in a sort of office with a memorable view over the bay looking towards Santa Cruz.

Ariss put out a hand and said, 'Pleased to meet you, Mr Young,' sparing me the usual 'How ya doin'?'

He gestured at the little room we stood in. 'This has become a sort of literary club now, as I expect John has told you. It burned down one terrible day in 1936 when Ed Ricketts had all his marine specimens stored here. It was soon rebuilt, of course, and he replaced his collection. After Ed's death in 1948, John Steinbeck sold it.'

'The Lab.' was a two-storey building facing the street, which at the back ran out over the water of the bay. Over its street entrance was a sign saying: 'Cannery Row Unlimited'. Once a room next to the one we stood in had contained microscopes and slides and drug cabinets and chemicals. It had reeked of formalin, and sea water, menthol and ether, the sharp pungent smell of rattlesnakes and the musty smell of rats. A backyard shed had been full of jars containing anemones, worms and shells, urchins and corals, and other lovely animals of the sea. Al these exciting creatures were gone now. The basement sink for embalming and injecting had disappeared, too. I remembered it from Steinbeck's description in *Cannery Row*.

'Ed was a very fine biologist,' said Bruce Ariss, 'Top-notch.' Ricketts had been Steinbeck's closest friend in Monterey, and Ariss, apart from sketching him, described him as he was in the 1930s as a 'compact, middle-sized, and middle-aged man with a fair complexion and a shock of reddish-brown hair. He had large,' said Ariss, 'expressive eyes which crinkled when he smiled.' Everyone called Ricketts 'Doc', and everybody loved him, and they mourned him bitterly when his car was hit by a train at a blind level crossing on Cannery Row – down the street to the left of where we were standing – on 9 May 1948. He died in hospital three days later.

In his life of Steinbeck, Jackson J. Benson wrote of Ed and *Cannery Row*, that in its 'onrush of recollected experiences and emotions of life once lived, [Steinbeck] creates a mythical land. And Doc – a mythical being'.

Elsewhere Steinbeck wrote of his friend quite simply:

> The statistics on Ed Ricketts would read: Born in Chicago, played in the street, went to public school, studied biology at the University of Chicago. Opened a small commercial laboratory in Pacific Grove, California. Moved to Cannery Row in Monterey. Degrees – Bachelor of Science only; clubs, none; honours, none. Army service – both World Wars. Killed by a train at the age of fifty-two.

Steinbeck was sentimental. He could have – but didn't – add something like:

> Missed by one and all and by none more than his devoted student, J.S.

In the sun outside, where the canneries had been, tourists parked their fleets of cars up and down the street, roaring their engines as they tried to manoeuvre themselves into impossibly small spaces. The excited shouting of children filled the air. Down the road was a waxworks museum, and numerous boutiques and fast-food outlets and all the attractions of a boisterous holiday seaside resort. The tourists were looking for reminders of Steinbeck. Apart from his statue, they'd be lucky to find him among the T-shirts, the hot dogs and the frozen yoghurt stands.

Ariss was saying, 'There were, oh, eighteen or more big canneries on Cannery Row in the Thirties. "Cannery Row" ceased to be Cannery Row when the sardines disappeared in 1945.' Ariss shook his head sadly.

'Ed warned 'em. He warned the fishermen, who sometimes took boats out of over 100 feet long, that they were over-fishing these waters. Every year they were forced to take their nets further and further out to sea. As they well knew. But they ignored Ed's words of wisdom. They shrugged and said, "Well, there's more in the sea than ever came out of it." And, you see, they were dead wrong. Ed knew best.'

He smiled. Then, holding his nose as if detecting a bad smell, 'Ouff,' he said through his fingers. 'The smell of the sardines – or rather the smell of the burning of the left-overs of the sardines – hung over the place like an evil smog. Overpowering. And when fishing was at its peak, the canneries operated right round the clock. So the smell was constant. Where you see all those smart Japanese cars belonging to tourists, the cannery workers wandered about – bindle-stiffs, that's what they were called then, hobos of all shapes and sizes; Italians and Sicilians working on the sardines, Japanese mostly on the abalone. Of course, the whorehouses and greasy-spoon restaurants did great business.' He laughed.

'But, phew! There was the Carmel Packing Company, the Monterey Canning Company, the Custom House Packing Corporation – oh, all sorts. Monterey sardines seemed to be particularly rank-smelling. Don't know why. The best ones were packed in mustard sauce, and they had red labels. But even that didn't help much. My wife, Jean, became so nauseated by the smell of sardines that after a while she couldn't touch 'em any more.

'On top of which, believe it or not, Ed produced some kind of horrible shark-liver oil. Insisted we drink some every day to ward off colds. It was god-awful. We preferred the colds, we told him.'

Bruce Ariss showed me his sketches. Done over the past fifty years, they give a perfect image of what the old Cannery Row had looked like. You can see in one of them, between the twin blocks housing the Monterey Canning Co. and the San Carlos Canning Co., Ed's little Lab. Ed himself is at the top of the outside stairway in waders, apron and baseball cap, waving to someone in the street. His old Packard is parked alongside, and in it John Steinbeck reclines in the back seat with his legs dangling through the window. Almost directly across the road is Dora Flood's Lone Star Restaurant (which of course served a good deal more than food), and Lee Chong, the Chinese grocer, is trotting down Ocean Avenue balancing two heavy containers on a pole across his shoulders. A big Hovenden Canning Co. truck is blocking the street while its driver, feigning indifference, waits beside his cab for two voluptuous lady canners fast approaching in gumboots, pants and head-scarves. One sketch Bruce gave me shows George and Lenny – the two 'bindle-stiffs' from Steinbeck's *Of Mice and Men* – walking towards Steinbeck himself, who is seated on the ground and making notes with a cigarette in his mouth. A sad-eyed spotted dog (an early forerunner of Charley, I suppose) sits beside him.

Bruce Ariss's book *Inside Cannery Row* (his words and his pictures) has everything in it: drawings of a Monterey fish-oil separator (whatever that was); of an incident in the murderous Salinas Lettuce Strike; of moray eels and sea cucumbers (trapped by Ed Ricketts); and of the Thirties' sardine fleet at sea in Monterey Bay (a sketch dated 1935, which I think is a particularly beautiful one).

One question above all I wanted to ask Ariss: what about the dead girl Ed had found trapped Ophelia-like under the water at La Jolla – was there more to the story?

Bruce Ariss shook his head. 'I don't know. There may be something in it,' he said. 'It may be a true story. With embellishments from Steinbeck, of course.'

I had had no idea, until I read Ariss's text, that *The Grapes of Wrath* had been banned from the library in Pacific Grove. It was mainly written there. Nor that it had been *twice* publicly burned in Salinas, Steinbeck's birthplace. *Publicly burned* – surely only the Nazis did that. *Twice*.

'*Grapes* was his peak, I think,' said Bruce Ariss. 'By far the best thing he ever wrote. I wouldn't have a word changed in it.'

Ariss stood on the staircase where he had placed Ed Ricketts in his sketch, and waved goodbye as John and I walked to our car. It was parked not far from the spot where Ed had been killed by the train.

Back in Carmel, I dug about and found my copy of Steinbeck's *Log from the Sea of Cortez*, a marine specimen-gathering trip he went on down the Baja Peninsula with Ed Ricketts. I wanted to find a passage he had written after Ed's death which I had found memorable. Here it was:

> Everyone near him [Steinbeck wrote] was influenced by him, deeply and permanently. Some he taught how to think, others how to see or hear. Children on the beach he taught how to look for and find beautiful animals in worlds they had not suspected were there at all.

It was typical of everything I have read about Ed that his only comment, having been invited by Steinbeck to read the typescript of *Cannery Row* and make any changes he cared to, should have been, 'Let it go that way. It is written in kindness. Such a thing can't be bad.'

> The important things in life are love and beauty, which bring joy to the process of living. Life and death – simply are.

And that was the Steinbeck-Ricketts philosophy as set out by Steinbeck.

I asked John Thompson if he could run me up to Salinas where *The Grapes of Wrath* was publicly burned twice; and possibly even to Fremont Peak. From that hilltop, in 1960, Steinbeck, with Charley at his side, had said a final farewell to his birthplace.

Thompson was a wonderful guide and a man of few words. 'Willingly,' he said at once. And he went on to suggest we stop *en route* at the cemetery in which both Ed Ricketts and Flora Adams – the original of Dora Flood, owner of the 'most central and best' whorehouse in Monterey – were buried.

Ed Ricketts's place of rest was simply a name on a wall full of plaques – they looked like labels on a series of walled-up drawers. Flora Adams, on the other hand, almost equally loved (though for different reasons, of course), had a small but independent plot on a wide flat lawn some way away.

'Dora Flood', as Steinbeck had named her in *Cannery Row* and *Sweet Thursday*, had died in her sleep a few years after the Second World War. Her girls, he said in *Sweet Thursday*, were broken-hearted; and to show it, they 'put on a lady-drunk that lasted three days', stuck a 'Not Open for Business' sign on the door; even, through the walls, you could hear them doing honour to Dora Flood (or Flora Adams) in three-part harmony – 'Rock of Ages', 'Asleep in the Deep', and 'St James Infirmary'. Those girls really mourned, marvelled Steinbeck – 'they mourned like coyotes'.

In his two tender, humorous, human novels about Cannery Row, Steinbeck showed himself to be loving, lyrical, sentimental and funny at the same time. In his fictionalised Monterey, Dora (or Flora) had wanted to name her place the Lone Star (in reality she did), because once in her youth she had spent a wonderful weekend in Fort Worth. Her sister insisted that it be called (which in reality it never was) the Bear Flag, in honour of California. 'For,' she said, 'if you were *hustling* a state you should *do honour* to that state.'

Now, searching the lawn for Flora's tomb, my eye was drawn to a small Stars and Stripes sticking up out of the grass. Sure enough it flew over Flora. 'Flora Adams', the inscription said on the small flat slab of greyish marble. And '1876–1948'. That was all. Except for one more poignant thing: under the little white wooden cross someone had left a pair of blue high-heeled shoes. They lay there – just anyhow – as if she had just that minute kicked them off.

'Salinas's temperature in the summer climbs into the hundreds,' said John. 'This brings in the cold air from Monterey Bay. And that leads to fog.'

There was a blanket of fog hanging over the northwest now as we ploughed our way across the Salinas River and the vast valley of dark, rich earth, the endless fields of artichokes and high-banked strawberries, towards Steinbeck's birthplace.

When we reached Salinas, a block from John Steinbeck's house, we stopped to watch a coffin being carried down a chapel's step through rows of young Mexican-looking mourners. John, who as a journalist followed events hereabouts, said it was the body of a Mexican gang member who had been recently murdered. Parts of the town were simply seedy patches of wiry uncut grass, among ram-shackle slums of garages. A shabby Mexican dive offered 'Pescado Frito'. In Chinatown we passed Salinas's Confucius Church. But there were some fine old buildings, too.

Steinbeck, once so hated and reviled, is commemorated in a number of ways. Bruce Ariss points out there's the John Steinbeck Library and the Steinbeck Festival, the Steinbeck Credit Union, the Steinbeck Mortgage Company, and, 'possibly to commemorate Steinbeck's somewhat exaggerated reputation as a two-fisted drink-er', the Steinbeck Alcoholic Treatment Centre.

More than that, Ariss is of the opinion that, as the name of Maxim Gorki's home town in Russia was changed to 'Gorki' in 1932, Salinas should one day – the sooner the better – become 'Steinbeck, California'. 'Our Nobel Prize-winning author, being the only famous person to come out of Salinas, will,' Ariss is sure, 'give his name to his home town.'

Salinas, California, USA! The town which, according to Bruce

Ariss, publicly burned one of the great American novels of the twentieth century, *The Grapes of Wrath*. Burned it *twice!*

As Al Joad used to say, 'God Awmighty, Ma!'

Part Six

Indian Territory

All the past we leave behind,
We debouch upon a newer mightier varied world,
Fresh and strong the world we seize, the world of labor and the
　　march,
　　　　Pioneers! O pioneers!

WALT WHITMAN: 'Pioneers! O Pioneers!'

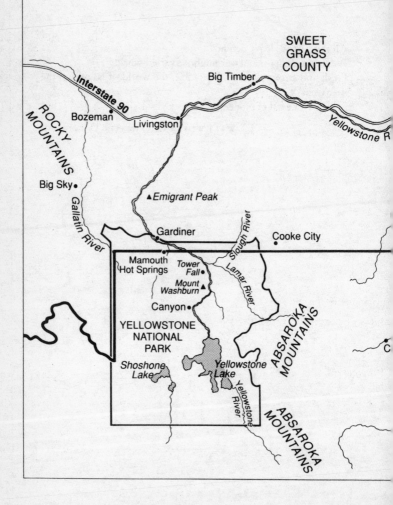

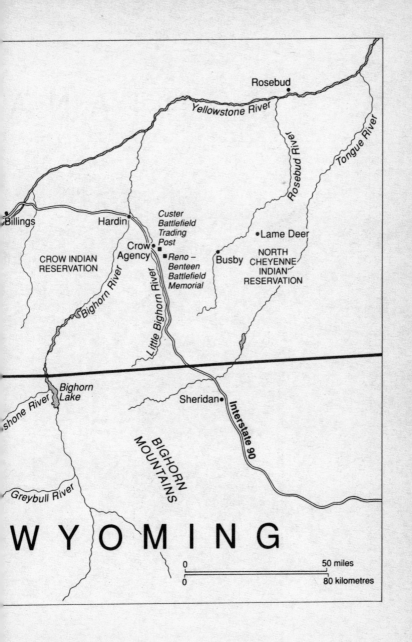

Rosebud

Yellowstone River

Rosebud River

Tongue River

Billings

Hardin

Custer
Battlefield
Trading
Post

Crow
Agency

Lame Deer

Reno –
Benteen
Battlefield
Memorial

Busby

NORTH
CHEYENNE
INDIAN
RESERVATION

CROW INDIAN
RESERVATION

Bighorn River

Little Bighorn River

Bighorn
Lake

shone River

Sheridan

Interstate 90

Greybull River

BIGHORN
MOUNTAINS

WYOMING

0   50 miles

0   80 kilometres

Chapter 15

From Oakland and San Francisco on the Pacific, I flew inland to Bozeman in Montana, changing planes in Salt Lake City. I had to see what is sometimes called the 'Great Divide' and at other times the 'Frontier'. It is the region, say what you like, where much of the 'old' American character of the 'True Grit' variety was formed. I wanted experience of the Rockies, of America just to the west of the hundredth meridian, of the rolling plains where the tall grasses of the East gave way to the short grass of the West. I wanted to see those plains; the ranges where millions – yes, *millions* – of buffalo really did once roam (mighty herds which, people swore, made the earth tremble); where once the grizzly bears stood on their powerful hind legs to sniff the untainted air as fearlessly as the prairie dogs of today; and where, like beautiful grey shadows flickering between the trees, wolves once lived at ease. These days representatives of farming timber interests, who can howl just as loudly as any wolf when their profits are threatened, have branded wolves vermin and driven them away.

Apart from that, I wanted to renew my acquaintance with those Civil War heroes now that they had recreated themselves in other 'heroic' guises. For example, Lieutenant-Colonel George Armstrong Custer's immediate boss in the Indian campaigns in the West leading up to his defeat and death at the Little Bighorn was the 5-foot 5-inch Civil War hero and general, 'Little Phil' Sheridan. Sheridan's boss was none other than my old friend from the plinth in Central Park, General William Tecumseh Sherman, who now commanded the United States Army under President (and ex-General) Ulysses S. Grant. These powerful palefaces, having polished off the Confederates, shared similarly murderous views on what to do about the West, particularly how to polish off the Red Indians.

Irascible Little Phil informed the white world that 'the only good Indians I ever saw were dead'. And Sherman, the man who had made Georgia howl, wrote to him agreeing that 'the Indians are the enemies of our race and our civilisation'. The white general with the Indian middle name now proposed to make the redskins howl as Georgia had done, before meting out the 'utter annihilation' he felt they deserved.

191

I also wanted to see what was left after what Ian Frazier in his book *Great Plains* calls the 'punch line' of 200 years of the white man's presence there. Here are extracts from Frazier's analysis of that 'punch line':

> We trap out the beaver . . . call the land a desert and hurry across it to get to California and Oregon; suck up the buffalo, bones and all; kill off nations of elk and wolves and cranes and prairie chickens . . . dig up the gold and rebury it in vaults someplace; ruin the Sioux and Cheyenne and Arapaho and Crow and Kiowa and Comanche; kill Crazy Horse, kill Sitting Bull; harvest wave after wave of immigrants' dreams and send the wised-up dreamers on their way; plough the topsoil until it blows to the ocean; ship out the wheat, ship out the cattle; dig up the earth itself and burn it in power plants . . . dismiss the small farmers, empty the little towns . . . dry up the rivers and springs . . . .

The list of symptoms of the white man's cruelty, blindness and stupidity is a long and dismal one. Would there be anything left worth seeing? The only thing to do was to have a look.

I decided to begin looking in the Yellowstone Park.

It is easy to mock the Yellowstone, and many have done so. Steinbeck, for instance, wrote that it is no more representative of America than is Disneyland. Nevertheless he drove there with Charley and enjoyed it. For one thing, it reminded him of the explorers Meriwether Lewis and William Clark, the first Americans to cross the Great Divide of the Rockies, to push through wild and unknown country to the Pacific Ocean and then back: real American originals. The Lewis and Clark expeditions started out from St Louis in 1804 and returned in 1806, and Steinbeck recalled that only one man of that truly intrepid, arduous and long-drawn out venture died and only one deserted. 'And we,' said Steinbeck contemptuously, 'get sick if the milk delivery is late and nearly die of heart failure if there is an elevator strike.'

I knew nothing of the Great Plains, so I took the advice of American friends who live in Missoula, Montana, and wrote to an obliging organisation in Bozeman called Off The Beaten Path. The founders of this splendid firm are Bill and Pam Bryan, and if they don't know everything worth knowing about the area, I don't know who does. When they wrote in answer to my letter asking what I wanted to see, I replied, 'I don't know what you've got to offer. But, in a word: Everything.' I said that because I knew next to nothing.

First I asked for a guide to take me camping and trekking in the Yellowstone Park. I wanted someone who could show me the mountains, rivers and rapids: bison, grizzlies and brown bear, and elk, pronghorn antelope and Bighorn sheep. Someone who knew the birds, too: the redtailed hawks and golden eagles, the ospreys and trumpeter swans, the kestrels and the falcons; and the geese, the herons, the cranes and the cormorants, the ravens and the black-billed magpies. In short, a first-class naturalist was what I wanted.

There was something called 'White water rafting' on the Bryans' list of Things to Do. I added that to my list, whatever it was. And I also asked the Bryans if they could arrange visits to the Custer battlefield at the Little Bighorn. They could do all these things they said – and they tacked on a detour to Wyoming to see Cody, the town Buffalo Bill built, and booked me into the Irma, the huge Victorian hotel he had put up in honour of his daughter. As if this was not enough, they added an extra guide for the Yellowstone; a former head game warden of the Yellowstone called John Good. In a postscript to my letter I had asked the Bryans not to forget to lay on a good Scotch whisky for cold outdoor nights in the Park. John Good, a first-rate fisherman and naturalist, turned out to be a cheerful drinker and a good talker as well. What did it matter if he preferred his own bourbon to my Red Label? As for the permanent naturalist and guide, Bill Bryan had arranged for Ken Sinay, a much younger man than either Good or myself, to take me into the Yellowstone. I couldn't have asked for a better companion. I believe Ken was born with the sort of outsized passion for watching wild animals and birds that amounts to an overwhelming obsession. When I first met him at our rendezvous in Bozeman, I happened to ask him if he knew anything about wild flowers as well as everything else. I had forgotten to mention flowers and trees in my letter to the Bryans, and people were saying it was a particularly good year for flowers.

'If you happen to know one or two of them –' I said.

Ken grinned. I was pleased to find that, unlike many Americans, he was a man of few words. 'Try me,' was all he said.

It would be pointless to recount exactly what birds and animals Ken Sinay did show me in our few days in the Yellowstone Park, and exactly where. Actually, I was surprised to find how many Bighorn sheep, bears and bison, leave alone ospreys and eagles, we did see at this 'punch line' time of American history.

All that we saw obviously couldn't come within a million miles of what Lewis and Clark found. For a start, experts think that, in about 1800, 100,000 grizzly bears roamed North America compared to today's dismal figure of fewer than 1,000. Lewis and Clark found grizzlies all over the place. Clark went out one morning quite casually and killed a bear of a size which staggered him. It was 'verry large', he noted in his eccentric spelling, 'and a turrible looking animal which we found verry hard to kill'. When he finally did kill it and had measured it from nose to heel, he found it to be '8 feet 7.5 inches tall' and '5 feet 10.5 Ins arround the breast'. It must have weighed, he thought, 600 lb., and Lewis thought it might be 200 lb. more. Whatever it weighed, that bear, every one agreed, was a real whopper. There were many others just as big; as well as 'Grown Wolves in every direction'.

To give an idea of what Lewis and Clark came across on their average day, I have only to quote at random from Lewis's diary. For instance, for Thursday, 8 August 1805:

> at Noon Reubin Fields arrived and reported that he had been up Wisdom river some miles above where it entered the mountain . . . he had killed a deer and an Antelope. great quantity of beaver Otter and musk-rats in these rivers. two of the hunters we sent out this morning returned at noon had killed each a deer and an antelope . . . .

Among other animals, large panthers, 'gangs' of elk, a good many 'burrowing-squirrels', and endless beavers cropped up along their way – all recorded in the captains' strange English. They regularly came across irate rattlesnakes, strident black woodpeckers, leave alone large herds of buffalo, their bones, and sometimes 'their excrement of an old date'.

Taking Clark's entry for Sunday, 19 May 1805, I read:

> I walked on Shore (of the Musselshell River) with two men we killed a white or grey bear; notwithstanding that it was Shot through the heart it ran at it's usial pace near a quarter of a mile before it fell. Capt Lewis's dog was badly bitten by a wounded beaver and was near bleeding to death. after killing the Bear I continued my walk alone & killed 3 Deer & a Beaver . . . Capt Lewis walked on Shore this after noon & killed an Elk, Buck, and & a Beaver. I killed three Deer at dinner . . . .
>
> We can scarcely cast our eyes in any direction without perceiving deer Elk Buffaloe or Antelopes.

And so they ploughed on to the Pacific Ocean, firing away at the animals as they went. Of course these intrepid men, isolated in an unmapped wilderness, killed in order to eat; the life of their expedition depended on the game they shot. Theirs was no fancy hunting party, the sort of thing that became only too common later and among other things finally did for the buffalo. It is worth remembering that by 1874 – only sixty-nine years after Lewis and Clark had passed through – there were probably nearly as many hunters as animals on the Great Plains.

Ken Sinay was in his element in the Yellowstone – and he was probably equally so in other parts of the Rockies. A born naturalist and fisherman, he was devoted to the outdoor life. In a burst of feverish activity, and with great excitement and enthusiasm, he would pull up his heavy four-wheel-drive truck at the roadside, and in a trice offload binoculars and powerful mounted 'scopes so that we could peer at the far-off shape of a lumbering grizzly or black bear, or a herd of elk or mule deer moving across this dramatic landscape.

Ken possessed the first-rate guide's priceless gift of making ignorant clients (in this case me) feel they were contributing to the good time he himself was having. This meant that if I spotted, by pure chance, across the valley a boulder that moved – and so obviously was a bear, not a rock at all – his delighted congratulations made the incident memorable for both of us.

One incident became memorable enough to stick in my mind for ever. I suspect Ken will have told the tale a good many times since it happened. And why not? It was a good chuckle for him, even if it was the sort of nightmare designed to turn my own hair grey on the spot.

That particular morning Ken and I had parked the pick-up by the roadside and set off on foot up a wide bare valley bordered on its right side by stands of pine trees. 'There are bear in there,' said Ken, indicating them. 'See the elk ahead,' he pointed. 'We'll probably see a few buffalo later.'

I could see the elk – a large herd of them was grazing on a low ridge ahead of us. To me the trouble seemed to be that we were horribly exposed, as we wandered down this open tract, to any grizzlies that might suddenly come charging out of those trees to our right.

We had walked several hundred yards, with Ken way ahead of me, before I expressed the nagging fear that was beginning to cause an empty feeling in my stomach.

'Ken,' I called as nonchalantly as I could, 'what does one actually *do* when an angry grizzly advances on one?' It was only sensible, I thought, to be prepared. 'Exit, pursued by a bear,' I remembered from *The Winter's Tale*. About Act 3, was it? I didn't want that scene repeated here.

Ken's reply was immediate. 'Run for a tree and climb it. Fifteen feet off the ground should do it.'

Was he serious? 'Fifteen feet?' I quavered. 'But, Ken, there are no trees handy at all. Of *any* height.'

'If there isn't a tree nearby,' Ken continued calmly, 'just lie down with your hands over your ears and your arms protecting your sides. Then, the grizzly stands less chance of disembowelling you.' He grinned. 'Of course, he has huge teeth. He'll most likely take a couple of big bites out of your ass. Painful as hell I would think.'

I hardly took my eyes off those trees after that.

I should have had eyes in the back of my head. No bears rushing from the treeline threatened to mow us down as we strolled unprotected in the open. Worse than that, it was a party of buffalo – led by an enormous thundering, snorting male – which came charging high-spiritedly down the very trail on which we were walking.

I have to explain here that buffalo, though not the biggest, are the most extraordinarily *massive* creatures I have ever seen. They can weigh over a ton. If you approach them when they are lying down, you seem to be standing beside an unbelievably huge shaggy boulder. Colossal shoulders grow out of a gigantic hump of muscle and end in a head covered with black curls in which are tiny eyes that look lazy, watchful and extremely mean. There is also in the offing a pair of extremely dangerous-looking horns. On its feet, a buffalo is so huge that you dwindle to the size of a diminutive Theseus standing beside a very large Minotaur. No wonder the Yellowstone Park has warnings to tourists at frequent intervals; warnings to give buffalo a wide berth and certainly not to touch them. The apparent apathy of these huge beasts is wholly false. These Tiger tanks of the animal world can move with the speed of an express train.

It was the pounding hooves of five or six of these enormous creatures that warned me that we were actually strolling in their chosen path. The fleeting thought crossed my mind that it was an impertinent thing for us to be doing. I actually felt the earth tremble just as writers of old have described it, as I scrambled, after the unperturbed back of Ken Sinay – had he heard and felt nothing? – while these terrible mountains of muscle thundered down on us. I find it difficult to believe now, I was simply too embarrassed to call out to warn Ken of my impending trampling (the buffalo would have got to me a few seconds before him). And when he did at last turn round and saw what was happening – he stopped in his tracks and, to my great annoyance, doubled up with laughter.

He *laughed* – just as the monster leading the charge uttered a tremendous snort, threw his horns in the air, and veered away to his left.

'They're only playing,' shouted Ken between explosions of mirth. 'High jinks,' he explained, still grinning. 'It's a great sight, though, isn't it?' It was a question I felt I could let go by me.

The group of lunging, plunging animals following their snorting leader charged off the track and headed for a low hill in another direction. Possibly to have a good laugh. On what sudden whim, their leader had diverted them, heaven knew. As Ken had said, it was a great sight all right. I stood there mildly trembling, and thought about it; I thought about how it might feel to be hammered into the ground by enormous creatures that looked like things seen in a bad dream. I faced up the track and directed my faltering footsteps to follow Ken once more across the open plain. And got back to worrying about the grizzlies lurking in the trees.

We drove next day to the Yellowstone tourist centre at Canyon to meet John Good. We found him waiting for us, leaning against the wall, a lean, trim figure in shorts. Bill had said he was about sixty-eight but he looked a good deal younger than that. He had a good-humoured look about him that I liked.

'Howdy,' he said, briefly, in the quiet voice I associated by now with this part of the country. He heaved a bedroll into the vehicle and we set off to our first camping place, Slough Creek, across the Lamar River. Chosen by Ken.

'Suit you, John?' Ken asked him politely.

'Slough Creek's fine, Ken.'

We parked the car up a track that ended near a stream, and set up our three tents. Mine, borrowed from Ken, was a diminutive affair, and he showed me how to put it up so that its entrance practically overhung the creek. When I woke in the night I could hear the sound of owls and the roar of the water. Straight ahead hills rose sharply behind the tall pine trees and above them was clear sky and the stars. It was a good spot.

In the morning we left the tents there – no one would steal them at a camp site – and set out for another noon trek.

A notice near the camp site at Slough Creek said: '*Warning*. Bear frequented area. There is no guarantee of your safety while hiking or camping in bear country.'

Another announcement was far more sinister: 'Have you seen this person? Daren "Franny" Dixon. 20 years old. 6'1". 170 lbs. Avid fisherman. Last seen: [the date was about a week before].'

'What do you make of that, John?' I asked.

John Good said, 'I think he's probably dead. Drowned or fell off a cliff. Maybe a bear got him. In my time here, people vanished. Just never found. There was a Swiss woman in the Eighties who obeyed all the camping rules – but even so a bear came in and took her. It happens.'

'I'll lace my tent up well tonight,' I said.

'It may help you none. A bear could come through the side of the tent. Don't let it spoil your sleep, though.'

You can easily lose track of the exact number of animals you see in the Park on even a single morning's walk. I know we saw mule deer with their fine spreading antlers and white rumps; and big herds of elk; a good many delicate pronghorn antelope with what looked like painted mask-like faces, anxious eyes, and hind legs that can propel them faster than any other animal except a cheetah. There were monstrous buffalo like mythical Minotaurs, and Bighorn sheep perched on impossible ledges like dirty grey outcrops of the mountainside itself. Bald eagles now and again flew slowly overhead, turning their white heads from side to side as they searched for something edible on the ground below.

We skirted coppices of lodgepole pine, spruce and fir, and waded through carpets of pink Indian paintbrush flowers, yellow-blossom sweetclover and high clumps of sage. I soon found I had given up meticulously making nature notes.

In any case, this account of the Yellowstone is not going to turn into a list of the Park's flora and fauna. Even so it seems important to give some idea of the whole point of coming here. Should one give equal emphasis to the crowds of tourists we found milling round the Park's geysers? Geysers vary. Some are huge steaming cauldrons of boiling, or near-boiling, water that spouts or drips on to terraces and there somehow congeals into frozen waterfalls of cream-white and pink like elaborate arrangements of ice cream. Other geysers are simply holes in the ground encircled by a brittle crust easy to fall through. There was something particularly alarming about these. No wonder notices tell you to be sure your children do not fall in: you could boil a lobster in some of these geysers in no time at all. But still the tourists crowd in, children and all.

How many of the car-loads of visitors I saw snacking on hot dogs and french fries, had any inkling of the past; of Lewis and Clark, of 'Little Phil' Sheridan and of the great Oglala war chief, Crazy Horse. Did it matter if they had never heard of these men? Perhaps it was enough that they were sufficiently interested in nature to have driven for their precious summer holidays all this way to Yellowstone.

Or perhaps that was not quite enough. For the Yellowstone

may not be there for ever. It matters, surely, that it is menaced by a number of threats to degrade and destroy it. Among those threats, probably the greatest are oil and gas exploration schemes originating in Washington; then there are logging interests, mining and geothermal energy projects and reclamation plans. Other obvious threats involve the use (and overuse) of poisons and herbicides; and the schemes, motivated by human and political greed, to sell public land and drive motorways into the remaining secluded areas. Not least, it would probably astound many of the Yellowstone tourists to hear, is the threat posed by burgeoning major ski areas and the growth of 'resorts', with all that goes with them – hotels, hideous second homes, condominiums and golf courses, for example. In 'free' America it is virtually impossible to keep human greed at bay. And, with the help of America's law-givers, greed could – quite soon – simply force out the animals. Often the right to be greedy seems, in effect, to be guaranteed by one constitutional amendment or another.

It was outrageous to think that those magnificent creatures, which only that morning had looked as though they would grind me into the prairie, could be banished to perpetual oblivion by a gaggle of martini-swigging, besuited men in offices in Washington, DC.

Darkness had overtaken Slough Creek. An owl cried over the tall dark trees; the pine-covered hills had vanished into the night. Overhead nighthawks – goat-suckers was their other name – flew eerily back and forth, like large shadows, on great silent, scythe-shaped wings. I sat with John and Ken at a table on a hard Park bench under the few stars that peeped out from ragged clouds, while the creek-water ran chattering beside us. Orion was overhead (always a good omen, I think). My Red Label whiskey stood on a rough wooden table, John's bourbon beside it. Ken drank coffee.

'John,' I said, 'did you notice there were no black tourists in the Park today?' There had been a number of Asians – who might have been American immigrants, or perhaps foreign tourists. I suppose my question somehow followed on from my musings about the future of the Yellowstone in the face of all those threats. Who cared, after all? John must have his own ideas; he had been a director of the Park.

'You know,' he said, 'once I went on a West Coast tour of black institutions of one sort or another. I asked black teachers, pastors and the like why more black children – and their parents, for that matter – didn't visit the Yellowstone? The reply I got most often was simply: "Well, that's not the sort of thing we do." '

An unsatisfactory answer. It seemed to me there must be more to it than that. If it had been me I might have repeated the question to those black teachers, pressing for a better answer. But it was too late now.

With John and Ken I knew I was with Americans who not only loved the fauna and flora that surrounded us, but who were the sort of Americans who had *always* been drawn to the Great Plains; the Great Divide; the Frontier. The prototypical American persona derived from the place we sat in now, listening to the chatter of water as Clark might have done, sitting under similar trees in which the remote ancestors of these same owls had screeched at him. Steinbeck had mentioned that Frontier element in the old American character – who had not? I fetched a torch and my copy of *Travels with Charley* and between sips of whisky began to read from it.

I read the passage when an old friend, 'a well-known and highly respected political reporter, a completely honest man', approached Steinbeck before he set off with Charley round America and said to him,

> There used to be a thing or a commodity we put great store by. It was called the People. Find out where the People have gone. I don't mean the square-eyed toothpaste-and-hair-dye people, or the success-and-coronary people. Maybe they never existed, but if there ever were the People, that's the commodity the Declaration was talking about, and Mr. Lincoln . . . .
>
> Wouldn't it be silly if the Constitution had been talking about a young man whose life centers around a whistle, a wink, and Wildroot?

'Or rap dancing, joints and Diet Coke, for that matter,' I added. 'Is that all that youth is interested in today? Maybe, John, I've got cynical since I came here; since I met you and Ken.'

I heard John chuckle in the gloom, and I poured some bourbon into his glass and a little whiskey into mine. A flashlight moved in the trees; a camper was dumping his garbage; he had seen the signs that warned that grizzlies were attracted by the smell of food and came sniffing round for it at night.

I went on, 'Maybe I've been over-influenced by those self-indulgent, big-buttocked holiday-makers I've been seeing too much of this summer in San Francisco, Los Angeles and Long Island.'

From John's reply – quietly non-committal – I gathered he understood and agreed with the complaint Steinbeck's friend had voiced all those years ago. 'Well, one must be thankful that there are as many sightseers in the Yellowstone as there are. We've seen quite a lot, really.'

Ken kept quiet. I think nostalgia for America's past seemed pointless to him. Yet Ken had told me he had deliberately escaped from an Eastern or Midwestern city to make his life in this Frontier world – the world of the Old America, the world that had been the inspiration of the Americans, of the Declaration of Independence and the Constitution, of the People 'Mr Lincoln' was talking about.

Who 'the People' were these days, God knew. But, sitting at night in the Yellowstone Park, with the owls calling in trees that stood in the dark like cloaked sentinels, with the stars overhead, and with a glass of whiskey in my hand, I was convinced then (as I am now) that Ken Sinay and John Good were 'people' as admirable as any America today can produce.

Worrying, though, that no black Americans came to this glorious place – still threatened admittedly by white business interests, but surely still capable of inspiring a nation's youth, whatever its colour. Could they not afford to? Yet there are rich black families in America. Was coming here really 'not the sort of thing black people did'? Could it be that they preferred to remain entombed in their inner-city ghettoes? If so, perhaps there was no hope for the idea of one nation here at all.

One night John Good told how he had once met a grizzly face to face.

'I was hobbling along a river bank,' he said, 'I forget which one – taking it easy because I had broken a leg skiing and I had a stick. I came to a biggish bush at one point and as I edged between it and the river, a grizzly came round it to meet me.' There they were, John said, nose to nose.

Luckily it was not a full-grown grizzly, but even an immature grizzly bear is a formidable creature. John immediately prepared to throw himself into the river.

'Broken leg and all?' I asked.

'Better, I thought, to try and swim for it with a broken leg than to be mauled to death on the bank. Anyway, they stared at each other; John looking closely at the bear's teeth and smelling its appalling breath. Luckily, the bear was just as astonished as he was to have met something coming round the side of the bush, and dropped to his all-fours position and ran off.'

'John, tell me, in that moment when you stood facing the bear,' I asked, 'did your past life go flashing by?' It was difficult to imagine John Good being really scared by anything.

'I'm not sure that it did. But I'm pretty sure I swore to turn over a new leaf in future if that bear went away. And it did.'

He shook his head as if he was reliving those seconds of peril, murmuring 'Phew!' I reached for the dark shape of the whiskey bottle.

'Have a taste of this,' I said, and he didn't shake his head again.

'We could walk along Specimen Ridge,' John said next morning. 'But I think Mount Washburn is a better bet. Ten thousand feet. Think you can make it?' He smiled at me.

'Of course,' I said boldly. But *could* I make it? I had climbed very few mountains (if any) in recent years and 10,000 feet is no molehill. True, John was a couple of years older than me. If he could do it without collapsing halfway up with a heart attack so, I supposed, could I. If not, what was I doing here? In any case, the only alternative was a humiliating backdown.

'Of course I can make it,' I repeated, more firmly still. And so that morning we clambered to the top of Mount Washburn. It was worth it, as reaching the top of a mountain usually is, for the view alone. Of course this view was deceptive. The sea of ridges, the uneven profiles of the far peaks and the spurs and valleys intermittently visible between them, seemed to stretch to infinity. In reality Yellowstone Park is relatively small.

Some valley sides were badly scarred by acres of burnt pines and spruces – sad relics of the disastrous fires of 1988, the result of human carelessness or perhaps lightning that burned nearly a million acres of trees. The ancient volcanic caldera – the high flat plateau – lay beneath us now, plainly visible. And, created millions of years ago by that volcanic cataclysm, the region had been prey to natural disasters ever since. Acres of 150- and 200-year-old trees had gone up with a roar in that summer of 1988, the driest recorded since President Ulysses S. Grant signed the act creating the Yellowstone Park.

The view of the Park from the summit of Mount Washburn will remain in my mind for a long time.

From this peak we overlooked ridges of basalt from the ancient volcano, and despite the fires huge, surviving fir forests faded far away, disappearing into snowy mountain tops.

'That's the Absaroka Range,' said John, pointing. 'Crow country. Years ago the Blackfeet Indians hunted here, although they wintered somewhere else. It was too darned tough for them up here.'

Low black clouds huddled over the ridges to the west; we could see rain there falling like fog. But just below us, as if in another world, golden eagles, resting on a cleft in the basalt, basked in the sun.

John, leaning against a rock, looked around him. 'I know a

good many parks, but I like Yellowstone more than any other,' he said. 'Why? Its size. Its naturalness; it's pretty well as it was when it was first discovered by white men. And then there's the variety and quantity of animals and birds here.'

Since that day he has returned to the Yellowstone to live. He couldn't bear to be away from it.

John Good left us to return home after that (he had some important meeting to address in Jackson Hole, Wyoming, where he lived then). But Ken and I still had a day or two together, and a few vignettes remain fixed in my memory as clearly as snapshots looked at only a minute or two ago.

There was the infant mule deer's head peeping at me, allowing curiosity to outweigh anxiety, over a tuft of sage; its wide astonished eyes on a stalk-like neck, and the huge mule-like ears which give it its name, pricked forward to hear to the best advantage.

At Tower Creek, Ken suddenly braked just before we reached a bridge. I thought he was avoiding a careless motorist; the park was full of cars in this holiday period. But that was not it. His unerring eye had spotted, high on a cliff above the road, two Bighorn sheep poised to scramble down at us. They hesitated on the brink, releasing a small shower of stones into the roadway, and then slowly followed the stones down the almost sheer side of the cliff. It was an amazingly bold descent down a crumbling cliff, into the path of the holiday traffic. Not all the drivers could see them coming. I got out of Ken's car and motioned to the oncoming traffic, warning drivers to stop. And for a while the sheep, their heavy ungainly horns curling about their ears, prowled about the road, quite unafraid of the lines of pick-ups and mobile homes, and of the people who clambered out of them, pointing and shouting. Evidently deciding there was no point in staying in this human bedlam, these strangely unperturbed wild creatures scrambled back up the perpendicular cliff, dislodging a further hailstorm of stones, and disappeared disdainfully into the trees.

What else do I remember? Ken's cries of 'Hey, that's real neat!' as he glued his eyes to the telescope to peer at the unusual sight of a family of coyotes gambolling round their den; Ken minutely examining an astonished Least Chipmunk from a distance of a few feet like a plastic surgeon with a magnifying lens analysing a birthmark; and a twittering ground squirrel that kept bobbing out at us from the verge of a grassy path. And the brown and grizzly bears. And of course the buffalo; I can never forget the buffalo.

But now that I think back to those enchanted few days, I

remember that there is something I have neglected to mention: the flowers. Because of the rain, it was a good year for wild flowers. And a few weeks after leaving him, I was glad to receive a letter from Ken. 'Howdy!' he typically began, and he enclosed a list of the animals, birds and flowers we had seen. Among the flowers, he mentioned balsamroot, sweetclover, Indian paintbrush, Alpine forget-me-nots, sticky geranium; and the names reminded me of the multi-coloured carpet we had walked through coming down Mount Washburn. Of the trees he included the slender silver-trunked aspen, the beauty of which I had somehow allowed to slip my mind.

Chapter 16

Then he told me, 'In the part I was reading it says the Word was in the beginning, and that's right. I used to think water was first, but if you listen carefully you will hear that the words are underneath the water.'

'That's because you are a preacher first and then a fisherman,' I told him. 'If you ask Paul, he will tell you that the words are formed out of water.'

'No,' my father said, 'you are not listening carefully. The water runs over the words. Paul will tell you the same thing.'

NORMAN MACLEAN: *A River Runs Through It*

'You'll need to borrow these waterproof clothes,' said David, as he and a colleague began to inflate the rubber raft they'd unloaded from the pick-up. 'The water's extra high in the Yellowstone just now. It'll be very wet. We might even tip over.'

Just my luck, I thought, and I said, 'Thanks for the warning, Dave. And for not adding "Have a nice day".'

He laughed, and pointed skyward. Vast sooty clouds were scurrying towards us over the Absaroka Mountain range that loomed above us to our right. I had chosen to leave the Yellowstone Park by the river. The Yellowstone River flowed – no, roared – from near the Park's northern entrance at Gardiner, and eastwards through Montana in the direction of Livingston and Big Timber and Billings. I wanted to stop the night in Big Timber on my way to the Little Bighorn battlefield, the place where General Custer had got his comeuppance from Sitting Bull and Crazy Horse. Dave, of the Whitewater Montana agency, based somewhere near Big Sky, had been designated to try to get me down the river without drowning. To judge from the state of the river and the sky he was going to have his work cut out. A nice day, it most certainly was not.

There had been exceptional rains. My visit to the Yellowstone's Grand Canyon falls had been especially spectacular as a result of them; a falling smoking plume of dead-white water, a solid fall turning to a startling white-flecked green as it levelled out below the first ledge, then hurrying on to the next drop as white once more as a newly starched shirt-front. Sending up a dense cloud of spray, it pounded away, far below an osprey's nest, a wide ramshackle affair perched precariously on the point of a mere needle of rock like an immensely tall and slender stalagmite which you thought the water might at any moment undermine and sweep away.

Most of the way from Gardiner to Emigrant, a diminutive hamlet some miles down the river, would be easy-going, Dave said – a chance as we floated down mid-stream to look about us and see whatever birds were on the wing that day. There might easily, he said, be an osprey or a trumpeter swan or two; certainly some hawks. I looked at the clouds and wondered.

When Dave and his friend had pumped up the heavy raft until its skin was as tight as a drum, they waited to get their breath back and then began to ease it with difficulty towards the water. It had two seats, one lashed behind the other, and canvas straps attached to its hard round gunwales to hang on to if things got rough.

Then Dave slipped a couple of oars aboard and gripped the raft in case it floated away on the current while I had one foot in it and one foot on the bank. To avoid that I took a swift leap and sat down quickly facing the raft's bows, holding a fistful of straps, while Dave followed me, picked up the oars and pushed off, gently spinning us mid-stream with the current.

The waterproof pants I was wearing and the orange life jacket had been a good idea. Already it was beginning to rain – heavily. Thick purplish-black clouds lay close overhead, and there were rumbles of thunder and occasional flashes of lightning. Raindrops bounced off the surface of the river like bullets. I seemed to have chosen a bad day for rafting.

Dave's companion appeared to agree with me. He held out his hand. 'Well, I'll say goodbye. Enjoy the river.'

'You're going?' I said. Deserting us, was he?

'Got a party waiting for me on the Gallatin near Big Sky. That's over the ridge there.' He waved. 'David will take good care of you.' He strode to his pick-up and was gone. Was one expert rafter enough on this swollen river? I wondered; suppose we snagged a sharp rock and sprang a leak in mid-river – in mid-torrent, more like.

'Well, I'll do my best,' said Dave, cheerfully. 'Just hold on tight when we get to Yankee Jim's Canyon, that's all. I'll tell you when we are getting near it. You'll hear the rapids anyway with all this water rushing over them. There are three falls, quite close together. Once we get past them, we'll be all right.' I thought, and if we don't –?

But we began to move quite steadily down the middle of the Yellowstone, using the current and speeded up by Dave's gentle oar-strokes. Now and again the broad, smooth back of a rock seemed to ease its way to the surface, but the raft slipped over it. There was enough water here for that. No unsettling bumps, no unnerving tilts.

'Any idea of the depth here?' I shouted to Dave.

'Probably six to eight feet on average.'

'Speed?'

'Umm. Eight miles an hour, about.'

After a while there were breaks in the rain, and in one such lull two ospreys followed one another upstream a couple of feet above the far bank, flapping languid white wings. A redtailed hawk swooped, then lazily hung, wings flickering, inspecting the grass for food, its streamlined silhouette posed against towering cottonwood trees that rose like puffs of green smoke against the threatening sky.

When there was a break in the rain, patches of sudden sunshine pierced the clouds. An unexpected spotlight of sun would catch us unawares, and then minutes later, equally without warning, came a drenching downpour or a jagged fork of lightning. In any case, sun or rain, the river carried us on swiftly and benignly between its high banks, skirting a prairie that faded into clumps of cottonwoods, or a line of spruces and willows or featureless acres of smoky-green sagebrush out of which came the trilling of meadowlarks, and where could be seen the stern profiles of kestrels and Swainson's hawks perched on fenceposts and wires. Dwarfing everything to our right was the 10,000-foot upward sweep of Emigrant Peak. It looked like one of the pillars of Hercules.

When the sunshine came through, everything was idyllic on this stretch of river. Here William Clark had enjoyed the most comfortable travelling of his and Lewis's long, arduous expedition. He had found trees suitable for making 28-foot-long dugouts 16 or 18 inches deep; and so in 1806, this river, the Yellowstone – the 'Elk River', to the Crow Indians – was first navigated by white men.

Later I would read the late Norman Maclean's novella *A River Runs Through It* which a movie company had recently filmed on the Gallatin over the ridge. I found a fine passage in it that reminded me of this morning on which Dave and I negotiated the Yellowstone in the unpredictable interchange of sunlight, shadow and rain amid the babble of its swollen waters. Indeed, I marked the page and the passage:

> The voices of the subterranean river in the shadows were different from the voices of the sunlit river ahead. In the shadows against the cliff the river was deep and engaged in profundities, circling back on

itself now and then to say things over to be sure it had understood itself. But the river ahead came in to the sunny world like a chatter-box, doing its best to be friendly. It bowed to one shore and to the other so nothing would feel neglected.

In *Travels with Charley*, John Steinbeck had written: 'I am in love with Montana.' Now I was floating down the green Montana valley under the ramparts of the Absaroka Mountains, as Thomas Jefferson's emissary, William Clark, had done 187 years earlier. And I was in love, too. Personally, I was heading towards Arrow Creek, home of the late, great Crow Indian chief, Plenty Coups, who as a boy had seen in visions the impending extinction of the immense buffalo herds of the Plains, and who as a young warrior had fought against General Crook in the bloody Battle of the Rosebud, only missing by a whisker the massacre of Custer and his men at the Little Bighorn. Of course it was impossible not to agree with Steinbeck about loving Montana, floating as I was through this beautiful world; this strange, beautiful world in which – as Graham Greene says of quite a different place – the past and the present leave equal traces, and the geography may belong to today or to 200 years ago.

On the map this section of the Yellowstone runs in a straight line until it reaches Livingston. And although its beauty is threatened by new settlers, what Norman Maclean called 'Moorish invaders from California' (by which he meant chiefly, I imagine, movie people), as well as by a crackpot 'church' whose members sometimes dig up whole segments of the valley to make deep shelters to hide them from the Apocalypse, the valley still deserves its name. Which is Paradise.

We were approaching by now the Yankee Jim rapids, named after some local character about whom I remember nothing at all. I remember the rapids, though.

'The water is very, *very* high,' shouted Dave, manically flailing the oars to keep us centre-stream, and incidentally to keep me facing the way the raft was heading.

'So much water,' he had time to yell, 'changes the face of the whole river.' A certain menace lay behind that remark, I thought. As it was, a good deal of all that extra water in the river was flooding over me. I could feel cold trickles of it running down under my shirt.

Water below, water above. The rain came down again, even heavier this time. Indistinctly through a screen of slanting drops I saw the razor-edge of mountain on our right sloping down towards the river ahead of us.

'Yankee Jim's Canyon and the rapids begin where that big spur meets the water, see it?'

I could see the spur, and now I heard the roar of the rapids, too.

Through the veil of teeming rain, the surface of the river rose up hissing in abrupt white waves like a choppy sea. Dave had to work the oars in a serious fashion to keep the raft from skidding sideways on to those angry waves.

'Hold on,' he suddenly yelled, and I braced my feet against the rubber gunwales and twisted my hands more tightly into the straps. The river banks narrowed approaching the rapids and the scurrying water chuckled wickedly and slid round or steeplechased over the dangerously large brown rocks that suddenly appeared out of the water like the backs of unsuspected monsters, or was sucked gurgling into the spaces between them.

The raft was tossed sideways in sickening lunges whatever Dave tried to do. And big white waves curled into the craft washing around our feet and threatening to have us over. Viewing the current I wondered if I would be able to swim against it. Forget about the rain; I had long since been drenched to the skin.

And then all of a sudden we had skimmed over the falls, rocking and spinning like a helpless crab battered by an incoming tide. And that was that; we floated into quieter water where the Yellowstone hadn't nearly as much to say for itself. And got ready for Yankee Jim's second lot of rapids.

The second lot were the most fearsome. Here the rocks were bigger and there was far less space between them, so that the danger of the raft getting caught up on one or more of them was considerable. What is more, the water pouring down the falls seemed to take on an oddly smooth look as if it had been mixed with oil.

That was sinister enough. But the worst part of these falls came when we had somehow lurched our way over the rocks and reached a point where the water seemed to turn back on itself in high frothing waves which easily overwhelmed the low gunwales of our little raft. The waves held us steady while at the same time they lifted the forward edge under my feet so high and effortlessly that I thought, 'Oops, here we go,' – and got ready to be pitched into the maelstrom. All I could hear behind me was Dave's frantic breathing.

We were not dumped into the Yellowstone after all. The raft righted itself at the last minute, and Dave's thrashing about with the oars somehow got us through that fearful choppiness right side up.

After a bit, he took a breather and said, 'That was what we call a "hole". That happens when deep water outruns water nearer the surface. A hole is left, which must be filled, of course. Water, like nature, abhors a vacuum. So the surface water curls back on itself to fill that hole. Well, we were sitting in that hole. So the returning water – the waves – became agitated and gave us a hard time.'

'Might we have overturned?'

'Oh yes, sometimes rafts overturn. That, I am sure, is what our audience was waiting to see.'

Our audience? I looked about me and he was right – we had an audience. On the high right bank, a cliff commanding the best view of the rapids and any craft trying to shoot them, three or four cars had drawn up and their occupants were leaning expectantly over the rail on its edge. No doubt hoping to see the real-life drama of two madmen being swept to their deaths in a downpour of rain. A man in a scarlet baseball cap actually had his camera at the ready.

The third set of falls – the last – proved to be an anticlimax. We sailed serenely over them. The only problem was one of humiliation. For instead of nearly capsizing, the raft simply spun giddily towards the bank where it was nudged by surface eddies in a gentle *backward* direction. It was astonishing. We began moving back the way we had come – that is to say, we headed slowly upstream. It was astonishing and bizarre and uncanny; as well as frustrating and, as I say, humiliating. It must have made an amusing spectacle for the onlookers on their cliff edge. Cursing angrily, Dave evidently found nothing amusing about wrestling with the oars to bring the errant raft back into the mainstream of the river. When finally he did so, we continued downriver more or less decorously until we drew into the bank near Emigrant, and squelched ashore.

There our excursion ended. We hauled the raft out of the water, let the air out of her, folded the heavy lengths of rubber, and man-handled the whole deflated craft (with difficulty – it seemed to weigh a ton) to the pick-up that Dave had left for us there. Our audience had vanished, wretchedly disappointed, I suppose, with our failure to sink (within camera range) beneath those furious waves in Yankee Jim's Canyon.

There remained only one thing to settle. Dave was embarrassed. He had misled me, he said, about the cost of the trip; I owed him about twice the sum he had originally quoted. That was no problem, I told him. We all make mistakes. I had had a thrilling morning, and I gave him without a qualm what he said was the true cost of our morning's expedition.

This led to two interesting developments.

A couple of months later, a letter reached me in New York. It was from David and it read:

Dear Gavin,

The morning after our Yellowstone Park trip, I woke with a bad nagging feeling. It stemmed from my acceptance of the cash at the end of the trip. I felt it was not the right thing to do, and it's been a thorn in my side. I have also dragged my feet in resolving the issue . . . .

. . . In the rafting business one does not discuss money with clients. I am still learning the ropes.

For my peace of mind, I'm returning the extra cash you gave me. I trust this letter finds you in good health and positive spirits. Until our paths cross again,

Your Raft Guide,
Dave

Enclosed was a cheque signed by Dave for the extra amount I had (quite willingly) paid him. I have seldom received a more generous letter.

The second development was less welcome. Two days later on my way to my New York hotel on 58th Street at two o'clock in the afternoon, I was relieved of my wallet, robbed very professionally and without violence. Inside the wallet was Dave's cheque.

I doubt if the thieves – three of them – were able to cash the cheque. I certainly could not. So Dave would not have been out of pocket, and, with his conscience assuaged, his noble gesture got the reward it deserved.

As for me – it amply fulfilled my high expectations of the people of Montana. And of New York, for that matter.

Chapter 17

In all your intercourse with the natives treat them in the most friendly and conciliatory manner . . .

Instructions of President Thomas
Jefferson to Captain Meriwether
Lewis, before the Lewis and
Clark expedition set out,
20 June 1803

As William Clark had noted in his journals, the 'Countrey on both sides [of the Yellowstone] is handsom and fertile'. And so it remains.

I could see why John Steinbeck had said he loved Montana. He wrote:

> It seems to me that Montana is a great splash of grandeur. The scale is huge but not overpowering. The land is rich with grass and color, and the mountains are the kind I would create if mountains were ever put on my agenda . . . It seemed to me that the frantic bustle of America was not in Montana . . . . The calm of the mountains and the rolling grasslands had got into the inhabitants.

If they were ever on my agenda, I would create mountains like this, too. And I agreed so strongly that the frantic bustle of America was not in Montana, that when I stopped at a gas station to fill my rented Pontiac, and the young man in a tall hat who topped her up, without being asked, directed me on my way to Big Timber, Billings and Hardin, I said, 'Thank you for your help,' and then added, hoping he'd not take it for impertinence, 'and for not wearing a baseball cap.'

He replied, 'You bet.'

I gave him a large tip then, explaining, 'And that's for not saying, "Have a nice day" or "How ya doin' ".'

'Yes, *sir*,' he replied.

As I turned back on to the highway I could see him in my rear-window looking after me with an astonished grin on his face. I think he'd remember what I'd said. I hoped he'd tell his friends.

'Handsom and fertile' the country certainly was along Interstate 90, the West-East highway that swings southeast to link Bozeman, Montana, to Sheridan, Wyoming.

'Handsom and fertile', yes. Luckily I took pictures to prove it; to disprove an idiotic notion that I might come to believe I had imagined the greenness of all this openness, the blue skies with their towering clouds like wisps of gauze. So there, in a photograph of our departure from Yellowstone, Ken Sinay stands on the edge of the road that sweeps white and flat through vivid green grass strewn with corn-coloured flowers. And here, in some snapshots I stopped the car to take on my way to Big Timber, is the Yellowstone River snaking through the plain, its low bed betrayed by a thick fluffy curtain of cottonwood trees, while in the background, rise and fall the ridges and escarpments of the Crazy Mountains of the Gallatin National Forest. Even the name of the county I stopped in to take those pictures was beautiful: Sweet Grass County, they call it.

It was those towering cottonwood trees that gave Big Timber its name. Bill Bryan of Off The Beaten Path had booked me into the Grand Hotel there. 'It's an old hotel,' he had said, 'recently refurbished with marble floors and pressed tin ceilings.' He was right to recommend the Grand. It was such a simple and charming place that I booked myself into it for a second night on my way back from the Crow Reservation.

The Grand had red brick walls, and green awnings that covered the windows that looked on to the street; old Victorian bedrooms with large springy mattresses; and a good, high wooden bar downstairs with the heads of an elk, a pronghorn, and a steer with amazingly wide horns staring from the walls. A large lady acted as the most genial of barmaids under a topknot of reddish curls. She was one of those well-endowed and still young women who are inclined to take pity on and 'adopt' lone passing strangers with funny accents like myself. I have a photo of the two of us standing by a fire hydrant in the street with the words 'The Grand' traced on the window of the bar behind us. She went with the other comforting things in that red old two-storey hotel in the middle of Nowhere: things like the elk head in the bar and the print of Landseer's *Stag at Bay* over my enormous sagging bed.

In the early evening the bar was crowded with men with lined faces in wide cowboy hats who talked to each other in low laconic bursts, if at all. The hats went with their belts with big buckles, jeans, string ties, and sometimes tweed jackets. I overheard one remark I jotted down as worth recording. From the nodding of heads with which it was repeated, it was clearly a heartfelt complaint. 'It's a problem finding real Montanans hereabouts now,' a man said. 'We're bein' Californicated to death.'

It was a remark that later that evening was dramatically borne out by a happily raucous party of eight or nine female tourists, who burst into the bar chattering and laughing. My friendly lady-bartender whispered that they came here fairly often. She thought maybe they were Californians on a fishing trip.

There was nothing to dislike about them. One of these loud ladies even invited me to join their table and I refused only partly because I wanted an early night and they looked like being here some time. Perhaps, as Steinbeck had said, the calm of the mountains had begun to get to me. At any rate these bright, gossipy ladies reminded me of a louder American world that in Montana with a certain relief I was beginning to forget.

After a final after-dinner drink, I excused myself to my plump friend behind the bar and went upstairs to my Victorian bedroom. I wanted to begin reading the reminiscences of Plenty Coups, the great Crow Indian chief. Next day I was going to make an early start to the Crow Reservation at the Little Bighorn.

I had a date to meet Angela Russell at the Custer Trading Post, just at the turning to the battlefield monument. Angela is a Crow Indian, a strong traditionalist, so it was said; she speaks fluent Crow, and Bill Bryan had told me she was involved in education, natural-resource protection and social work, apart from being a long-time member of the Montana House of Representatives. 'A day with Angela,' said Bill enthusiastically, 'will be a highlight of anybody's trip.'

I reached Hardin, where I was to stay that night, quite early. It sprawls untidily at the confluence of the Little Bighorn and the Bighorn Rivers. I simply noted the guesthouse I would put up in, and then drove due southeast into the Crow Indian Reservation. I kept the Little Bighorn River on my left until the road crossed it at the township of Crow Agency, the tribal community centre.

I turned into the Custer Battlefield Trading Post hungry and thirsty, with still half an hour in which to wait for Angela Russell.

The Trading Post was a long, well-built, two-storey wooden building with a verandah. It seemed to be part coffee shop and part Indian curio-store. I sat down in the coffee shop, watched the tourists manoeuvring their overweight hips between parked tables and listened to the Indian tribal music (drumming was a predominant feature of it) swirling about me from the speakers in the corners. 'Indian Tacos and Fry Bread' the menu said, but I ordered a cup of ham and pea soup and half a common or garden ham and cheese sandwich. When I added a beer, my Indian-looking waitress looked at me severely, 'No liquor is sold on the reservation. You can have alcohol-less beer.' So I ordered iced tea. And examined the menu, back to front.

The back of the Trading Post's menus (a good touch) are in the form of the front page of the Bismarck (Dakota Territory) *Tribune* for 6 July 1876, the edition which first announced Custer's death to the wider world. 'Massacred', it read. 'Gen. Custer and 261 Men The Victims'. The names of the dead followed and they filled quite a lot of space.

The same sensational issue of the *Tribune* printed a good deal of balderdash about the battle. On the other hand, this was probably designed to keep up the morale of folks back home who would have been stunned by news of such a military disaster. 'The Indian dead were great in number . . . . The Indians were severely punished. The hostile assaults were each time repulsed with heavy slaughter' – none of this was true. Evan Connell makes this clear in his wonderfully readable reconstruction of the events leading to, during and after the Custer battle. However you look at it, the Little Bighorn affair was an out-and-out military disaster for the palefaces. Sipping my iced tea at the Custer Battlefield Trading Post, the *Tribune*'s reportorial 'snow-job' reminded me of nothing so much as optimistic interpretations nearly a hundred years later of any number of horrendously costly American 'victories' in Vietnam.

Angela Russell turned up soon after I had paid my bill. She was a large Crow lady, and if, as Bill Bryan had said, she was fluent in Crow she was equally fluent in English.

'Well,' she said at once, 'I should tell you something about myself. I went to Hardin College, and it was tough.' She'd studied anthropology and sociology, she said. 'Thirty-six went in and only four of us graduated.' She proudly admitted she was a three-term member of the Montana House of Representatives. ('How on earth did you know that?' she asked me with a coy giggle.) Now she was eager to get moving so that she could drive me to see a little of the reservation and then take me to a dedication ceremony of some sort at the memorial to the famous Crow Chief, Plenty Coups. The old chief had been alive during the Custer battle and, with those lethal memories in his mind, made his peace with the Great White Chief, the President of the United States in Washington, DC, and lived on until 1933, finally leaving his house with its fine view of the Pryor and Bighorn Mountains to the state.

Angela drove a Toyota expertly and at some speed. She laughed out loud on a sharp bend in the road when I told her she didn't look how I had expected a Crow Indian lady to look.

'You expected me to have a feather in my hair? No, Gavin, I'm Crow all right. My Dad's name had been Medicine Rock. I asked him to change it back to that from Russell. But he was old by then. He didn't care any more.'

She added, 'A pity. I'd like to be called Angela Medicine Rock.'

We circled north through the hamlet called Crow Agency and then followed the Bighorn River, which ran in a shallow valley between two low escarpments. Thunder-clouds were gathering over distant hills.

'See the clouds? That's Bighorn Canyon.'

The Bighorn Valley, where we were, was green with what looked like sugar beet; was this rolling landscape – after all it was part of the reservation – farmed by Crows? I hoped it was: it looked as 'handsom and fertile' as anything seen by Lewis and Clark.

Angela sounded offended by the idea of Crows farming. '*That* wasn't part of our lives,' she said. 'We Crows were hunters and free spirits. Never into farming at all. Although we do have a small token buffalo herd,' she admitted, softening. 'And there *are* some people who keep steers.'

'There are about nine thousand Crows,' she went on. 'But I tell you Crows die young – at thirty-something.'

When I asked why – although I thought I knew the answer – she said, 'Alcoholism's one cause.'

It was the predictable answer. The tragic answer. I hadn't mentioned alcoholism – even though the Indians of America (and South America) are known for their alcohol addiction. But I remembered the wretched shambling figures by the roadside in Arizona.

I mentioned them now. 'Alcoholism is an Indian problem,' Angela sadly agreed. 'The Crows are no exception. Maybe it's a bit better now: there's programmes and cures. On the other hand, drug-taking may be on the rise. You notice there's no liquor sold on the reservation. Hardin's just off the reservation so it's the nearest place people can go to drink. You're sleeping there, right? So you'll see them.'

Plenty Coups was Chief of the Crows for longer than most people could remember. The name Plenty Coups was a rough translation of his Indian name which in other words meant Many Achievements. Before he died in 1933, the great Crow Chief made over his house and land at Arrow Creek to the government to be a 'Nation's Park' and, just as important, a memorial to the Crow nation.

Driving with Angela Russell to his house for the dedication ceremony she had mentioned, we bumped over mile after mile of grazing land, all of it conspicuously empty.

'All this is Crow land?' I asked Angela.

'Well,' she said, 'the old wheatfields are farmed by a non-Indian company, a corporation. As I said, it is not in the Crow nature to farm. I regret to say that, in hard times, some Crows who own land sell it to non-Indians. We should work out some tighter control.'

If they didn't, I thought, there would soon be very few Crow grazing lands left in Crow hands. 'Wouldn't the Federal Bureau of Indian Affairs help you?'

'That,' Angela snorted, 'is just about the most inefficient government office. We need a really good lawyer, that's what we need.'

We were approaching a cluster of tall cottonwood trees; under them on a broad lawn stood a fairly large two-storey wooden house with dormer windows on the second floor and with a stone structure a little way away. 'That stone building's our museum,' said Angela. Facing the wooden house four rows of folding chairs were drawn up, all occupied by middle-aged Crows and younger whites, one of whom had a camera. In shirts and jeans, the elders of the Crows prepared for their ceremony.

They stood facing the seated audience, waiting for the 'off' like musicians at a jazz concert. A pipe as long as a clarinet was solemnly produced and lit in the breeze with some difficulty. As the sun went slowly down behind us and the shadows of the cottonwoods lengthened across smokers and watchers, the pipe passed: each man offering the stem of the pipe to the north, south, east and west; to the sun, to the sunrise, the sunset, and to the Earth, the mother of all things.

'What's in the pipe?' I whispered to Angela who was busily talking to her neighbours in the Crow language.

'Tobacco,' she said briefly, and her eyebrows, frowning, seemed to add, 'What do you think it is: buffalo dung?'

Donations were offered and, to make amends, I produced a $20 bill. Angela could smile again.

The ceremony, it turned out, was to raise money for the restoration of Plenty Coups' house, and it ended when the elders had stalked in solemn procession round the house itself. 'That's that, then,' beamed Angela, moving away. I took it that I was free to go and look at the museum.

Part of the museum was given over to the long life of Plenty Coups. A fine picture of him, taken years before, caught my eye.

It showed him seated in his chiefly finery with other Crow chiefs — Pretty Face, Long Elk, Medicine Crow and Two Belly: they were named in the caption. Bearded white men stood at the back looking awkward in dark three-piece suits; presumably officials of the Indian Affairs agency. In those days Plenty Coups had had a particularly fine, young Indian face: hooked nose, chin held high, strong humorous mouth. It was the face of the man whose influence on the Crows had been strong enough to induce the tribe to make peace with the white men's government.

Crows had served with Custer as scouts. They were not, therefore, part of the vast Sioux and Cheyenne warrior band which had wiped out him and the men of the 7th Cavalry at the Little Bighorn. The secret of Plenty Coups' extraordinary influence stemmed from visions he had had as a young warrior. As I said, the visions predicted many things that would soon come to pass: including the disappearance of the buffalo herds on which Indian life so much depended. Millions of buffalo then roamed the Plains — and Crow country was the very heart of the northwestern buffalo range. Because the land of the Crows was so desirable and so fertile, enemies were continually trying to take it from them — enemies like the Sioux and the Striped-feathered-arrows (the Cheyenne) to the east, the Shoshones and the Arapahoes to the south. Some of these enemies even had guns.

'There is no better weapon than the bow for running buffalo, but in war the gun is the best,' advised Plenty Coups. In later life, when some paleface asked: 'Which of all the Indian tribesmen our people have met in war are the bravest?' the chief answered instantly from his own experiences, 'Cheyennes; and next the Flatheads. A Flathead will die where he stands.'

The chief went on, still looking into the past: 'The Absaroka [Crows] were obliged to fight alone, and we *could* fight. When I was a boy our chiefs were able men.' He listed them. 'They were Long Horse, Sits-in-the-Middle-of-the-Land, Thin Belly and Iron Bull. How they inspired me!'

From the window of Plenty Coups' museum I could see an escarpment and the Pryor Mountains against the dying sun. Long Horse, Thin Belly — even Plenty Coups — were gone, and with them the great days had gone, too.

Plenty Coups, remembering, had said, 'We followed the buffalo herds over our beautiful plains, fighting a battle one day and sending out a war party the next. My heart was afire. I wished so much to distinguish myself, so that I might wear an eagle's feather in my hair . . . .'

The name Plenty Coups, pronounced 'Plenny Coos' by American

palefaces, means, as I have said, Many Achievements. It derives from an Indian habit of 'counting coups' in battle.

> To count a coup [according to Frank Linderman, the old chief's best white friend], a warrior had to strike an armed and fighting enemy with his coup-stick or bow before otherwise harming him, or take his weapons while he was alive. Or strike the enemy's breastworks while under fire, or steal a horse tied to a lodge (wigwam) in an enemy's camp . . . . To strike such a coup a warrior would often display great bravery. An eagle's feather worn in the hair was a mark of distinction and told the world that the wearer had counted coup.

As for the stealing of horses, the early explorer William Clark, to whom the Crows were 'Ravin' (Raven) Indians, not Crows at all, said the Crows were honoured by all the other Plains tribes as the most expert horse thieves. He knew about that expertise from experience: one night they got away with half of his horses. A little later he sent ahead of his party a Sergeant Pryor (the soldier who gave his name to the mountains that overlook Plenty Coups' house). On Pryor's second night out the 'accomplished Crows' (Clark's expression) stole every single horse he had with him.

As for the life-shaping visions Plenty Coups experienced as a youth, they came to him like this. One night sleeping out on a peak in the Crazy Mountains, he dreamed a strange dream: countless buffalo poured out of a hole in the ground – hundreds of them – bulls and cows and calves. They spread across the Plains and in such numbers that they blackened it. And then, all at once, they were gone – all of them quite *gone*. And in their place, out of the same ground came pouring innumerable cattle: steers, cows and calves replacing the buffalo.

When Plenty Coups reported this vision to the Wise Ones of the Crows, they had no doubt of its meaning. 'The dream of Plenty Coups means,' they said, 'that the white men will take and hold this country and that their spotted-buffalo [cattle] will cover the plains.' It also meant, they added, that Plenty Coups should make sure that the one tribe of the plains that had never made war against the white man would never do so. No one could defeat the white men in the end – no one, however much they wished to. Certainly not the Crows, the Absaroka. So said the Wise Ones.

There was more to the vision than that, but that was its essence. And Plenty Coups was able to add, bitterly, in old age:

> We saw that those who made war against the white men always failed in the end and lost their lands. Look at the Cheyennes. Most of them are living where they hate the ground that holds their lodges. They cannot look at the mountains as I can or drink good water as

I do every day. Instead of making a treaty with the white men and by holding their country which they loved, they fought and lost all, taking whatever the white man would give. And when the hearts of the givers are filled with hate their gifts are small.

He went on that he was sorry today for the Cheyenne – and even the Sioux 'who fared a little better'. For he said: 'When I fought with the white man against them it was not because I loved him or because I hated the Sioux and Cheyenne, but because I saw this was the only way we could keep our land.'

Yet, sadness lies in the fact that, despite Chief Plenty Coups' policy of peaceful coexistence, the Crows, too, suffered unimaginable anguish. So much so that back in 1909 the Chief, sadly recalling his forecast of the white man's victory and its aftermath, said:

I see no longer the curling smoke rising from our lodge poles. I hear no longer the songs of the women as they prepare the meal. The antelope are gone; the buffalo wallows are empty. Only the wail of the coyote is heard. The white man's medicine is stronger than ours . . . we are like birds with a broken wing.

My paleface landlord at the Hardin guesthouse was a psychiatrist who worked with Crows. He liked them. He confirmed what Plenty Coups had said: the Crows, he said, *were* better off than the Cheyenne – possibly than the Sioux as well.

'In the towns Busby and Lame Deer on the Cheyenne Reservation east of here,' he told me, 'there's no store, no gas station (or if there is they are always out of gas). The kids just hang out and drink out of boredom, as a way of escape. The Crows are rich compared with the North Cheyenne.'

But not as rich, evidently, as they might make themselves. In his view the Bureau of Indian Affairs was spoiling the Indians. 'Why don't they farm? Because of the system. Without the Bureau's support, their handouts and perks, the Crows will have to fend for themselves. There's coal under the Crow Reservation. Yet no one digs it up.'

As far as the coal was concerned, I personally was glad the Crows *didn't* dig it up. True, if they did they might possibly make money. But has anyone seen the depressing shambles open-cast mining can make of a landscape? The sight of *that* spectacle might drive people to drink far quicker than anything else.

Hardin, just outside the Reservation, was a depressingly normal town with the usual bars and liquor stores. Forbidden to drink on the Reservation, that is where some Crows went off to. On Hardin's street corners I saw much the same shambling –

sometimes pugnacious – figures, Crows this time, that I had seen in and around Seligman, Arizona. The lurching drunks and the general rundown look of Hardin, a rail junction with not, I think, much else to its name except the high school that Angela Russell had graduated from, made me glad I was staying at an untypically charming bed and breakfast pension called the Kendrick House Inn, managed by the psychiatrist's wife.

In my bedroom, rummaging among a pile of old books, I discovered George Barr McCutcheon's humorous novel *Brewster's Millions*, which I vaguely remembered from an old movie (was Fred Allen the star?), and *Great Expectations* which I sat up rereading for much of the night. I wanted to rid my mind of the pathetic images of the down-at-heel Indians I had seen lolling about the streets.

What had my psychiatrist-landlord meant by the handouts and perks the Bureau of Indian Affairs so lavishly dished out? Next day he explained: 'Free homes. Free medical and dental services. Free commodities like reconstituted eggs, flour, peanut butter – which sometimes the Indians try to sell.'

Could this be true? Was such official generosity really 'spoiling' the Indians? There was no way of knowing. At least this white man lived here through his own choice; so he should know. After all, no one could bring his wife and child here and live and work close to an Indian reservation and not sympathise with Indians.

After the ceremony at Chief Plenty Coups' house, Angela huddled with the Tribal Elders, and I walked about under the tall trees that spread their branches over Plenty Coups' last resting place. And later a strange thing happened. It was almost as if what Plenty Coups had said in 1909 had come true.

The sun had long since dipped out of sight of Arrow Creek behind the mountains to the west. Plenty Coups' house, the museum, his Medicine Spring, everything lay in darkness. And from the empty Plains, from the dark sea of low green ridges that surround the Chief's cluster of cottonwood trees, I heard the rising cry of a coyote. Once, twice: closer . . . closer . . . .

I stood stock-still, listening. Sometimes it was more like a low groan. Sometimes the howl soared into the night sky and expired abruptly into a shimmering silence. It was a melancholy sound in that shadowy empty space. It might have been some mournful Indian spirit wailing for the beautiful, lost time that will never return.

Chapter 18

Do not be anxious about me . . . I hope to have a good report to send you by the next mail . . . . I send you an extract from General Terry's official order, knowing how much you appreciate words of commendation and confidence, such as the following: '. . . The Department Commander places too much confidence in your zeal, energy, and ability to wish to impose upon you precise orders, which might hamper your action in contact with the enemy.'

Letter from General George Armstrong Custer to his wife
22 June 1876
(three days before the Battle of the Little Bighorn)

On the evening of 25 June 1876 General George A. Custer and his men of the 7th US Cavalry lay dead, scattered on the bluff above the Little Bighorn River like the regiment's carelessly discarded refuse.

When Custer fell he appeared, according to the first white man to find his dead body, to have died a natural death. Or at least that's what the white man wrote later for a newspaper.

Custer had been stripped down to his socks, he said, and so had the men dead around him. The bottom of one of his boots lay nearby – so it looked as if the squaws who scoured the fields after every battle to pillage and mutilate had cut the uppers off to make moccasins for themselves.

Evan Connell, the author of the most convincing and comprehensive book (and the liveliest) on Custer's death, believes that unpublished letters somewhere detail various disfigurements inflicted on Custer's body: thighs slashed to the bone, ears slit, arrows driven into the groin. Before those alleged mutilations, Custer had been shot twice, once beneath the heart, and once in the left temple. Probably the shot near the heart was the one that killed him.

Not far from the Custer Trading Post where I had met Angela Russell and now waited for Patrick Hill, a thirty-two-year-old part-Pawnee and part-Crow guide, to take me around the battlefield, are a clump of white marble tombstones half-buried in tall grass. On one white stone an inscription reads:

George A. Custer
Lieut. Colonel
Bvt. Major General
7 U.S. Cav.
Fell here
June 25, 1876

The other tombs carry other inscriptions but most of them have nothing to show but 'Unknown Soldier' or simply 'Unknown'. The positions of the tombstones do not even prove that the troopers named actually died there because, as Connell says, 'Indians frequently amused themselves by roping enemies – alive or dead – and dragging them around'. The white tombstones are set on the slope of the long spur inside a black iron fence, and from them you look across the wrinkles, dimples and indentations in what seems to be an unending stretch of plain and watercourse. The day I was there, I could see, down below me to the west, the Little Bighorn River washed by a golden surge of sun, as it splashed its way through low unchanging banks and a curtain of cottonwoods.

Looking down the slope from where I now stood, Custer had presumably been shocked to see, on this very hot 25 June, an immensely large conglomeration of Sioux and Cheyenne lodges – in fact, it has been said, 'the greatest concentration of militant Indians in the history of North America'.

To return to the subsequent massacre: it is hard to know the true number of the 7th Cavalry's dead at Little Bighorn. General Terry, Custer's immediate commanding officer, wrote of 268 officers, men and civilians killed and 52 wounded. But there are other estimates.

At any rate, the actual scene of the massacre was certainly not pretty. One of the first men to arrive there commented, of all things, on the contrasted colours: 'The marble white bodies, the somber brown of the dead horses ... the tufts of reddish brown grass on the almost ashy white soil'. That was a poetic view.

In fact, it was such a sorry sight that rough-and-ready soldiers detailed to bury what was left were soon vomiting and retching as they dug. Some of the dead could not be identified because of their agonised expressions of terror or pain. Some faces had been pounded with clubs or stones. Many corpses, says Connell, had been mutilated 'in every conceivable way'.

How long did the Little Bighorn massacre take? An Indian who took part in it said it took as long as it took the sun to travel the width of a wigwam pole: fifteen, twenty minutes. A Cheyenne warrior called Wooden Leg described what he was able to see in the mêlée. When the soldiers stopped shooting, he recalled,

> the warriors who had crept close to them began to call out that all of the white men were dead. All of the Indians then jumped up and rushed forward. All of the boys and old men on their horses came tearing into the crowd. The air was full of dust and smoke. Everybody was greatly excited. It looked like thousands of dogs might look if all of them were mixed up together in a fight. All the Indians were saying these soldiers also went crazy and killed themselves. I do not know. I could not see them. But I believe they did so . . . .

Wooden Leg was about eighteen at the time of the battle.

Tom Custer, the general's young brother and the commander of 'C' Company, lay face down, bristling with arrows, his skull crushed 'as that of a man's hand'. His abdomen was slit – Connell says – both horizontally and vertically. His throat had been cut and the scalp almost completely ripped off, leaving just a few hairs at the nape of the neck. There are other details, too. But enough is enough.

Connell convincingly explains these hideous mutilations – of which Tom Custer was not by a long chalk the only victim – as expressions of bottomless Indian grief and bewilderment. In a masterly analysis of the emotions that overwhelmed the original inhabitants of the Plains, in those days of Indian defeat and disaster, when for the Indians the end of the world seemed to have come, he has this to say:

> They [the Indians] could not even understand why soldiers pursued them when all they ever wanted was to be left alone so that they might live as they had lived for centuries: hunting, fishing, trailing the munificent buffalo. They failed to see why they should live in one place all year, why they should become farmers when they had been hunters. They did not see how the land could be divided, allotted, owned. They thought the earth was created for everybody, that it could not be appropriated by individuals or groups, and to destroy vegetation by plowing was to contradict the obvious plan of a supreme deity.
>
> Wasichus [palefaces], convinced of their status as the Almighty's Chosen, followed these people insistently – threatening, promising, cajoling – and far from the settlements, Custer's regiment fell upon a summer camp. So the squaws, weeping for a dead husband or a dead brother or son, hacked at naked white corpses with butcher knives and axes . . . .

'They thought the earth was created for everybody' – that phrase, above all, stands out. It seemed to me to explain a great deal. How many of the *wasichus* agreed (even if they didn't feel convinced of their status as the Almighty's Chosen) with what appeared in a famous telegram? General William Tecumseh Sherman, by then General-in-Chief of the Army, sent the telegram to President Grant, and it read: 'We must act with vindictive earnestness against the Sioux, even to their extermination, men, women and children. Nothing less will reach the root of the case.'

As Evan Connell remarks, 'If one word of this extraordinary telegram is altered it reads like a message from Eichmann to Hitler.'

As I have noted, Sherman knew *Hamlet* by heart, as a good many amateur dramatic societies performing the play in army towns he visited had learned to their cost. Thus he must have known the line 'Conscience doth make cowards of us all'. No one ever accused Uncle Cump of cowardice, so what then of his conscience? Did he think he was one of the Almighty's Chosen? I remembered what the old Georgian lady had said about Sherman's church attendance as we stood together in the General's requisitioned house next door to the church in Savannah. 'Ah don't believe,' she snapped, 'that *Mister* Sherman was much of a church-goin' man, Mr Young.' Of course, the old lady was a Southerner, so – like the Indians who killed Custer at Little Bighorn, who only wanted to live more or less like Ken Sinay or the author of *A River Runs Through It* – she may have been biased.

There is a bitter irony in the fact that Sherman's namesake, the Indian chief Tecumseh, the Shawnee leader who fought the British in 1790 and 1791, turned against the American settlers whom he saw inexorably encroaching on Indian lands. Tecumseh's vision was that of a great alliance of Indian tribes from the Great Lakes to the Gulf of Mexico to resist colonisation by the newly arrived white man.

For he said: 'Brothers – the white people are like poisonous serpents: when chilled, they are feeble and harmless, but invigorate them with warmth, and they sting their benefactors to death.' And: 'The white men are not friends to the Indians: at first, they only asked for land sufficient for a wigwam; now, nothing will satisfy them but the whole of our hunting grounds, from the rising to the setting sun.' And again: 'Brothers – the white men despise and cheat the Indians; they abuse and insult them, they do not think the red men sufficiently good to live.'

Tecumseh had spoken.

And Tecumseh – the Shawnee Indian chief – was killed in 1813 fighting *with* the British against the American Governor of Indiana, William Henry Harrison.

At least one American writer has claimed that Custer's Plains life is simply a wonderful example of a swashbuckling sort of person having 'fun'. He quotes an extract from Custer's book, *My Life on the Plains*. In it Custer tells of finding the bodies of twelve Americans who had been caught by hundreds of Sioux while on a mission to find Custer himself (as was his wont, he had been irresponsibly wandering far from the beaten track). The bodies of these troopers, who died simply because they were out searching for Custer, were so mangled as to be unrecognisable: 'shot with 20 to 25 arrows each, limbs hacked, genitals cut off and stuffed into mouths, eyes cut out and laid on nearby rocks'. And so on.

Of this terrible scene and the men's frantic effort to escape the Sioux, Custer remarks, 'How painfully, almost despairingly exciting . . . !' Did he feel that excitement when he and his men, owing to his own vain folly, were, in their turn, pinned down, massacred and mutilated on the spur overlooking the Little Bighorn?

And how many of Custer's fellow victims – simple troopers in the 7th Cavalry – felt the 'almost unbearable excitement' of that day? To me it seems that if he thought of the Indian wars as fun, Custer was unbalanced to the point of mania. Fun, maybe, for cinema audiences watching the many films of his Last Stand. But Custer – not Errol Flynn – was responsible for losing the battle commemorated by all those pathetic tombstones around a Trading Post that now serves 'Fry Bread' and iced tea 15 miles from Hardin.

The romantic vision of George Armstrong Custer was immeasurably enhanced by nineteenth-century paintings of the Little Bighorn battle. They tend to show Custer, reddish curls flowing (he was nicknamed 'Curly' at West Point), dying gracefully among troopers in trim blue uniforms as they tried to fight off the well-muscled Indian hordes. In these paintings Custer is not of course scalped; the blond locks are in place. Nor, in fact, *was* he scalped. Yet most of the dead troopers were, so why not he?

The truth seems to be that, as Connell says, 'from an Indian warrior's point of view, the Son of the Morning Star (as some Indians dubbed him), had an unattractive head'. Custer, 'the chief with the yellow hair', in Whittier's poem, had cut his hair short and he was going prematurely bald. So, 'a number of braves might have inspected him and decided the hair was not worth keeping'.

But 'a short-haired general commanding what might have been mistaken for a limping drunken mob of itinerant farmhands' (in

Evan Connell's phrase) would hardly be acceptable to Americans brought up on Hollywood movies with Errol Flynn as hero. The brutal, unheroic fact is, though, that on as hot a day as 25 June 1875, the troopers would have rolled their blue tunics up and tied them to their saddles. Some thus exposed white shirts, some, grey pullover shirts; others, their own checkered shirts, or indeed any old clothes they happened to be wearing, including straw hats and kepis on their heads. As for the officers, the Army in those days was often led by cripples and alcoholics, 'officers who would not be commissioned today or who would be removed from field service'. Some were half-blind or deaf from Civil War wounds, some had a limb missing, a good many were regularly soused. 'One gets the impression,' Connell says, 'that half the paleface commandants were physically limited and/or drunk, to say nothing of their neuroses and obsessions' – of which Custer had his share. Yet, fed by America's rage at the death of the 7th Cavalry, the myth of Custer's glorious Last Stand widely persists.

For many, Custer – valiant, dashing and certainly gallant – but a West Point cadet who had graduated thirty-fourth in a class of 34 (with no fewer than 726 demerits) – and who in the Civil War became one of the youngest generals in the Unionist Army thanks partly to the patronage of General Phil Sheridan and partly to his own madcap bravery – is still the hero of the Little Bighorn battlefield, that corpse-strewn ridge in Montana.

It was a sunny, sparkling morning when I turned left across the Bighorn River by the Hardin flyover and headed towards the more modest Little Bighorn. The cultivation started to enfold the roadside before Crow Agency, and to the right the derelict Bighorn Carpet Factory Inc., a failed Indian enterprise crumbling away there since 1972. The Little Bighorn itself is a gentle stream today; you can often wade across it. It has been diverted somewhat since the battle, by the railroad to Billings.

At the Trading Post, Pat Hill was waiting with his car, a tall, pleasant man in his early thirties, with a lugubrious manner of speech. He looked about him as we set out for the battlefield, saying, 'All this is the Crow Reservation, of course. "As long as the sun may shine and the winds may blow", eh? You have heard of the Black Hills?'

I had heard of the Black Hills of Dakota.

'The Black Hills were sacred to the Sioux like the Vatican to Catholics or mosques to the Muslim peoples.' Pat Hill turned to me his deadpan face. 'Men like Sitting Bull and Crazy Horse, the greatest Sioux, refused to negotiate or accept agreements with the US government. They said, "Why should we negotiate the surrender of what was always ours?" '

I had heard of that, too. And I had also read what negotiations had achieved: fifty years of treaty-signing eventually left the Sioux with only one small strip of land to call their own. As Connell says, that caused resentment intense enough to nourish them for a century. (One paleface years ago who ignored that resentment was on record as having remarked carelessly of the Indians, 'If they're hungry, let them eat grass.' Perhaps somebody was listening. When that paleface's mutilated body was found, his mouth was stuffed with grass.)

The humiliation of the Sioux started in 1874 with a government-sponsored expedition. Led by Custer, it set out to explore – 'to study' was the official word – the Black Hills of Dakota, a region seen as yet only by Indian eyes, on the lookout for gold. (The idea was that, once gold was found, white prospectors would be followed by white settlers. At that point not much room would be left for Indians of any sort.) Through beautiful, flower-covered valleys – all sacred to the Sioux – Custer and his expedition ploughed on, accompanied by a cavalry band on white horses playing Custer's favourite march 'Garry Owen'. The General took his hunting dogs with him and his Indian scouts. He had a grand open-air life. Another Plains' personality, Calamity Jane, had attached herself to the expedition. Dressed as a man, covered in lice and smelling to high heaven of dirt and drink, she occasionally helped out with the troopers' laundry in return for shots of whiskey. Connell comments, 'It sounds less like military reconnaissance than a summer excursion through the Catskills,' but in any case, needless to say, some gold was 'discovered' – though whether it came from the Black Hills is questionable. In such dubious ways are colonies founded.

Apart from the band and 'Garry Owen', Custer and his men were accompanied as usual by a heady commentary of justification from the white man's press. The Bismarck *Tribune* urged on the imperialistic pace: 'The American people need the country the Indians now occupy; many of our people are out of employment; *the masses need some new excitement* [my italics] .... An Indian war would do no harm, for it must come, sooner or later ....'

The American attitude to their Western frontier was that the white government in Washington, DC had a *mission civilisatrice* to perform – a civilising mission, like the one the French boastfully claimed justified their colonising incursions into Africa and Indo-China. '*The masses need some new excitement.*' It is ironic that these days for many Americans – particularly from Hollywood – the Plains have become a refuge from excitement, from the claustrophobia and violence of the rest of the United States. As the Montanan at the bar of the Grand Hotel in Big Timber had said, 'Montana is bein' Californicated'.

When I repeated this to Pat Hill, he laughed at the last remark, then nodded. 'It was like this. Sherman said to Sheridan, "Phil, we'll have to do something about these Indians. We have railroads to build, people to settle." That was it in a nutshell.'

He went on: 'See, the Custer Little Bighorn campaign of 1876 was three-pronged. First, the Montana column of Colonel Gibbon would march from Bozeman down the Yellowstone; then General Terry and Custer would go southwest from Fort Abraham Lincoln on the Missouri near Dakota Territory; and finally General Crook marched forth out of Fort Laramie in Wyoming.' Crook met Indians; so the Bighorn battle of 25 June was preceded by the Rosebud of 17 June, a little below it.

Pat asked rhetorically, 'Who won the Battle of the Rosebud? No one seems to know.' Perhaps both sides; it has been said in any case that Custer's fate was already sealed there. The fight at the Rosebud occurred when Crook, advancing north to trap a combination of Indian tribes in a sort of nutcracker – between Terry's and Custer's troops and those of Gibbon coming south – ran into at least a thousand warriors – Cheyenne, Oglalas, Sans Arcs, Miniconjoux, Blackfeet and Unkpapas. The fight took place between the Little Bighorn and Rosebud Rivers, and in the end thirty-six Indians were killed (according to the great warrior chief Crazy Horse), and the rest of them were chased back seven miles. Crook lost nine troopers and an Indian scout. But he too retreated. This helped both sides to claim success. Obliged to return to his base, Crook was soon happy to go fishing. He caught seventy trout, it is said, in one afternoon.

'So Crook was no longer part of the campaign,' said Pat Hill. 'Pretty dam' smart. He just went fishin'.'

Custer was unaware of Crook's withdrawal. He was forging ahead with the 7th Cavalry into Indian territory, over-confident, a match in his view for any alliance of Indians – but at least half in the dark about their whereabouts. We stood on the gently sloping hillside among the odd sagebush and contemplated a dusty track winding towards us from another range of hills to our south. Behind it was the Rosebud River.

Despite Crook's retreat, Custer had had plenty of warning of the enemy's strength. His Crow scouts had told Major Marcus Reno, who commanded a battalion of Custer's 7th Cavalry, that they could see, from 14 miles away, a hillside 'moving like worms' – meaning alive with Indian warriors. But because they saw no teepees, they thought the Indian tribesmen were on the run.

'From 14 miles it must have been hard to get a clear view.'

'Indians can see things by intuition,' said Pat Hill, as we followed Reno's trail down to the Little Bighorn Valley, 'much better than purely by sight.'

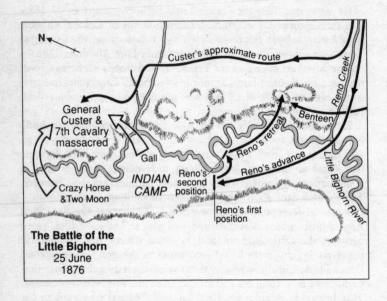

N

Custer's approximate route

Reno Creek

General Custer & 7th Cavalry massacred

Benteen

Reno's retreat

Gall

Reno's advance

Little Bighorn River

INDIAN CAMP

Reno's second position

Crazy Horse & Two Moon

Reno's first position

The Battle of the Little Bighorn
25 June
1876

But as he turned into the Little Bighorn Valley as we turned now, Reno could no longer have been under any misapprehension: he, and the forty Ree Indian scouts with him, could see very clearly right before him 'the greatest concentration of militant Indians in the history of North America'. Their massed teepees ran closely packed up the line of cottonwood trees I could see below me; way up the bank of the Little Bighorn River, which is no more than a deep trout stream (people fish for bass and catfish in it now). They would have run a long way, as far as Garry Owen where Harry Real Bird stables the horses on which I was to tour the hidden dips and ridges of the battlefield next day. It was strange. On the map distances on the battlefield – the northern ridge, for example, on which Custer rode to attack the Indian encampment while Reno's skirmish line opened fire from where I stood – appeared very short. In fact that ridge is four miles long and, because of the uneven terrain, Custer's men were out of sight of Reno all the time they advanced along it to their deaths.

It didn't take Reno long to realise he had bitten off more than his men could chew. It was as if they had kicked over a swarm of hornets. Indians poured from the tents. Dismounted, the troopers retreated in panic under a furious assault from the Indian camp, and the retreat very soon turned into a mad race for safety led by Reno himself. In utter panic, the troopers dropped guns and cartridges as they ran, pursued by hundreds of Sioux. Reno was scared witless. His conduct later became the subject of a Court of Inquiry. In his defence, Reno's chief of scouts testified that if Reno's column had continued its advance on the Indian camp it would have been demolished in five minutes. As it was, a good many of his soldiers were shot to death with arrows, or brained with stone-headed clubs; others were scalped. One could imagine – looking down on that narrow valley – the terror in the dust and smoke, the infuriated yelping of the Indian warriors, the shriek of their eagle-bone whistles, the shots, the screams of dying horses. No wonder the panic-stricken troopers were delighted to follow their utterly demoralised leader back across the Little Bighorn and up the bluff the other side.

Next day as I was riding on horseback with Harry Real Bird, my second Crow guide and a rougher type than Pat Hill, along the ridge that leads northward – the one followed all those years ago by Custer himself – he was to say, 'Custer's men had killed everybody: old men, women, children.' And he bitterly echoed what Indians who fought against Reno had said in the aftermath of Custer's death: 'It was our country.' A simple statement: they had made it again and again.

Harry was to put it bluntly: 'The Sioux hated Custer because he made shish-kebab of Indian babies.' Harry was more certainly brutal than Pat Hill. He felt strongly about Custer; after all, shish-kebab applied to babies is a particularly nasty image. But, shish-kebab or no, for a number of reasons one could see why Indians hated the guts of Sheridan's golden-haired pet.

Abandoning his ill-considered attack on the vast Indian camp and pursued by furious warriors, Reno had retreated as best he could to the cottonwoods by the river bank. He had already emptied his revolvers and flung them away.

I had seen the bluffs his men had had to climb to reach the safer, higher ground behind them. The bluffs were steep. So steep that Edward Godfrey, who commanded troops at the battle, commented that it was surprising what steep inclines men and horses clambered up under the excitement of danger. Here, nevertheless, Lieutenant Donald McIntosh was killed, and Dr De Wolf, and another of Reno's officers, Lieutenant B. H. Hodson, had his horse shot from under him – and was himself shot dead shortly afterwards.

According to Godfrey, Reno's retreat was a major reason for Custer's massacre. 'Indians say,' wrote Godfrey, 'if Reno's position in the valley had been held they would have been compelled to divide their strength . . . . That would have prevented the concentration of every able-bodied warrior upon the battalion under Custer.'

Some white witnesses said Reno was drunk at the time of his panic and rout. Maybe; maybe not. He had a reputation as a drinker. 'Drunk or sober, Reno would try to flee back across the Little Bighorn – just there,' said Pat Hill, pointing from his car window as we started up the road that runs up to Crow Agency and Hardin. He pointed to a sort of abrupt lowish cliff that at the beginning of the valley formed a bridge to the bluff above it. 'That is where Reno established a defensive position,' he said, 'and was joined by Captain Frederick Benteen, Custer's other battalion commander. Benteen loathed Reno and both officers lacked any confidence at all in Custer.'

A happy little team, I thought.

'Benteen ran into Reno retreating in panic. They formed a defensive position. Accordingly they and their men were pinned on the bluff for two days by the Sioux and Cheyenne, suffering many casualties. They hadn't the remotest idea of what had happened to Custer.'

Nor, to this day, have we any clear idea. Perhaps he had been dreaming, as he pressed on up the ridge and out of sight, of the glory of scattering the 'greatest concentration of militant Indians in the history of North America'. Perhaps he had seen himself riding in triumph through Washington, DC on the strength of his forthcoming victory over the great Indian warrior-hero, Crazy Horse. Who knows? He was vain – and perhaps mad – enough for that.

Crazy Horse, whom many Indians regard as their greatest chief, more important even than Sitting Bull, was a slim man of medium build. He was quiet, reserved to the point of reclusiveness, and his eyes were said to 'look beyond things'. He seldom spoke at tribal council; he preferred to be a listener.

Sioux admirers of Crazy Horse depicted him as a

kind of being never seen on earth: a genius in war, yet a lover of peace; a statesman, who apparently never thought of the interests of any human being outside his own camp; a dreamer, a mystic, and a kind of Sioux Christ, who was betrayed in the end by his own disciples.

Some loved him for the wonderful reason that 'he remained himself from the moment of his birth to the moment he died and because he knew exactly where he wanted to live, and never left; and because, unlike many other people all over the world, when he met white men he was not diminished by the encounter'. (This is one of the many perceptively honest remarks by Ian Frazier in his book, *Great Plains*.)

At Little Bighorn, at any rate, Crazy Horse, Two Moon and the gigantic Sioux chief named Gall led their warriors up the lumpy ridge scattered with sagebushes, to massacre to the last man the troopers of the 7th Cavalry and their leader. Of the explosive Gall, even Custer's widow, Elizabeth, said: 'Painful as it is for me to look upon the pictured face of an Indian, I never in my life dreamed there could be in all the tribes so fine a specimen of a warrior as Gall.' Some who saw him were reminded of Daniel Webster by his 'tremendous character, great commonsense and massive physiognomy'. Gall had to survive several attempts by white men or their Indian scouts to arrest or kill him, and he died many years after Custer.

Not so Crazy Horse. In 1877, a year after Custer's death, Crazy Horse was tricked by white men and their red allies and killed; he was bayoneted by an American sentry named Gentles as other soldiers were leading him into a prison cell at Fort Robinson. He had realised too late that the bars on the little room he was being led to meant that he had been betrayed. He drew a knife and tried in his despair to stab the officer who was leading him to it. Soon he lay dying on his back, 'grinding his teeth and frothing at the mouth': a terrible death. Yet in dying he may have escaped a worse fate. Some say that General Sheridan intended to have him sent to the Dry Tortugas, an atoll off Key West in Florida where the Army had prison cells that were really nothing more than holes dug in the coral with bars placed across them. How long could a Plains Indian like Crazy Horse survive that? Perhaps, after all, a couple of bayonet thrusts in Fort Robinson, Nebraska, did him a good turn.

The words Crazy Horse is supposed to have muttered as he lay dying are moving in their simplicity. He said, in part:

We preferred our own way of living. We were no expense to

the government then. All we wanted was peace and to be left alone. Soldiers were sent out in the winter who destroyed our villages. Then 'Long Hair' [Custer] came in the same way. They say we massacred him, but he would have done the same to us had we not defended ourselves and fought to the last. Our first impulse was to escape with our squaws and papooses, but we were so hemmed in that we had to fight . . . .

I came here to talk with the Big White Chief, but was not given a chance. They tried to confine me. I tried to escape, and a soldier ran his bayonet into me.

I have spoken.

No photograph of Crazy Horse exists. 'Why should you wish to shorten my life by taking from me my shadow?' he said. And Ian Frazier adds another perceptive remark on the subject of the greatest Indian. I read it when I returned from the Little Bighorn, lying on my bed in the psychiatrist's house in Hardin, and it held my attention as firmly as the Ancient Mariner's grip on the Wedding Guest. 'Once,' Frazier wrote, 'America's size in the imagination was limitless. After Europeans settled and changed it . . . its size shrank . . . . Just as people finally came to the Great Plains and changed them, so they came to where Crazy Horse lived and killed him.' Frazier then wrote this memorable sentence: 'Crazy Horse had the misfortune to live in a place which existed both in reality and in the dreams of people far away; he managed to leave both the real and the imaginary place unbetrayed.'

The real and the imaginary place . . . 'unbetrayed'.

In his life as with his dying breath, Crazy Horse has spoken.

The romance and reality of Crazy Horse have exercised a magnetic pull on many Americans. That is a healthy thing, and hardly surprising. Yet Pat Hill, talking to me, gave it a dismal perspective: 'Every ten or fifteen years,' he said sadly, 'the Indians become famous in the land. We've never been a political power. People come here and express sympathy, but it's only for the moment. They've got other concerns – you know, taxes, education, their kids.'

'Do most young Indians know all about their glorious past?' I asked. 'Are they proud of it?'

And his answer came back to me. 'No. Not really.' And more sadly still, 'I would say no.'

As for the unfarmed grasslands the Crows owned, Harry Real Bird had his own rough word on that.

'Shit,' he said, swinging his massive bulk from his horse's saddle to the ground, 'I could learn farming if I had to.' And he angrily added, 'And I may f— have to at this rate of loss on this business.' The guiding business, he meant. It would be a pity if he gave it up, because Harry Real Bird had given me a unique view of the battle-field. Riding around it on horseback makes you realise its great size and all its unsuspected and hidden dips and creeks: the geography of the various parts of Custer's campaign as well as the actual battle itself.

I wanted to run over to the Trading Post and tell all the tourists to get over right away to Harry's stable, heave themselves on to the back of the nearest compliant horse – and take a good look at the scene of Custer's Last Stand as a trooper of the 7th Cavalry would have seen it. Because only Harry Real Bird has had the sense to arrange this, and he and his Crow friends deserve success, not one more Indian failure.

I didn't do that, of course. I left the paleface tourists in peace to mull over the other side of their menus, the side that carries the replica front page of the Bismarck *Tribune* of 6 July 1876 that told of the massacre. 'Squaws Mutilate and Rob the Dead', one headline said; and others asked, 'What Will Congress Do About It?' and 'Shall This Be the Beginning of the End?'

That's what it was, all right. The Beginning of the End.

Chapter 19

I felt sad leaving the Custer battlefield. For some reason a deep depression settled on me when I came to drive south, and the beauty of a splash of pink roses on the lower Bighorn Mountains did nothing to raise it. The Crow tribe's buffalo herd was sometimes visible, I had been told, on those slopes – from that distance a mere collection of black dots. Today, I couldn't even see the dots.

After a few miles, I looked back at the rolling plain and the hillside that had 'moved like worms'. The Plains – the 'Frontier' – swept green and smoothly uneven away from me: the once untouched place which Crazy Horse had 'had the misfortune to live in – a place which existed both in reality and in the dreams of people far away'.

The dream had faded now; the Frontier had moved somewhere else – but where to: to the moon? Today's reality at the Little Bighorn was tourists, fry bread, and an X-tra large iced tea for $1.50.

There seemed to have been a certain aura of romance here once upon a time. Perhaps it was a hangover from that that accounted for my present depression.

Custer's life on the Plains had somehow achieved in city-bred Americans' minds a sort of glamour: spurious, maybe, but glamour none the less. What had been here to make a soldier's life seem so romantic? What was that life but a mixture of fighting and fear of capture and subsequent horrendous mutilation, interspersed with weeks of deadly boredom? Is it surprising that the suicide rate among American soldiers was astoundingly high; the alcoholism rate even more so? Connell put it like this: life in the Army out here, he said, was a hellish mixture of 'vicious punishments, loneliness, boredom, booze, fleas, maggoty bread, tarantulas, blizzards, deserts, psychotic sergeants, incomprehensible officers, and yipping savages anxious to part your hair'. Army doctors in military posts spent a good deal of their time treating the clap. Grace notes were mad wolves and gigantic mosquitoes that swarmed around one in temperatures of 90 degrees. And, of course, there were raddled old lushes like Calamity Jane, who hung about the ranks and stunk to high heaven.

236

A fine romance.

The soldiers' arduous and unrewarding task – the real task – was to make life safe for the real white predators: the hunters (both professional Americans and well-heeled European amateurs), the buffalo-skin merchants, the railroad magnates, the settlers – and all the rest of the gold-seeking riff-raff to whom the Indians were nothing more than vermin doing their damnedest to separate the 'innocent' newcomers from profits the neglected earth 'owed them'.

Even Mrs Custer noticed that Plains life had its drawbacks. 'The life of an enlisted man,' wrote Elizabeth Custer in her book *Boots and Saddles*, 'was very dull during the cold weather.' In the hot weather too, she might have added. A photograph shows the Brevet General and his wife in his study at his base in Fort Lincoln three years before the last battle. He is writing – or is so posed; she just sits, holding a book. On the wall above them are large portraits of Custer himself and a smaller likeness of his mentor, General 'Little Phil' Sheridan. Two pronghorn heads protrude into the room – shot perhaps by Our Hero in company with Bloody Knife, Custer's favourite scout – also to be killed at the Little Bighorn.

'Everyone relied on cards as the unfailing amusement,' wrote Elizabeth Custer. 'I used to dread the arrival of the young officers who came to the regiment from West Point, fearing that the sameness and inactivity of the garrison life would be a test to which their character would succumb.'

Melancholy, I had discovered, can coexist with a sense of liberation on the Plains. Driving over the Rosebud Mountains, across the Tongue River to the town of Sheridan, I felt only the melancholy. Sheridan would have been bored by the town named after him. It was an unattractive place; its modern, uninteresting hotels, gas stations and fast-food 'outlets' did nothing for the spirits. Cody, though, was better. It was on the way back to Yellowstone – and that fact in itself made me feel lighter-hearted. In the city that Buffalo Bill founded and in particular in the hotel, the Irma – a delightful Victorian 'folly' – he built for his daughter, and in his magnificent Wild West museum, I felt better still. My bed in the Irma had four posts and was made of dark carved wood. Queen Victoria might have slept here. The bedside desk, with its Gideon bible in the drawer, was wooden and might have been a trophy of Buffalo Bill's forays with his circus and re-enactment of Custer's Last Stand in Victoria's England. The leather-covered seat of the armchair could easily have accommodated Colonel Cody's spacious bottom; and over the bed hung a picture of snowy mountains, a lake and spruces that might have been anywhere from the Rockies to Scotland.

Remington's prairie paintings covered a good many feet of wall in the museum. Two stuffed bison stood lowering among the glass-cased relics of Buffalo Bill – his rifle, his buckskin jacket, his hat (Cody had worn a stetson, not an affair of racoon-skin) – and the souvenirs of Annie (*Annie Get Your Gun*) Oakley, the lady sharp-shooter, who had accompanied him to Europe (with Chief Sitting Bull) as part of his Wild West Show.

Cody was certainly worth a visit, I thought next day as I drove on westwards past the Church of God Animal Home, Ron's fishing tackle store, and the usual string of used car lots.

Accelerating along the road that would take me to Cooke City and down the familiar trail to Mammoth Hot Springs and the Yellowstone at Paradise Valley, I found that my melancholia had quite slipped away from me.

I was aiming for Bozeman, but I made a short diversion to spend one more night in the Grand Hotel in Big Timber. I couldn't resist it. I had taken a fancy to Big Timber, its small size, its unpretentiousness, its valley of cottonwoods; even its name. It didn't matter that this time there was no stetsoned Montanan at the bar talking indulgently of the 'Californication' of his state. The wide-horned bull glared down from the wall like an angry colonel, and my plump barlady friend was behind her counter as cheerful as ever and she even agreed to be photographed with me outside in the street.

Two days later, when my Delta jet had lifted off from Bozeman, and was heading southwest through the clear summer air to our first stop at Salt Lake City, I opened the *Journals* again, this time at the page where it said that the 'Red Haired Chief' (that is, William Clark) became, because of his decency and fairness, a kind of 'culture hero' among the Indians. As the white man 'whose tongue was straight', the even-tempered Clark was, De Voto says, to accomplish more for Indians than anyone else in Western history.

Before John Steinbeck had set off with his dog Charley, I remembered, he said his friend, the 'highly respected political reporter', had implored him: 'If anywhere in your travels you come on a man with guts, mark the place.' Alas, Steinbeck missed William Clark and Meriwether Lewis by a good number of years – about 157 to be more or less precise. Men like them had the guts he was looking for.

Even General Phil Sheridan, who for a long time did his professional best to harry Indians to a living hell, did later have second thoughts about what he had done in the name of duty. In old age he wrote sadly: 'We took away their country and their means of support, broke up their mode of living, their habits of life, introduced disease and decay among them, and it was for this and against this that they made war. Could anyone expect less?'

What Alan Moorehead called the Fatal Impact – in his book of this title concerning Western man's disastrous intrusions into the Pacific Islands – came to the Plains many years ago. Phil Sheridan had mentioned two elements in that catastrophic Western impact – disease and decay. There are others: gunpowder and drink, for example, and an obsessive materialism that cuts down trees, implants missiles, and kills wildlife. Every summer we can witness Fatal Impact II: mass tourism. And now, finally, for Montana there is Fatal Impact III: the imminent arrival there of settlers from Hollywood.

Above Gardiner, I had stopped the car and taken a long last look down the Paradise Valley; had seen on my right-hand side the Yellowstone River rushing down to Livingston, and had thought of Dave and the moment when our raft seemed about to throw us into the foaming and freezing water. Yankee Jim's falls were out of sight under the dark spur of familiar cliff that sloped down from Emigrant Park.

A redtailed hawk, inspecting the ground, hovered over the left bank. Crazy Horse had worn a redtailed hawk on his head before going into battle. And it was as if the quiet man for whom every Indian feels respect, the chief 'who looked beyond things' and who was railroaded to his death at Fort Robinson by treachery, jealousy and unreliable reports – it was as if his spirit hovered along the green banks of the sunlit river; and, as I watched, swooped, fluttered and soared away from me down one of the most beautiful valleys I have ever seen.

Part Seven

The Call of the Wild

There's a land where the mountains are nameless,
  And the rivers all run God knows where;
There are lives that are erring and aimless,
  And deaths that just hang by a hair;
There are hardships that nobody reckons;
  There are valleys unpeopled and still;
There's a land – oh, it beckons and beckons,
  And I want to go back – and I will.

ROBERT SERVICE: 'The Spell of the Yukon'

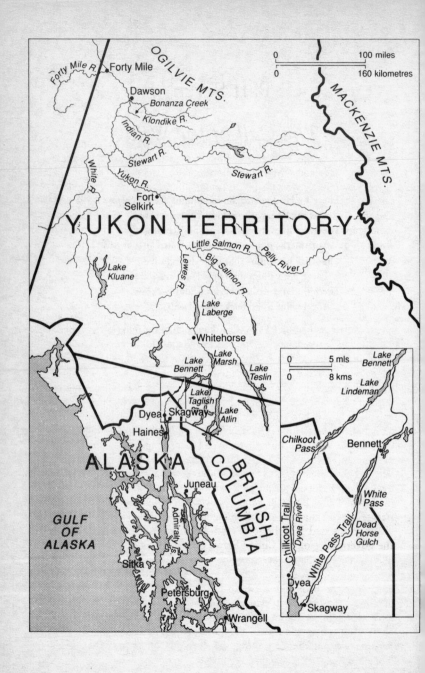

Chapter 20

In these days of political correctness it is strange to come unexpectedly on the extreme political *in*correctness of that great
left-wing American writer, Jack London.

John Steinbeck was no revolutionary in spite of the anger that
seethes through his Depression-time books, *The Grapes of Wrath*
and *In Dubious Battle*; that wonderful anger with the bosses of
America who ruthlessly harassed migrants seeking work in their own
country. Jack London, who made his way to Carmel and Salinas a
good many years earlier than Steinbeck, was a real revolutionary,
and this went a long way to explaining his great popularity in the
former Soviet Union.

To start with, circumstances forced London to work like a
boy-slave first in a jute mill, then in a cannery for ten cents an
hour, and later with a railway company. During the Depression of
1893–7, he enthusiastically joined the Socialist Labour Party, and
went along with the so-called Industrial Army of unemployed and
angry men, which was setting off to Washington, DC, to demonstrate
on the steps of the Capitol. London himself deserted the hard-pressed
Army in despair and near-starvation, but the names Karl Marx and
Friedrich Engels had stuck with him; speakers he cheered at meeting
after meeting back in Oakland called for nothing less than immediate
revolution. When he himself took to climbing on to soapboxes, he
became known as Oakland's 'boy socialist'. All this revolutionary
fire and brimstone was far from the comparatively moderate political
outlook of Steinbeck (although even he, as I have said, had heard of
his books being burnt in Salinas). Events and his own adventurous
nature saved London from doing anything too ill-advised.

What diverted Jack London from his youthful desire to overturn
the government of the United States by force was the arrival of the
SS *Excelsior* in San Francisco: she sailed through the Golden Gate
with the galvanising news that a lot of gold had just been discovered near the Klondike River in northwestern Canada. In no time
at all the boy socialist was up and away in the Gold Bug's grip.
And although he found no gold up in Yukon Territory, he found
something more valuable – enough inspiring material to make his
fortune writing the best things he ever put on paper: the novels

The Call of the Wild and *White Fang*, and his Klondike short stories.

London described in his semi-autobiographical novel *The Valley of the Moon* his escape from the Depression-ridden city of Oakland. He described the enchantment of his wife Charmian (Saxon in the book) with Carmel's 'genial, human atmosphere'.

> She was no longer pent in the narrow working-class environment of a Pine Street neighbourhood. Life had grown opulent. They fared better physically, materially, and spiritually; and all this was reflected in their features, in the carriage of their bodies .... Mrs Hall and several other of the matrons had enthusiastically admired [his wife's] form one day when in for a cold dip in the Carmel River. They called her Venus, and made her assume different poses.

As for his love for her – 'it was the love that lasted – if only they did not go back to the city where the beautiful things of the spirit perished and the beast bared its fangs.'

This sentimental rigmarole was an example of London's later writing and was published three years before his death aged forty in 1916. Whatever Steinbeck might have thought of that kind of prose, it is pretty certain what he would have thought of the description of how Billy and Saxon (Jack and Charmian, if you like) came into a village in which 'everything seemed un-American. The names on the strange dingy shops were unspeakably foreign. The one dingy hotel was run by a Greek. "Huh! – this ain't the United States," Billy muttered.'

Fresh revelations of the horrors of multiracial aspects of American life lay ahead for Billy and Saxon in the fruit-growing valleys in the Salinas areas. ' "What are all the Chinks doin' in the valley?" Billy asked.' 'It was our folks made this country,' he went on to reflect. 'Fought for it, opened it up, did everything.'

When about twenty-three years later John Steinbeck came to write his furious indictment of the iniquitous fruit growers of exactly the same area, did he mention the 'unspeakable foreignness' of the fruit growers' associations of the regions? I don't remember that he did.

Recently returned from the Great Plains, my faith in America well shored up, I settled for a few days in San Francisco. Jack London, whose yarns had gripped me when I first read them as a youth at school, was the man I was following now. I knew he had finally settled in the Sonoma Valley (his Valley of the Moon) north of the Bay area of San Francisco. Sonoma, I saw from the map, runs parallel to the Napa Valley famous for its wines. London's Wolf House, burnt down and never rebuilt, lay up there, and I wanted to visit the ruins. But first there was the First and Last Chance Saloon to call on; the little one-roomed bar on the waterfront at Oakland which Jack London, having bought his sloop *Razzle Dazzle* there from an oysterman called Frank French, fondly described as 'a saloon for the transactions of men'.

The Saloon has stood on that same spot since a sailor named John Heinold came ashore from a windjammer in 1876 – the year of London's birth – and turned an old bunk house for oystermen into the bar that in 1883 became known as Heinold's First and Last Chance. It was only one room with a single longish bar, and was so small that it stood, and still stands, a good chance of being overlooked by the tourists who stream past it in summer. 'Beer on Draught' signs say outside it. But even they don't necessarily cause the penny to drop.

The whole point of the First and Last Chance Saloon is, I suppose, that not only Jack London used it, regularly throughout his life – a friendly message from London to 'Dear Johnny Heinold', dated only about two years before London's death, appears on the flyleaf of a first edition of *John Barleycorn*, one of his last books. The saloon also became a West Coast writers' 'hang-out'. A good many other writers took it up over the years, including Robert Louis Stevenson, who was forced to wait about while a hundred feet away his ship, the *Casco*, was being prepared for the South Seas. Ambrose Bierce came here, too, and Robert Service (author of 'The Shooting of Dan McGrew'), and later Erskine Caldwell, Erle Stanley Gardner, and other more or less well-known writers. But you can see why Jack London's photograph hangs behind the bar: he was far more intimately connected with Heinold, and knew him from way back, having gone there first as a very young man. As some regular drinkers said, 'London used up quite a lot of whiskey in his day', which was a polite way of putting it, and he started learning to write as a boy in the saloon's back room. It is even said that Heinold put up the money for London's tuition fees at Berkeley – and the tradition is that he made notes on a few novels at a table near the old stove with the crooked chimney. Johnny's son, George, took over as owner-operator of the Last Chance on his father's death in 1932, and carried on until 1969. It has been run, as far as I know, since 1984 by a lady called Carol Brookman. It is said to have remained exactly the same as the San Francisco earthquake left it.

That means that it is the same as it has been ever since 1906. So that when I stepped into it with Brian McGarry – 'Mac', who had once been skipper of the ketch *Fiona*, in which I had tracked the ghost of Joseph Conrad through his Southeast Asian world in 1977, and was now married and living in San Francisco – we stumbled down the eight-inch drop from front step to the bar-room floor, almost landing on our knees. This unexpected drop is one of the unique features of the place. Another is the bar, which slopes away into the room at an angle that is very steep indeed – perhaps 45 degrees, though I wouldn't bet on it. The slope of the bar, the tilt of the room, coming after that eight-inch drop at the entrance, unbalances you, so that you feel suddenly like W. C. Fields or a character out of *Alice in Wonderland*: all are relics of the famous San Francisco earthquake. Heinold simply left things as the earthquake had left them – all lopsided; he didn't bother to shore the place up again. It makes the place much more memorable.

Once Mac and I had fallen into the Last Chance, we had time to notice the slope of the floor and the fascinating way in which one's glass tended to drift away from one, if you didn't take a firm grip on it immediately it was served to you. I noticed, too, the old pot-bellied stove at which Jack London had warmed himself, and an incongruous tank of oxygen behind the bar under an old Italian military helmet from the North African campaign. The whole ramshackle room was covered with a clutter of mementoes; the ceiling, too. Over the bar in a tangle of bric-à-brac hung the boxing gloves Bob Fitzsimmons and Jim Jeffries had used in their title fight in Oakland – oddly diminutive gloves, without the stuffing packed into them today to protect fighters.

At the bar the day I was there, my next-door neighbour turned out to be a large Russian tourist with a flowing moustache. The barman poured my scotch and I had grabbed it before it floated off down the bar, when the Russian said in a deep voice,

'We, in my country, we read much Jack London. We like him very much. Not in America. Americans don' read eem. *We* read Jack London. You read *Martin Eden*?'

'No,' I said. 'That's one I haven't read.'

He turned eagerly towards me. 'What you think is best, most optimistic book of Jack London?' He looked at me intently as though my answer was of the greatest importance.

'Optimistic?' I thought. 'What can that mean?' Aloud, I said, 'I don't know about optimistic, but the best thing he wrote, I think, are his Yukon short stories.'

'His short stories? *Da?* They are most optimistic?'

'What's this about "optimistic"?' I wondered again. Stupidly I didn't ask the Russian to be more specific. Nor did I ask Mac, although later I suggested to him that perhaps the Russian had meant 'popular'.

'You should read his novel about – here.' I indicated the general area of San Francisco with an encircling finger. 'It's called *The Valley of the Moon*.' Plenty of revolutionary talk in that book, I thought, if that's what he wanted. The brutal beating of 'scabs' in workers' demonstrations; that sort of thing. Plenty of optimism there, perhaps, if this was an old Soviet kind of Russian.

'About here? Ah, *Valley of the Moon. Da!* I understand. Now I go to Glen Ellen: very interesting. Thank you, thank you. I read *Valley of the Moon*.'

He clambered off his stool and, stopping only to borrow a cigarette from Mac, staggered into the street. Soon after that I downed my drink and followed Mac up the slope to the Last Chance's front door, and we walked down to the wharf for a hot dog and a beer.

From my hotel in San Francisco, the Washington Square Inn, it was a short walk to the waterfront and the famous Eagle café on Pier 39. From here I could sit at a table on the terrace in the summer sun, eat the sort of American food I most preferred – chili con carne and eggs and bacon – and listen to the soothing racket of the seals barking in the marina at the end of the pier. From the terrace I could see the red girders of the Golden Gate Bridge and the light winking on the former prison island of Alcatraz that sits in the water like a fortress barring the way to Oakland and Alameda. Behind me the skyscrapers climbed the hill. Baghdad-on-the-Bay, a prominent newspaper columnist, Herb Caen, had dubbed the city. I could see why.

Out of my sight but not much further away to the north lay the Sonoma Valley, and up there was Glen Ellen. On a hillside nearby, Jack London had built the home of his dreams – Wolf House. He had built it to die in, but was doomed never to pass a single day in it.

Two policemen chased a couple of small black boys through the crowds of holiday-makers. The boys swiftly disappeared into a car park; there had never seemed much hope of them being caught. The sun shone on the whitecaps in the Bay, and on hordes of holiday-makers who strolled, shrieked and laughed about the waterside sidewalks. I noticed for the first time how enormously overweight most of them were, and thought how odd it was that in a country in which people spent inordinate amounts of time reading about diets and tips on how to avoid obesity the sheer mountainous girth of men and women of all ages was such an unavoidable feature of the landscape. One was almost overwhelmed by the buttocks, bosoms and thighs around one, often in summer weather displayed in the flimsiest of cotton shorts and T-shirts.

I was delighted when Mac offered to drive me to the site of Wolf House, and we set off across the Golden Gate with him behind the wheel.

Wolf House is a colossal wreck. Many people seeing it must be as surprised as I was, and asked themselves as I did: why did Jack London – in essence a simple, idealistic soul – want such an absurdly grandiose house? It was intended to have twenty-six rooms, bathrooms, a roof of Spanish tiles, a pool, and a refrigeration plant; it was constructed of heavy slabs of volcanic stone and redwood timber. Now it lay, like the hulk of a great burnt-out ship, stranded on a hillside among the eucalyptus, pines and oaks. It was very quiet on the hillside. A buzzard silently circled the trees and a small plane faintly grumbled far overhead. I read the two notices near the burnt house. One said: 'Residence for Jack London, Glen Ellen, Sonoma Co., California' and gave the name of an architect in San Francisco. The second read: 'My house will be standing, act of God permitting, for a thousand years; Jack London'.

That God did not permit, the ruins show. Shortly before London and his wife could move in, Wolf House burned to the ground. It was a total loss. 'I shall rebuild,' said London; but he never did so.

The ranch next-door, which the Londons named the Beauty Ranch, to me has the look of a much more desirable place to live in. A huge live oak stands guard over a cottage there, and although it is surrounded by a forest of eucalyptus, which are said to be dangerous to other trees because they burn easily, at least they were not the tomcat-smelling variety.

He had a shrewd idea about the origins of the fire at Wolf House. It was a case of arson, he thought. Some radical, he suspected, had considered the huge house far too pretentious for a man who had once proclaimed himself a revolutionary socialist. No one will ever know the answer to that conundrum. London, that sentimental and strangely naïve man, resigned from the Socialist Party shortly before he died, embittered because the workers had ignored his advice to rise up and overthrow the system.

Jack London was generous to a fault; the sort of easy-going fellow who finds himself surrounded by spongers and conmen in no time at all. A man who was at his happiest in the no-nonsense masculine atmosphere of the Last Chance Saloon with Johnny Heinold and his cronies, or planting thousands of eucalyptus trees or raising fat hogs on the isolated hillsides of Sonoma.

As a very young man London's happiest days had been spent trekking through the snows of the Yukon Territory or floating down that great river through Alaska to the Bering Sea. His finest – anyway his most memorable – writing came out of the world of ice and snow, of silence and solitude, of huskies and the Canadian Mounted Police, of lonely deaths from cold, hunger and violence.

In the scent of the manzanitas I looked around me at this fine green place, and thought: that's where I will aim for now – the land of *White Fang* and Buck in *The Call of the Wild*; the land of the Malamute Kid and the *White Silence*; of the Klondike and Snookum Jim.

I said to Mac, 'I may be gone some time.'

He looked startled. 'Eh?'

'The Yukon, that's where I'm going. That's the side of London I remember best. I'll go there now in summer. And later go back when there is snow and ice about the place. I may even try to mush a few huskies. The call of the wild and all that, you know.'

Mac looked at me sceptically. 'Aren't you a bit old for that?' he said. It was something I had wondered myself.

'Well, we'll see,' I replied.

As soon as I could, I booked myself on two steamers that took passengers at this warmish time of year from Vancouver up to Prince Rupert in British Columbia, and from there to Skagway at the foot of the Chilkoot Pass, once the gateway to the former goldfields. From there I would somehow get to Whitehorse, the capital of Yukon Territory, and to Dawson City where the Yukon and Klondike Rivers meet.

Having struggled up the Chilkoot Pass, London had spent the winter of 1897–8 in an abandoned cabin, 80 miles south of Dawson at the mouth of the Stewart River. Part of the cabin had been taken apart and rebuilt in Dawson itself; the other reconstructed part stood just by the Last Chance Saloon in Oakland.

From Vancouver I kept a rough-and-ready diary of my progress to the Yukon. I started it in the plane between Vancouver and Port Hardy, the little port of Victoria Island at its northernmost point.

A drunken logger sat just behind me. He was on his way back from Hawaii for some reason. His snores were deafening. A businessman next to me whispered: 'These loggers often fly with me round here. Always drunk. Always try to get me involved in their banter. I smile

– and try to ignore them.' At that moment the drunken logger woke up. 'Hey,' he cried, 'the spotted owl. The f— spotted owl. They want to bring it back. Like hell! They can't stop the loggin'. And the ravens – where have they gone?' No one answered him. 'I don't know where they've gone. But I do know we'll cut down all the f— trees they might want to come back to. There'll be no trees for the f— spotted owl to nest in, or whatever f— thing they do in them!'

When we land in Port Hardy he staggered off, swilling something from a bottle hidden in a paper bag.

Port Hardy is a small place scattered round a flat grey shield of water. At the North Shore Inn's bar lounge fishermen and miners from the local copper mine play billiards and drink. In the restaurant I look for fresh fish. But a pretty waitress says, 'Only frozen halibut.' I sit looking glumly at a stretch of water full of fresh fish, eating a solid, tasteless slab of frozen halibut. [Halibut, I learned, is to be a regular feature of summer on the west coast of Canada.]

Apropos. Down in the North Shore Inn's bar I meet a big man with a well-trimmed beard in a smart baseball cap. 'Kypp' Lantz is an important man in the International Union of Operating Engineers (what is a non-operating engineer?) in Port Hardy. He also buys and sells Finest Quality Balsam Firs for his 'Lantz's Old Tyme Christmas Trees'.

'Fish,' he says. 'Trouble is Port Hardy may look like a little god-forsaken place, and in some ways it is. In some ways. But it is also possibly a place where the average man has the highest per capita income in Canada.'

'Really?'

'The mine, y'see. Copper. Mining. And fishing. The mine may close sometime soon – used up. But the fishing community packs their catch into containers and ships it off to Vancouver, Seattle, other cities. Halibut, now; salmon, later; oysters; crabs – you name it. So you have to eat frozen fish. It's a shame. You see, they don't take the tourists seriously yet. But when the mine begins to pack up, maybe the people will change their attitude.' He went on: 'Of course, the supermarkets in the cities are to blame. Getting townspeople used to old frozen fish. They don't want to taste the fresh lot any more.'

Two bald-headed eagles perch on a tall pine over the other hotel. Others wheel on huge wings over the fishing boats.

Lantz says: 'We say here, there's more eagles than seagulls.' The 'bald-heads', I notice, are really white feathers; not bald at all.

'What's that?' I ask the bar girl as she mixes a pint of beer with tomato juice. 'Red-eye?' she answers with a question as if she expected me to know.

The *Queen of the North* is a car ferry. Does 19 knots. She will leave Port Hardy for Prince Rupert at 07.30 a.m. and arrive at 10.00 p.m. A Canadian vessel, full of Canadians, quiet-spoken folk.

An American woman becomes quite hysterical over this, shouting, 'Are you Americans? I feel like a minority here.'

Today is rainy and foggy. The channel north widens and narrows between cliffs covered with a dense pelt of trees. Clouds rise out of them like wisps of an old man's beard. The water is flat and grey; the distant mountains dark blue, and the even more far-off mountain peaks almost black – they peer over the foremost ranges like curious onlookers at a football match.

Some nice names from the map: Cape Caution, Swindle Island, Goose Bay, Desolation Sound, Poison Cove, Blubber Bay.

A little history from my guidebook: Captain Cook came here in the 1770s, Captain George Vancouver a little later. Vancouver started the sea-otter fur trade with the Far East. A number of the many islands here are named after Hudson Bay Co. vessels and masters.

Prince Rupert, BC, was built, I read in the guidebook, when there were plans to make it the terminus of the Canadian Grand Trunk Pacific Railway. It would have rivalled Vancouver. Now it has a population of 17,500. Its name derives from its first governor, the cousin of Charles II and first boss of the Hudson Bay Co. (One president of the CP Railway, Charles Hays, went down on the *Titanic*.)

Now P. Rupert exports grain, lumber and wood pulp. As we come into port and slide alongside, the crew of a Panamanian freighter stop loading timber to watch us in.

The Punjabi from Chandigar who drove me to my hotel, The Moby Dick, says: 'I have been here since 1969. We have over 100 families in P. Rupert – that is over 400 Punjabis.' Also a number of Chinese and Vietnamese: I saw them walking the streets next day.

The first night in P. Rupert was gloomy, cloudy and cold with a stone-grey sky. You can see the mountain ranges going back and back – the highest sprinkled with the merest flecks of snow. I ventured down the street to something called the Highland Bar, crossing the road to avoid a desperately staggering old wreck. He might have tried to talk to me – and who would want to end up in the gutter of Prince Rupert at 11 p.m., pinned down by a helpless and pungent old geezer too drunk to move?

In the Highland Bar men with wide hats, shaggy beards teetered between the bar-stools, and the barmaid winked at me and whispered, 'This is a heavy drinking town, I think you'll find.' Not to let her down I ordered another Genuine Canadian Draft Ale, and she added, 'They come off the fishing boats. That does it, I guess.' I said I guessed it did. The next morning in the sunshine, the whole place looked different. The bay reflected the sky and led the eye to the thick belt of trees across the water. Mount Oldfield rose behind the town, all green and spiky with fir trees. A long, rusty freighter with a blue funnel lay in the bay, waiting to load. A seaplane droned overhead. Towards dark, one after the other, little fishing boats scurried up the bay, their crews eager to offload and get into the bars, I presumed.

In the bar of the Moby Dick, a plump and ageing 'cowboy' in a stetson sang a sentimental ditty:

> '. . . No old flames can hold a candle
> To yee-ee-ooo.'

Two or three Vietnamese girls in jeans danced on a postage-stamp floor. They looked petite and charming. Canadian girls – or Americans – were dancing, too, waggling their bejeaned buttocks like barrage balloons. The Vietnamese men looked like a rough bunch – like deserters from the Vietcong – and there were some abnormally fat Chinese, sinister-looking, with scarred unsmiling faces.

A statue of Charles Hays stood in the main street of P. Rupert. 'The founder of our city', said an inscription. And, 'President of the Grand Trunk Pacific Railway. His memorial was unveiled by Jim Ciccono, the last survivor of the crew which in 1914 drove the last spike at Fort Fraser'.

Things had changed here since Charlie Hays's time, I thought. Asians are coming to Canada in droves. Apart from all the Chinese and Vietnamese in the street and in the Moby Dick's bar, I had seen a tall, very upright old Sikh striding along the street. White turban, white moustache, imperious eye, he swung his umbrella like a cricket bat. The ghost of C. Aubrey Smith in disguise. And a taxi driver (white, originally from Toronto) told me as he drove me to a restaurant called Smiles (the best for fish), 'When I first came here, the taxi drivers were one-third East Indian [i.e., not Red Indian] and the rest whites. Now, it's pretty much reversed.' He didn't seem at all worried.

I had several days in Prince Rupert, waiting for the next ship, this one American, the *Malaspina*, the oldest vessel of the Alaska fleet: thirty years old and 3,585 tons.

The schedule says:

Port Rupert to Ketchikan	6 hours
Ketchikan to Wrangell	5 hours 30 mins
Wrangell to Petersburg	3 hours
P'burg to Juneau	7 hrs 45 mins
Juneau to Haines	4 hrs 15 mins
Haines to Skagway	1 hour

How I will get from Skagway (Alaska) to Dawson City (Yukon) remains to be seen. At least winter has not set in, so there is no snow or ice up there.

A footnote on my schedule says that Alaska is the largest of the United States of America, and twice the size of Texas. I would never have known that.

Chapter 21

We reached Ketchikan at about 2.30 in the afternoon. The mountains here had bald tops and the landscape a treeless look. There was also an odd feeling of bustle. A hissing tug drew barges that in turn drew rafts of logs after them. Sea planes took off and landed around us, and small yachts sliced through the waterways and roaring motor-boats churned them up.

Further west an island rose into ridges so high that their peaks were often in cloud: Prince of Wales Island, the map said. Later, between Ketchikan and Wrangell I saw an amazing effect of the light. Ahead, the skyline, above blue ridges of islands, was the colour of a freshly opened mussel: a clear pale pink and pale yellow. Behind us, our wake ran away through darkened blue water. Then all at once – and for what reason? – the water became an icy blue which persisted to the southern horizon. The contrast between mussel-yellow and the ice-blue was extraordinary. But at sunset, which up here came later, at 10 p.m., purple islands stood like cut-outs against the pale pink of the horizon while silver threads seemed to shimmer silkily through the blue of the sea. It was a beautiful place.

In the bar of the *Malaspina*, muzak rose to smother us: 'Da-a-a-vy, Davy Crockett, King of the Wild Fronti-ee-rr'. The barman, raising his voice above the racket, told me that the ship is named after a glacier which is in turn named after Captain Don Alessandro Malaspina, an Italian navigator who explored the northwest coast of Canada for the Spaniards in about 1791.

Talk of greedy guts. Long before the cafeteria opens its doors for lunch at, I think, twelve o'clock, the ageing tourists start piling up, as if ready to storm the joint. When the doors fly open, the stewards and stewardesses jump smartly aside. I don't blame them; they might be trampled to death under the feet of these elephantine tourists. Americans, I notice, jabber about food as English people do about the weather.

There was one old man who held things up dreadfully. Not his fault, because he was deaf. Whenever he asked the serving stewardess what a certain dish contained he was, through no fault of his own, unable to hear the answer. The scene suddenly reminded

253

me of an imaginary incident in P. G. Wodehouse's autobiography *Over Seventy*. He is speculating on the embarrassment for a man inclined to shyness of holding someone up in the street. One would go all pink and flustered, he says. And just suppose you happen to run across somebody deaf?

You say, 'This is a stick-up.'
He says, 'Huh?'
You say, 'A stick-up.'
He says, 'Huh?'
You say, 'A stick-up. A *stick*-up. S. for Samuel –'
He says, 'I'm afraid I couldn't tell you. I'm a stranger in these parts myself.'

This wasn't a stick-up in the ship's cafeteria. It was simply a long, long hold-up.

Now the mountainsides fall straight down into the water. Sheer lines of rock stick up in irregular lumps, and most of the higher ones are lost in thick billows of grey cloud. The long flank of Admiralty Island is nearest. Beyond it – out of sight – is Sitka on Barabov Island, once Russian. London's 'Sitka Charley' came from here in *The Wisdom of the Trail*. It had been a Tlingit Indian village.

Then came Juneau, the capital of Alaska (not Fairbanks). From here London's brother-in-law left him to turn back to San Francisco. Many gold-seekers hired Sitka Indians here to tackle the Chilkoot Pass. They impressed London with their staying power. 'To be almost as good as an Indian,' he wrote, 'was a new ambition to cherish.' We pressed on to Haines and Skagway, near which slopes of what look like pure, green grass soar up sharply into dense-packed spruces and ragged-edged precipices riven with deep clefts and waterfalls that plunge down hundreds of feet. The rock faces are hard, dark rock, crevassed and grey like the wrinkled skin of an old elephant. Formidable ramparts dividing the continent from the cold waters of these North American fjords. Thick layers of snow are caught up in huge crevices beneath the summits of these miniature Matterhorns. They have the deadly pale blue forward edges of glaciers, and look like avalanches ready to slide down and crush whatever disturbs them.

Having one last look round at my fellow passengers I see one ancient tourist on board staggering around in a red baseball cap with 'Sammy's Pizza' written on it. Another wears a T-shirt stencilled, 'People say I don't believe in anything, but I believe I'd like another beer'.

At Skagway on the mainland of Alaska, the jumping-off point for Dawson and the Klondike, the houses, hotels and shops are made of wood. The idea is to give the place a 'period' atmosphere, I imagine. Luckily I have only one night there. What I really want to do is to go up to Whitehorse and the Gold Rush area as quickly as possible.

So the next morning I take a minibus in that direction, climbing up a narrow and very steep-sided valley, green with spruces, and a river that gradually falls away among a deep cleft of forested crags. It is a sombre valley, like a print of medieval Italy or Edgar Allan Poe country ('the dim, mid-region of Weir'). In any case it is a relief to be ashore again – and an even greater one to be once again alone.

According to Pierre Berton, the Canadian historian who is *the* ultimate expert on the Gold Rush, 5,000 men and women tried to cross this valley – the White Pass – in the fall of 1897 – the time of the stampede. He writes, 'None who survived it ever forgot it, and most who remembered it did so with a sense of shame and remorse.' The shame of the Skagway trail, says Berton, lay in the fact that 3,000 pack horses, loaded to the breaking point, accompanied those stampeders, many of them ready for the glue factory.

Jack London described the scenes of horror:

The horses died like mosquitoes in the first frost and from Skagway to Bennett they rotted in heaps. They died at the rocks, they were poisoned at the summit, and they starved at the lakes; they fell off the trail, what there was of it, and they went through it; in the river they were drowned under their loads or were smashed to pieces against the boulders; they snapped their legs on the crevices and broke their backs falling backwards with their packs; in the sloughs they sank from fright or smothered in the slime; and they were disembowelled in the bogs where the corduroy logs turned end up in the mud; men shot them, worked them to death and when they were gone, went back to the beach and bought more. Some did not bother to shoot them, stripping their saddles off and the shoes and leaving them where they fell. Their hearts turned to stone – those which did not break – and they became beasts, the men on the Dead Horse Trail.

That's what the White Pass became known as: the Dead Horse Trail. That was what I was following now: Dead Horse Gulch.

There was another gold-rush trail to Klondike. It started at Dyea, Skagway's twin on the coast, and although it looked tougher, it was actually easier. All the winter of 1897–8 the stampeding gold-seekers poured through this pass – the Chilkoot Pass – and I suppose the image of the men and women on the Gold Rush struggling up the mountains is one that everyone knows who saw the Chaplin movie of that name. Twenty-two thousand people, each carrying a ton of supplies, made it and were checked by the Mounted Police as they crossed the Canadian frontier. They came from all sorts of places, Berton says; they were Scots, Americans, Greeks, Swedes,

Australians, Japanese and even Kanakas from the South Pacific islands. Some carried 50 lb., a few managed 100 lb. At any rate the Mounties insisted that everyone who crossed to Dawson must take a year's supplies with him or her, to avoid the real danger of a famine at this remote, brand-new and suddenly overcrowded township on the Klondike.

The most highly valued cargoes were whiskey and silk,

the one [says Berton] for the Klondike dance halls, the other for the dance hall girls. Whiskey and silk, steamboats and pianos, live chickens and stuffed turkeys, timber and glassware, bacon and beans, all went over on men's backs. If the man was too poor to hire a packer, he climbed the pass forty times before he got the outfit across.

Blizzards blew in the pass practically continuously, making a bad situation much worse.

The Gold Rush was no picnic.

A number of smaller valleys ran off the main trail, and roadside pools of water began to appear of an unpleasant reddish colour. Soon to increase the sombre effects of the gulch, the clouds began to close in lower, with the sun struggling to come through more and more like a dim moon. At the summit, the clouds actually came down to the road. We crossed from Alaska into British Columbia at the Customs Post at Fraser Lake. Not much further on more big lakes began to appear: 'The headwaters of the Yukon River,' said the driver, pointing to them. The sun came out and the valleys suddenly were bathed in a strange blue mist, as if the sky had slopped over the distant mountains and spread into the gulches and canyons.

A short time later we were in Whitehorse, the capital of Yukon Territory, among willows and poplars and spruces, and pulling up outside the Gold Rush Inn.

'This will be all white in January, you know,' said the driver, putting on the handbrake. 'Jesus, but it's cold then.'

The oldest Royal Canadian Mounted Policeman in Whitehorse was named G. T. Cameron. He had been posted to Whitehorse from Vancouver as long ago as 1924. When I called at Mounted Police Headquarters round the corner from my hotel, Sergeant King, a relative youngster in Public Relations, took me to see him. 'He'll interest you,' he said. 'He knows a lot about the Yukon.'

In fact, Cameron, a smiling, good-natured old man, seemed to remember everything that had happened to him since coming to the Yukon seventy years before. He was pleased to tell me about it, he said, sitting us down in the living room of his neat little suburban house.

'We had horses in Dawson then,' he began, 'horses in teams. And of course huskies. In fact, they had dogs in Old Crow up north on the Porcupine River until 1950. You know, we used to run behind the sleds in those days. It was the life!' he added proudly. 'Tough, but everybody did it. Well, we were in good shape.' He grinned. 'And let me tell you, we were the government out here. We did *everything*. Pulled teeth – a lot of that. Attended to births and deaths. Buried people. *Everything*.'

And Cameron sat smiling in his armchair in that living room, remembering those famous days, those great days before everyone became soft, and everything became confusing.

'We had a few Indians on the force. They spoke English. It's a pity that the native languages are almost lost. There were four or five dialects. They are teaching them now a bit. Trying to bring them back, you know. Good idea, really.'

'I suppose there's more crime up here now. Like everywhere else,' I said. 'Drugs.'

'We had no drugs then,' he said. 'Drink, though, that's always been a problem. They made their own then – apple soup they called it. But the people could just walk away from their homes – not even bothering to take their keys from the doors. Leave alone lock anything. Of course Dawson was really off the beaten track. Everything was done in Whitehorse. Dawson's so changed, though.' He shook his head. 'I get lost there now.'

'Did you prefer Dawson to Whitehorse?' I asked him.

'Dawson was a nice posting. We were very close to the community; good relations. The war changed it rather – the Americans made it a busy place. The Alaska Highway came through it, you see. The old pioneers' trail is now a tourists' trap in the summer. You'll find that when you go down there!'

'*Down* there?' I asked. 'But Dawson's north from here!'

'Well, yes. But you see, the Yukon flows *down* to it before turning west and running through Alaska and coming out into the Bering Strait. So you should say "down", by rights.'

'Of course,' I said. 'Stupid of me.'

Talking again about the Indians, Cameron added, 'The Coast Indians were quite numerous. And the Indians round Sitka and Hain were tough babies. Tough physically. They were the top-dogs and had an easier life, living on fish, with no extremes of temperature. Oh, yes, let me tell you something – in the old days, the Indians below Fort Selkirk [on the Yukon between Whitehorse and Dawson] had bows and arrows; yes – bows and arrows! They made kettles from small fibres of the roots and trees. And they dressed themselves from moose and reindeer skins, ornamented with coloured beads, porcupine quills or long hair. Of course, that was way back.' Cameron smiled at the recollection.

'When I first came here you never saw a drunken Indian. Drink was illegal, and usually came illegally from some white man. When the Indians named their suppliers the white men who supplied it would go to jail. Later, after World War Two, everyone was allowed to go to beer parlours, and then even cocktail lounges. And then there was an awful lot of drinking going on. Of course there are good natives and bad ones like there is good and bad in everyone. Maybe the Indians on the Coast are, er, a better class. But they started off better. You know there are good and bad white men, too.'

Sergeant Jim King apologised in advance for the mosquitoes that he warned me would make life a misery as soon as we stepped out of doors. I didn't see any here. Later they clustered round one's mouth and swarmed round one's eyes; they were particularly bad near Lake Lebarge and even worse in the trees and swamps round Dawson.

Lake Lebarge, where, in the poem by Robert Service, 'he cremated Sam McGee', is not far from Whitehorse.

> The Northern Lights have seen queer sights,
>   But the queerest they ever did see
> Was that night on the marge of Lake Lebarge
>   I cremated Sam McGee.

From the marge of Lake Lebarge, at this time of year at any rate, the lake reminded me in size of Lake Tiberias between Israel and Jordan, but I suppose it was really a good deal smaller.

There were plenty of flies here now. Plenty of flowers, too: gentians and forget-me-nots, pink roses and the pink of the fireweed flowers and small, blue lupins. Grey jays flapped from tree to tree; and in a tributary stream I saw a beaver's 'lodge', and near it on the bank, the pointed stubs of willows that had been gnawed away by the beavers, who drag the trunks away once they have felled them. Nearby there were moose droppings – surprisingly small for such a big animal – like a handful of dark cough lozenges. The sun shone, and it was hot under the trees.

When I returned to Whitehorse I mentioned to someone – was it to Jim King? or old G. T. Cameron? – that I'd like to come back in the winter. To do a dog trek. When there'd be no grass everywhere and no tourists; but lots of snow, and ice on the lakes, and a nip in the air.

'Well, March is a good month,' replied whoever it was. 'The ice doesn't break up on the lakes until late April.'

Still, I thought, it would be a long way to come.

The bus to Dawson from Whitehorse had a sign: 'This coach is rest-room equipped for your convenience'. A fat woman was eating popcorn from a big bag and filling the front of the bus with the sweet sickly smell of it. The highway was two-laned and ice-free, and even the distant hills showed no sign of snow. We made good time.

At Stewart Crossing the river was as wide as the Thames at Westminster, and clouds began to billow up into the sunny sky like steam from a steam engine. An hour and a half later we reached the valley of the Klondike and a wide but shallow river with large round rocks showing above its surface and willows and threadbare spruces lining its banks.

I had reached the Klondike! And somewhere here was Bonanza Creek – the goal of all those stampeders.

And in a moment there was Dawson on the Yukon River, which was here a deep canyon of fast-flowing water swinging north past the mouth of the Klondike and veering towards the Arctic Circle, but preparing to twist westwards through interminable mountains into Alaska on its long journey to the Bering Sea.

Dawson, before the Gold Rush stampeders arrived, was a mosquito-ridden swamp (and is still able to provide a few formidable biters). It is a small place of mostly wooden buildings, some of which, on Front Street bordering the river, date back to about 1900. I was to see quite a lot of Dawson in the future – and in all weathers. But now in summer it was hot and bustling with visitors, mostly Canadian or American. On Front Street, the elegant square tower of St Paul's Church dominated the junction of the Yukon with the Klondike. Further down, and a block or two inland, were the hotels: the Eldorado which stays open all year round; and the Westmark, the Triple J and the Midnight Sun, which open only for the summer tourist season – May to October. Diamond Tooth Gertie's Gambling Hall with its blackjack and roulette tables and its garter-snapping can-can dancers also opened up for the summer and the tourists – who swarmed in from Vancouver, Seattle or San Francisco via Skagway or Fairbanks, Alaska.

At the back of the swamp that was all Dawson was once, and wrapped round it like a muffler, rises a 1,000-foot bluff of land that surrounds the little town on its north and east sides. This bluff is called the Dome.

Thinking it might give me a good view of the surrounding countryside, I drove up it. I was right. The view from there was superb.

To the west the Yukon swept, wide and majestic from south to north, vanishing round the corner of the hills that covered the entire region. Below me, to the south, I could see the Klondike, whose water flowed into the Yukon, sometimes disappearing among many sandbanks. I could just see the site of the origin of the Gold Rush – Bonanza Creek – no more than a stream in a sandy valley between two bumps of green hills that ran way up into the greater angle of hills still further south, and led into the once even richer golden Valley of Eldorado Creek. At the junction of the Yukon and the Klondike had once stood Klondike City or Louse Town, which swiftly became the largest red-light district of North America when the gold-seekers arrived. Not a hut – not a stick or stone, leave alone a red light – remains today. Merely virgin stands of spruce trees.

Across the Yukon I could easily see the Top of the World Highway which runs off to Alaska, and to the east the peaks of the Ogilvie Range were light blue in the haze. But, clear as day below me, the town of Dawson lay like a grid beneath the Dome. A hundred years before, thousands of cabins, shacks, saloons, hotels, shops and brothels had cluttered that small shelf of land by the river.

Coming down the hill, a young brown bear wandered lazily on to the road and stopped there to look at me. I slowed down for it.

Behind Front Street, behind Madame Zoom's Ice Cream Parlor and the Bank of British North America, even behind the Nursing Station and something called Klondike Kate's Diner, were two wooden cabins almost side by side.

One was reputed to be Robert Service's former house, and in the summer – which meant now – an actor called Tom Byrne sat in a chair in the compound in a frilly shirt reciting a few of the best of Service's poems to entertain groups of tourists. He did it very well; looking a little like Edgar Allan Poe and reciting in an attractive Irish-Canadian accent.

The other cabin, a short walk away, was Jack London's old cabin – a replica of the one I had seen in Oakland beside The First and Last Chance Bar. There were actually three wooden structures here, and the whole place was called the Jack London Centre. The cabin on the right was the Jack London museum; and in it I discovered the curator of the museum, Dick North, a bulky American, no longer young but extremely genial, who came up here every year from Whitehorse where he lived with his French-Canadian wife, Andrée. It was his job to look after the collection of London memorabilia in the museum, and to answer the tourists' questions about London.

Dick was the ideal man for me to find in Dawson. He was amusing, practical and helpful – apart from knowing everything there was to know about London and his writings. He had supervised the building of this cabin.

And more than that. The London cabin in Dawson as well as the one in Oakland had been made from logs that formed London's original cabin on the Left Fork of the Henderson River upstream from Dawson. Dick North had not only arranged for the cabin to be moved to Dawson; he had actually rediscovered a slab in it with London's signature on it. The message attached to the signature is not a long one. It said, simply: 'Jack London, miner author, Jan. 27, 1898' and Dick good-humouredly commented that it might have been London's ironic reference to his own lack of success in both fields up to that time.

According to Dick North, London had first of all moved into a cabin on Stewart Island, near the mouth of Henderson Creek. That was in early October 1897. He went down to Dawson after that; and there chanced to meet Louis and Marshall Bond, from Louse Town, who owned a magnificent dog, part-St Bernard, part-Scotch shepherd, called Jack. Jack was later to become the prototype of Buck, the dog-hero of *The Call of the Wild*.

London moved back to one or two other cabins near the Stewart River in early 1898, and staked a gold-mining claim on the Left Fork of Henderson Creek. He found little or no gold; very few of the 100,000 stampeders did.

'I think the most amazing thing of all,' Dick North said, 'was that Jack London never wrote a non-fiction autobiography of his adventures in the Klondike.'

This, Dick thinks, may have been due to the fact that London was primarily writing fiction about the frozen north, and figured that non-fiction would destroy the aura of romance and mystery which enveloped his story about the great sub-arctic area.

Dick added, 'The cabins, by the way, were typical of the style necessitated by few carpenter's implements and long, cold winters.' He had uncovered an unpublished story of London's in which he describes an almost identical cabin.

> It was a snug little cabin in which he sat. Built of unbarked logs, measuring not more than ten to twelve feet on the inside, and heated by a roaring Yukon stove, it seemed more homelike to him than any he had ever lived in, except – of course always the one real home. The two bunks, table and stove, occupied two-thirds of the room, but every inch of space was utilised. Revolvers, rifles, hunting-knives, belts and clothes, hung from three of the walls in picturesque confusion; the remaining one being hidden by a set of shelves, which held all their cooking utensils.

I sat in the museum listening to Dick telling me how hard he had worked to rescue the cabins and get them rebuilt. He is one of those good-natured big men, who smiles easily through his glasses. He had trekked or mushed dogs up innumerable frozen creeks and down countless snowy valleys, carefully checking on cabins on the way to make sure he got the right ones, and at last he had the permission and the money to move the cabins – one to Oakland, California, by truck and ship; the other to Dawson City by cargo boat.

I could find Dick any morning in the Jack London Centre, and later, at about twelve o'clock, down the road in the Westmark Inn where he liked to lunch with Tom Byrne, the actor who, for the benefit of tourists, recited the poems of Robert Service, the Bard of the Yukon.

'The Shooting of Dan McGrew', one of Service's best-known poems, begins as follows:

> A bunch of the boys were whooping it up in the Malamute Saloon;
> The kid that handles the music-box was hitting a jag-time tune;
> Back of the bar, in a solo game, sat Dangerous Dan McGrew,
> And watching his luck was his light-o'-love, the lady that's known as Lou.

Malamute means a very large husky of a type that's bred near Norton Sound in Alaska on the Bering Sea. There is no Malamute Saloon in Dawson; nor, as a matter of fact, has there ever been one. But there happens to be a bar that must be wonderfully like the one Service envisaged.

These days it is the bar of the Westminster Hotel and it is known to most Dawsonites as the 'Snake Pit'. No wonder. It is rough and tough, I love it. I found it by chance as I wandered one evening down 3rd Avenue, following a group of elderly tourists – Americans, I think. A few steps ahead of me, they put their heads briefly into a doorway, quickly withdrew them. They hurried on, as if they had seen or smelled something utterly shocking.

What could it be?

I looked in myself. The sound of raucous voices poured into the street, and smoke, too. Smoke also largely obscured a bar against the far wall. There were people at tables between it and the door: a lively scrum of people with fur caps, whiskers and dungarees, who could have been trappers or miners. Drink was flowing – and it looked as if it had been doing so for some time. But I suppose the main thing that lured me in was the clever fiddler playing exceptionally lively music – half jig, half square dance – in one corner under a skull and crossbones flag. Boisterous customers were heeling and toeing it on a minute dance floor to what the fiddler and his group were playing, a group consisting of the fiddler himself (an Indian, it turned out, from Yellowknife on the Great Slave Lake), a girl in a top-hat playing an electric piano, an unshaven guitarist in a baseball cap, and a shaggy-headed pianist called Barnacle Bob, who was wearing a dirty top-hat.

Of course, I went in through the smoke and noise of music and up to the bar. Dawson, I thought, should have just such a bar as this. If it didn't exist, one would have had to invent it. I could see why the tourists had shied away from it, but to me it was perfect.

I spent the rest of the evening there. I was waved to a table by an affable, tipsy Englishman called Duncan who seemed to own the place, and who had wandered through Australia on his way to the Yukon and was now determined to stay in Dawson. He took me upstairs to show me the hotel. There, I saw for certain that this was the hotel for Dawson. The bedrooms were large and vividly furnished in scarlet plush; they reminded me of some slightly seedy San Francisco hotel at the turn of the century.

Outside, the three-storey hotel had, like so many buildings in Dawson, a wooden false front with large bow windows that protruded on to the street. The whole façade was painted an attractive shade of strawberry. I sat with Duncan and said, 'This is perfect. It's like something out of an old Western movie, starring Barbara Stanwyck, John Wayne and Joel McCrea.'

'It is rather,' said Duncan, putting back a scotch and looking gratified. 'I'm glad you like it.'

'Love it,' I said.

Time and whiskey have blurred any exact recollection of that first evening in the Snake Pit bar. I remember the wonderful swirl of the fiddle music – I even remember dancing to it on the tiny, smoky dance floor with someone, possibly the lady known as Lou. Above all, I distinctly remember the sudden entry into the bar on two or three occasions of massive Mounted Policemen, who without uttering a word would hoist some struggling drunk out of his chair and toss him into the street.

Next day I completed my inspection of Dawson and the Klondike. I walked up Bonanza Creek, and found in it a good many stone slag heaps, disfiguring the valleyscape. A track runs up one side of the creek down which a little muddy stream trickles into the wider Klondike.

The spruce copses that now line the side of the creek were not there at the time of the Gold Rush. They were needed then for firewood in the long freezing winter, or were used for building miners' shacks and cabins. Mining still goes on. A brochure told me that as recently as 1992 gold produced in the Yukon was worth $32,763,000.

'There are a fair amount of bugs here,' said the guide I had taken from Dawson. 'So we won't stick around too long.' He was right. Big flies – known here as bugs – settled on my cheeks and forehead by the dozen. They are a kind that leave large painful lumps where they bit you.

On the eve of my departure I visited the Snake Pit for one last drink with Duncan.

'You know, you should come back in the winter,' he said. 'That's when you see the true Yukon. Without the tourists. The population's about 2,000 maximum then. You could come in here and you'd be almost one of the Dawsonites.'

'Well, I'd like to come back in winter. Apart from anything else to see if Jack London wrote the truth about the silences and the whiteness and the dogs. But it's a long way to come.'

'All I can tell you,' said Duncan, 'is that that's the time to come.'

When I went to say goodbye to Dick North, I said:

'You know, I'm half thinking about coming back in the wintertime. March, perhaps.'

'That's a good time,' he said. 'Of course, I won't be here then. I'll be in Whitehorse until the end of May. Take my address and phone number there. If you want any help in arranging things, let me know.' He wrote out the address, and I shook his hand.

I wasn't at all certain I would go in winter to the Yukon. It was only a vague idea. But it grew. And that brief conversation with Duncan in the Snake Pit bar in the end led me to Paul and Cathy Wylie's Dog Camp at Forty Mile River the following year in a temperature of −40° C.

Chapter 22

Had I made a fatal mistake?

I hadn't got anywhere near the Klondike and at Whitehorse airport it was well below freezing already. A blizzard was blowing ferocious gusts of snowflakes across the runway. And when I arrived there early one March morning to catch the DC-3 to Dawson City, 300 miles or so even further north, the weather forecast was saying it would be at least 30° below freezing that night in Dawson itself – and I was headed 40 miles north even of Dawson. Despite my silk thermal underwear, my thick calf-length woollen stockings and the heavy boots with ridged soles, it was going to be a very chilly trip.

In London, before I set out for the Yukon I had jokingly replied to friends who asked me how long I would be gone with Captain Oates's farewell to Robert Falcon Scott as he left his doomed party in their tent near the South Pole: 'I may be gone some time.' I was only partly joking.

The thing was, they unnecessarily pointed out, that I had spent most of my life in tropical climates – the Middle East, Africa, and places like Vietnam, Thailand and Indonesia. How was I going to cope among sub-zero temperatures, snowdrifts and frozen rivers? Well, I said, I would have a go and find out.

The Air North flight was a 'no frills' one lasting over two hours. One side of the plane was stacked with miscellaneous baggage; seats occupied the other. Below us were spruce-covered hillsides and deep valleys white with snow; occasionally there were ribbons of writhing white ice as rivers snaked their way north through this desolation, their waters frozen solid.

An air hostess forced her way between muffled passengers to hand out trays of steaming coffee and pancakes spread with maple syrup. Near Dawson, a child cried and was sick as the plane began to dip and then to slide skilfully between white ridges. And at last I saw the Yukon in winter, half a mile broad and its water a solid sheet of ice, and then the frozen Klondike and snow-filled Bonanza Creek – and suddenly we were on Dawson's white runway and in the tiny hut that serves as its waiting room.

'Custer' was waiting for me in the snow. Dick North had assured me that he would be there, and he was. Not, of course, the long-haired 'Custer' Crazy Horse had done for on the plains of Montana. This Custer, standing by the hut, was a rough-looking, weather-beaten man with torn mitts on his hands and worn dungarees held up by braces, and a curious cap of reddish-brown beaver fur that stood up in a ridge all round his head. The untidy strands of long blond hair that poked out of the back of it had, I supposed, earned him his nickname.

He put out a hand and introduced himself. 'Brian McDonald, I've come to fly you up to Forty Mile River. To the Wylie Dog Camp. About twenty-five minutes in this weather,' he added, waving a mitted hand at the curtain of falling snow around us.

Custer's Cessna had a single engine and makeshift skis mounted on its undercarriage. I hoisted my bags into it and squeezed myself into the front seat next to him. A few minutes later we rose into the air over the Klondike and the entrance to Bonanza Creek, and then over the small wooden houses of Dawson itself, banking to follow the Yukon, a pure white ribbon. 'That ice is seven or eight feet thick,' said Custer, pointing down at it.

It was a good thing that ribbon was there. It soon became the only signpost we had to follow. The weather closed in until we were flying virtually blind between the vague outlines of hills that formed the river valley – now mere smudges of greenish black in the murk that enveloped us more thickly the further we ploughed north. Custer had to press his nose almost against the windscreen in an effort to keep his eyes on the white river highway below us and the hillsides that drew ever closer – dangerously so, it seemed to me – to the wings of the aircraft.

I said nothing. I wasn't going to make myself ridiculous by suggesting we turn back only ten minutes out of Dawson. I gripped the side of my seat and fought off thoughts of Will Rodgers and his pilot, Wylie Post, who I seemed to remember had perished in a small plane somewhere very near here.

After several minutes of this, Custer, too, had had enough. Without a word, he banked the Cessna sharply to the right; and soon we were on our way back to base. When he decided to turn back again towards the dog camp, the sun had come out and, turning left and swooping low over Forty Mile River, we saw three people standing near what looked like a sled in the centre of the river-ice.

'There we are,' said Custer, and dropped the Cessna neatly on to the ice by the sled.

Paul Wylie, the dog camp's owner, was there on the ice and snow wearing an old fur-lined cap with earflaps. He had a Skidoo – a kind of snowmobile – with him and a small sled on which he piled my light bags. The other two people with him would return to Dawson with Brian McDonald in the Cessna, and they piled into it now.

'Snow's about 24 inches,' Paul told Brian, and the Cessna roared down the ice in a cloud of whipped-up snow, rose and turned away from us down the river.

'Can you drive a motorbike?' Paul unexpectedly asked me, pointing to the Skidoo. It was a bit like a motorbike, though it had tracks where a bike's rear wheel would have been. 'Or shall I drive you back to the cabin?' And when I agreed to that, he added, 'Put these on in any case,' handing me a pair of large mitts and a heavy old coat, 'they're warmer than what you're wearing.'

I put on the mitts and the coat. I could already feel the sting of the cold on my cheeks. I wished I was wearing my balaclava helmet and the woollen cap I could pull down over my ears.

Paul, I noticed, had dark glasses, plenty of bushy hair that protected his cheeks, and a heavy moustache. His jacket was zipped up to the chin and his boots came high up his calf and were tied there like Roman soldiers' leggings. I sat on the back of the Skidoo, holding tight, as he drove up the steep side of the river bank, then on a looping, jolting, bucking ride along an uneven and narrow track of snow between the trees. It led eventually to a branch in the trail. There I heard the sound of dogs barking. Big dogs, they sounded like.

'House first or the dogs?' asked Paul over his shoulder. Well, I had come all this way to meet the ghosts of Jack London and the gold-rushers – and, of course, huskies. So I said, 'Can we see the dogs?'

'Right.'

I flapped my arms to keep the circulation moving inside the mitts Paul had lent me.

The dogs were large, excited – and beautiful. They tugged at the loose chains that moored them to metal stakes in an open patch of snow near a copse of spruces. They stood barking (not howling) at me – the stranger on the sled, and when I did the rounds to take a closer look at them, some dived forward, tongues lolling, lips drawn back, mouths grinning, trying to jump at me in welcome; while others, more cautious or nervous, cringed away at the end of their chains.

I pulled off a mitt and fumbled for a pencil and my notebook. I wanted to get their names down quickly before the intense cold reached my fingers. Then I would be forced to wrench my gloves back on in a hurry.

I wrote to Paul's directions.

First, Lobbo. Lobbo was one of Paul's biggest and also his favourite dog; his lead dog. He was big – 90 lb. – bearlike, in fact; with a wide wolf's face, a hard square head and a wise, solemn expression. I knew for a certainty that if Lobbo ever got his fangs round one's throat he'd never let go.

'You can stroke his chin,' said Paul. 'Try not to touch the top of his head. He's sensitive.' I avoided the top of Lobbo's head like the plague.

Later I used to squat beside Lobbo on the packing-case he liked to sit on, perhaps to get away from the snow, and we became friends. He actually presented the top of his head for me to scratch. And I found he liked his ears pulled, too.

Smithie was next – the smallest dog in Paul's camp; probably not over 50 lb. She had a curiously sad expression on her little face. She looked at me as if she might burst into tears at any moment. Paul said that despite her size she worked very hard, and I was later to see her at it – careening down the trail with an odd crablike movement that didn't seem to slow her down.

Galoot – a big dog, so called because he was always falling over himself.

Jack – perhaps the biggest dog there; approaching 100 lb., I should think, with very distinct black markings on his head and body, a white muzzle, and sharp, friendly eyes under two white marks about the size of a man's thumbprint.

Buck – with Jack – was, I think, the liveliest dog there; at any rate the perkiest. On his head, back and upper legs, he had well-defined black markings similar to Jack's. Like Jack, he appeared to enjoy posing as if in a dog show, fluffy tail curled up like a proud plume over his back.

Bag was a bitch: and 'a pretty smart dog', Paul said. Apart from that, Jack was in love with her. He was forever stretching his chain to get within reach of her; and once or twice in the next week he did reach her, to the excited howls of the other huskies.

Of all Paul's dogs – twenty-one of them – Truk had the most wolf in him. He was perfectly white – the only dog without any markings at all. He was also lean and strong; and he had a specially long tail, which he carried up when he was taking it easy on the trail. If it was down, Paul said, it meant he was really doing his best to pull the sled.

And then there was Big Lurch – a fluffy puppy of immense size, who had huge feet and legs and a tail like a plume of smoke from an express train. Later on the trail, I noticed that Lurch never seemed to rest: he was far too excited. Unlike most of the other dogs, who liked to lie down in the snow whenever a halt was called, Lurch remained on his feet, straining to go on, often barking impatiently at Paul and the other dogs. Poor Lurch suffered cruelly from the ice that gathered between his toes. He hadn't yet learned how to pull it out with his teeth, so Paul had to do it for him.

'Lurch will make a very big, good dog,' said Paul.

From Paul I discovered that, although one could talk of 'mushing' dog teams, the word 'mush' was not among the words one used to make dogs start pulling a sled. Paul had his own vocabulary with which to direct the dogs. They had learned to obey him. 'Pick it up, Lobbo!' he'd say, 'Pick it up, goddam it!' And Lobbo, at the head of a team of seven dogs, would jump forward with the others going hell for leather after him. Of course, you could simply shout, 'Go!' and they probably would go, but to stop a team you had to yell 'Ho!' Then they would stop – if they knew you well enough; if they didn't take to you, they would pay no attention whatsoever. The same thing applied if you shouted 'Ha!' (meaning 'left') or 'Gee!' (meaning 'right'). Or 'Stay!' (meaning, of course, 'wait') or 'Down!' (meaning 'sit down'). Some people, said Paul, could shout any damn thing they liked and until they were blue in the face – and the dogs would simply pretend not to hear them.

'Jack London hadn't prepared me for anything like that,' I said.

'No,' said Paul, smiling. 'I don't think he mentioned it.'

Paul's cabin – at this time of year – was surrounded by a deep blanket of snow that now more or less covered it and a few other buildings, including a chicken house and a rabbit hutch. It was a small one-storey building under the spruces with an upper room casually tacked on to it. It was all wood; the walls of logs mostly, although some were made of planks of white spruce. Icicles a foot long hung from the eaves. A number of cats occupied the front doorway, lying huddled among a variety of discarded objects: a saw, a coil of twine, and a pile of kindling-wood for the stove inside.

Paul's wife Cathy was in charge of cooking, and of making sure the stove was kept burning; without that stove the temperature inside the cabin would have been the same as it was outside; which on the day I arrived fell after sunset to not much above 40° below zero. A huge kettle of hot coffee stood permanently on the main cooking stove. This stove was a collector's item – an ancient and most handsome affair, all silver and black doors and hinges which Paul said they had found in Ontario and was a copy of an ancient model. The water (melted snow) was heated on something much more ramshackle. This was simply a 45-gallon drum Paul had set up into which Cathy fed thick spruce logs; spruce when green would last a long time. Drinking water came from a nearby creek. Cathy or Paul sprinkled it on the dogs' food every evening: fishmeal or beef-meat in biscuit form.

Paul drank an amazing amount of this coffee every day. In that cold, dry weather it was difficult to resist. Brian McDonald had delivered – apart from myself – a quart jar of Royal Wedding rye whiskey for the Wylies and two pints of Johnnie Walker Black Label scotch for me. We got through most of it during the time I was there – a week – even though Paul, who knew everything there was to know about living in these far-flung and icy conditions, swore that the best liquid for keeping the nerve ends from closing up in such bitter cold was actually strong, hot tea with plenty of sugar.

Apart from Paul and Cathy, there were two other occupants of this isolated cabin. One was the Wylies' son, Peter, a black-haired sturdy 15-year-old part Indian, part Eskimo and part white Canadian, whom they had adopted some years before on a visit to the extreme north of Canada. To make room for me, in the main cabin, Peter slept in a cruder wooden cabin 50 feet away.

The other occasional occupant was a tiny and very lively black dog with fluffy hair more like a pig than a dog and therefore known as Piggy. Because Piggy was playful and irritated Paul, he was frequently removed from the cabin and chained up in his own diminutive lean-to in the snow, well away from the big huskies, of whom he was afraid.

I myself occupied the upper room in the main cabin. This could only be reached by a vertical wooden ladder that shot straight up through an open trap door. In that small room were a bed and a good deal of junk belonging to Peter: toy aeroplanes, a big wall-poster of Batman and a tangle of books, among them a paperback version of Jack London's *White Fang*. There was also a basin, and an oil lamp. The Wylies' cabin had no electricity and no running water, so every morning Cathy would heat a bucket of water on her stove and hand it up to me through the trap door.

The great thing about that tiny ramshackle attic room was that the cabin's wood-burning stove was immediately beneath it.

'I suggest you sleep up there,' Cathy had said. 'It'll be a degree or two warmer.' She looked at me appraisingly. 'As long as you can manage the ladder . . . .'

It *was* a few degrees warmer there. So I made it my business not to fall down the ladder. This was important. If a call of nature made it imperative to go outdoors during the night, I had to negotiate the wooden ladder in the dark, both going and returning, having fumbled my way into the freezing backyard. Piggy in his little lean-to (who thought I was a burglar) would utter warning yelps, and that would start the howlings of the huskies his yapping had aroused. When I had a night-pee the whole forest knew it.

Possibly the greatest single annoyance in that cold climate was the number of clothes I had to wear. I tugged on *layers* of clothes. Corduroy trousers covered thermal underwear; waterproof and chillproof pants covered the corduroys; thick woollen socks covered smaller socks called liners inside my boots. My top half was protected by a waterproof anorak worn over a second anorak – both zipped up in a number of wondrous ways. And inside everything was a pocket containing my spectacle-case. So that to read (or write) anything I had first to find the means to get at and extricate my spectacles. This was easier thought about than done.

Later, when I explained this difficulty to someone in Whitehorse, he asked if these layers of clothing didn't make peeing a problem. And he added, thoughtfully,

'I suppose it depends how big the thing is you're looking for?'

'Whoever you are, nothing's very big in a temperature of minus forty degrees.'

Cathy reacted differently to this problem. 'Well, how do you think it is for us women? Frostbite on the buttocks. How would you like that?'

It said a good deal for Jack London that Paul Wylie was a great admirer of his Yukon stories. He had one or two bones to pick here and there, but generally he agreed that London was accurate. Coming from Paul, this was high praise, since Paul knew exactly what he was up to in this remote place. He was the sort of man anyone could have trusted his life with however much frost was lying around.

The matter of temperature was one that came up almost at once. I was sitting at the table near the stove drinking coffee with him and his son Peter when I asked him a question that I really wanted to solve. It arose when the radio-telephone which served the Wylies' cabin and one or two other homesteads on this out-of-the-way river suddenly erupted into life.

A voice said: 'How are things? Snowed in?'

We couldn't hear the reply, but the voice continued: 'Great Scott, it was 30 below here last night. We heard it had been 40 below with you.' And the conversation went on for some minutes.

When it ended, I asked Paul if he had ever read the Yukon short story by London called *To Build a Fire* – one of his finest. In it London had written: 'No man must travel alone in the Klondike after 50 below.' And:

'When it is 75 below zero a man must not fail in his first attempt
to build a fire – that is, if his feet are wet. If his feet are dry, and
he fails, he can run along the rail for half a mile and restore his
circulation. But the circulation of wet and freezing feet cannot be
restored by running when it is 75 below. No matter how fast he
runs, the wet feet will freeze the harder.

Those passages come in a story dealing with the death of a solitary
traveller in freezing temperatures who does accidentally get his feet
soaking wet. He tries to light a fire under a spruce tree loaded with
snow; and the snow falls on the fire burying it and putting it out.
That is a disaster that also in effect buries the man. Unable either
to get dry or to move on he freezes to death.

Paul sniffed. 'He should have known better than to try to build
a fire under a loaded spruce,' was his comment. As he spoke one
of the Wylies' cats leapt on to the table: a strange animal, I noticed,
with no ears.

'A cat with no ears,' I said. 'What happened?'

'They froze off. Froze and dropped off. She don't miss 'em. But
see what frost can do?' Paul wagged a finger and grinned. 'So don't
go wandering off, y'hear.'

That evening the same cat, as if to draw even more attention
to herself, produced a litter of three kittens in a cupboard behind
the stove. Cathy made sure she had a blanket to lie on. 'Ears or no
ears, life goes on,' she shrugged.

It was difficult on Forty Mile River in sub-zero temperatures
to leave the subject of cold. When London talked of 75° below he
meant Fahrenheit. Paul explained that that would mean 107°
below freezing point. 'At 40° below, you can hear your breath
freezing. Like steam,' Paul said. 'Your spit freezes in mid-air. So
does pee. London says somewhere that it "crackles". So you see,
that's the time of winter when you make sure to lay in a lot of
wood. Luckily, we've got lots of it growing round here.'

The official record for North America came in 1948 in Snag,
Yukon Territory, when the temperature dipped to 81° below. That
was Fahrenheit.

The first afternoon Paul took me out with the dogs. To give
me an idea of what it was like to drive a sled in deep snow he
loaded me into the sled, a long canvas-lined coffin-shaped vehicle
with a narrow ledge at the back for the driver or musher to stand
on, and a metal flange he could push down with his foot to slow
the sled on dangerous corners.

Paul, the experienced musher, made it seem very easy. With

Lobbo as lead dog and six other dogs harnessed one behind the other we raced off through the trees down to the river, the sled sliding and skidding round sharp turns in the trail, and Paul shouting instructions to the dogs in general, and Lobbo in particular.

Sometimes threateningly: 'Yah-hee! Ya-hee! Pick it up, Lobbo! What the hell are you doin'? Pick it up! You son of a f— bitch!'

Or, encouragingly: 'Good dawgs! Good dawgs!'

Or (when Jack decided he would stop to urinate on the trail – a manoeuvre that threatened to impede every dog behind him): 'Jacky, what the hell you think you're doin', you dumb a—? You'll be peeing on ya own foot, next!'

Sometimes when one or two dogs were obviously disobedient, Paul shouted 'Ho!' to stop the sled, seized up a short length of nylon cord, and ran up the line to whack the guilty ones. The nylon was soft, and the long-haired dogs were not really hurt: the cord's effect was mainly psychological. The dogs cringed at the time, but soon recovered, and continued smiling with tongues lolling, and their tails held high like triumphant banners. Then, in no time at all, Paul was shouting, 'Hut! Hut! Hut! Pick it up!' and the dogs were racing away hell-for-leather as cheerfully as before.

Below us, if the trees fell away, Paul would stop the dogs to say to me, 'Look down there. That's the mouth of the Forty Mile River. That's the Yukon joining it on the right, see? Beyond are the Ogilvie Mountains.' And looking the way he was pointing, I saw the smooth white unmoving surfaces of the two rivers as they came together, and behind them the great white-dappled wall of mountains that run in a southeast–northwest diagonal behind Dawson City, the Yukon and the Klondike.

In the bitter cold of this white solitude the trees, rivers and mountain ranges stood out as brightly and clearly in the snow as it was possible to imagine.

This breathtakingly beautiful, utterly calm scene was the appeal of London's 'sad and lonely north'. Even now, writing this, I haven't yet quite recovered from the experience of it. And when in the still cold dead of night I crept out of the Wylies' cabin and the dogs pointed their noses at the bright and enormous stars and howled long and wolf-like, it was as London had written in *The Call of the Wild*, their ancestors, dead and dust, pointing their noses at the stars and howling down the centuries and through them.

From the short story called *To Build a Fire* I had learned one easeful and painless way of dying: drop off in a snowdrift.

In the story, the man I have mentioned who dies of cold in that story thinks in his last moments it is 'a good idea to sleep off to death. It was like taking an anaesthetic. Freezing was not so bad as people thought. There were lots worse ways to die.' And quite soon he drowsed off into what seemed to him the most comfortable and satisfying sleep he had ever known. Of course he never woke up.

The first day, after I had tried mushing a team of dogs, I was halfway to believing all that myself. Nothing in Jack London had warned me of the sled dogs' way of 'dumping' their musher into a snowdrift. Paul was far too expert, of course, to have to submit to that indignity. He reminded me of Captain Lingard, who in the novels of Joseph Conrad, 'made light of his skill [as a seaman] with the assurance of perfect mastery, and feared the sea with the wise fear of a brave man'. The sea in Paul's case was the Wild and the Cold.

Five times in one day – the first day I followed Paul on a sled drawn by seven dogs – I bit, not the dust, but very soft and deep snow. Little Smithie was my lead dog, and Truk (the white wolf-dog) and big Jack were on the team, and I recalled later when we set off in pursuit of Paul and his dogs, how some of *my* dogs glanced back at me over their shoulder in a coyly speculative and furtive sort of way that I see now boded me nothing but evil. Even then, I think I had somehow divined enough about huskies to guess that often they have a wicked sense of humour. After that day I knew it for certain.

What happened was this:

We set off at a spanking pace, the sled moving smoothly in a straight line in the trail already carved out by Paul and his team. There was no trouble at that point. But we were aiming for the union of Forty Mile and the Yukon, and it was when we descended towards the steep bank of the Yukon that the sharp bends in the piled-up snow did for me. The first time we came to such a bend, we were travelling at considerable speed and I noticed that Truk (who had been cantering along with his tail disdainfully in the air and deftly both defecating and breaking wind as he ran) gave me a quick surreptitious glance which should, I suppose, have given me warning of husky mischief to come.

It came with a sudden wrenching corkscrew turn that hoisted the sled sharply up the right-hand bank of snow. There was no way I could hold the sled upright. It was far too heavy. In a half second, the sled was over on its side and I was tumbled ('dumped' is the technical word) into one of the deepest drifts on the trail. I was shouting 'Ho! Ho!' ('Stop!') as Paul had told me to, when I was sent sailing through the air. For all the good those 'Hos!' did me I might have been singing 'God Save the Queen'. The dogs raced on, totally ignoring my plight. They came to a halt about a mile away; and sat down on the trail. There they waited – looking back at me as, buried in soft, yielding snow, I struggled to get to my feet – lolling their tongues, their lips drawn back over sharp white teeth in soundless, contemptuous grins. 'Look at that 200 lb. dolt,' those grins seemed to convey. 'Well, we got rid of him once. We can do it again.'

They did. Exactly the same sequence of events was soon repeated. High speed – the abrupt curve – the sled riding up the bank – me shouting 'Ho! Ho! Ho!' like a maniac. And – 'DUMP!' And the long, infinitely exhausting struggle to clamber out of deep, soft snow weighed down with all those clothes. In time, Paul became used to looking back to find a driverless sled following him down the trail. And a pair of heavy boots sticking out of a snowdrift.

I had to give Paul his due. He never blamed me. He never laughed. He never tut-tutted in sorrow or anger. He simply shouted at my dogs to behave, and then waited for the next time they dumped me.

It was a humiliating experience – and, as I say, exhausting, too. And one, what's more, for which I was quite unprepared. London hadn't mentioned dumping. Nor, for that matter, had Paul.

Despite these delays, eventually we reached the junction of the two rivers, and pulled up our two sleds by the relics of a small village that stood in trees on the very edge of the ice-covered Forty Mile River.

'An interesting place, this,' said Paul, unscrewing the top of a thermos of hot coffee. 'Forty Mile village. See the church and the North West Mounted Police cabin. Here's where the man who started the Gold Rush, George Carmack, registered his discovery claim in Bonanza Creek.'

The Gold Rush had started *here* where we stood – with the registration of that claim!

Handing me a mug of coffee, Paul said, 'It's a good story. Pierre Berton's account is best.' I had a copy of Berton's book on the Klondike Gold Rush in my haversack in the Wylies' cabin. When I got back I opened it, read it, and this is the gist of what he said.

On 16 August 1896, three men – George Carmack (known to many as 'Lying George') and two Indians, Skookum Jim and Tagish Charley – stumbled on gold 'lying thickly between slabs of rock like cheese in a sandwich'. This was in Rabbit Creek, just by what is now the town of Dawson City, which was then nothing but a mosquito-ridden swamp. The creek ran (and still runs) down to the tributary of the Yukon called the Klondike River. The subsequent rush of gold-seekers was to make the name Klondike famous throughout the world.

The immediate reaction of Carmack, Jim and Charley was to dance a sort of mad jig of joy on the valley floor, but next morning Carmack staked three claims on the spot for himself and his two companions. 'I do this day, locate and claim, by right of discovery, five hundred feet, running up stream from this notice. Located this 17th day of August, 1896. G. W. Carmack.' That was how he worded his stake (see p. 284).

That day in 1896 Rabbit Creek acquired a new name: it was renamed Bonanza. Carmack himself lost no time: he hurried down the Yukon to Forty Mile to register the claim, although taking time to inform every other prospector on the way about his find. There were those who doubted the word of 'Lying George'. One French-Canadian spoke for many of them when he said, 'I think hees wan beeg bluff.'

There was a mining camp at Forty Mile in those days (there had been a modest strike ten years before), and a saloon that belonged to a man called Bill McPhee.

As Berton tells it, Carmack 'was no drinking man, but on this occasion in McPhee's bar he felt the need for two whiskies'. When he had downed those he was ready to break his astounding news once again.

'Boys,' he said, 'I've got some good news to tell you. There's a big strike up the river.' To fresh cries of disbelief, he pulled out a cartridge full of his Bonanza gold.

'In texture, shape and colour it was different from any gold that had been seen before in the Yukon Valley,' writes Berton, and when William Ogilvie, the respected Canadian government surveyor, instead of dismissing Carmack as a liar, observed gravely, 'Well, Carmack must have found the gold *somewhere*,' the rush was on. By morning, says Berton, Forty Mile was a dead mining camp. Even the drunks, he says, were dragged from the saloons by their friends and tied down, protesting, in boats speeding for the Klondike.

Now from where I stood with Paul and the dogs, looking across the frozen river I could see the high mountain range named after William Ogilvie. It was easy to imagine that southward helter-skelter of boats towards Bonanza Creek that began from the old North West Mounted Police headquarters that stood on the bank of the Forty Mile River.

It wasn't much harder to imagine George Carmack – no longer, or ever again, called 'Lying George' – excitedly scribbling on a piece of paper in the log building behind me, registering his claim with Inspector Charles Constantine of the NWMP, a power in the Territory, Justice of the Peace, land agent, Customs officer, postmaster and Indian agent, as well as the man responsible for keeping law and order throughout the whole Yukon. For all his official posts, Constantine from now on would be frantically busy simply registering and regulating the flood of mining claims that followed George Carmack's find when the news of it leaked into the outside world.

By the fall of 1897 the rush was truly a stampede. Among those who would join the rush to the Klondike goldfields was a tough young man from Oakland, California, called Jack London. And when he left it the next year, 1898, to return to San Francisco by following the Yukon through Alaska to the Bering Sea, he would ride down the river passing the very point on which Paul and I now stood.

Chapter 23

Shamefaced, I apologised that night to Paul for my humiliating incompetence with the sled. He shrugged it off.

'Forget it,' he said. 'I was dumped once and had to walk five miles to catch up with the team. Five miles! Luckily the sled stopped. It had got tangled up with some trees on the banks of the river.

'By that time my clothes were frozen solid. It took a quarter of an hour under a hot shower at home to thaw them out. Then a hot tub to thaw *me* out.'

To this day I wonder whether Paul knew how grateful I was to him for telling me that story. How glad I was not to be the only man in the Yukon to have been 'dumped'!

Paul said: 'Dogs must know the boss is, well, God. You must be harsh with them; but kind, too. You notice I never carry a whip. Never.'

London writes of mushers controlling their dogs with 30-foot caribou-gut whips. But Paul said, 'Dogs are entirely dependent on man – for food, work, everything. So they seldom, if ever, wander off into the forest to hunt on their own. They just might if they really *feared* their master. If not, they certainly would not.'

He was telling me this as we sat at the table in the Wylies' cabin, at which Peter did his homework for the educational correspondence course he was taking. In order not to disturb him, Paul and I went back into the living section of the cabin. There I asked him, 'Can sled dogs become fond of their master as pet dogs can?'

Paul said, 'Oh, yes. They can *love* their master; be extremely faithful to him. Once my lead dog – not Lobbo – saved my life. I'd fallen through the ice on Forty Mile. I was up to my chest in 34° below. Thank God I was able to grab the dog's collar and he backed off up the bank. Dragged me out. Lucky he was a big dog.'

Paul went on: 'You know, another time I crashed my sled going fast downhill. Crashed into a tree. The shock knocked me cold for, I don't know, perhaps twenty minutes. I woke up to find my lead dog sitting over me, licking my face.'

I smiled. 'I wouldn't mind,' I said, 'curling up in a nice, cold, comfortable snowdrift and slipping off to sleep – or perhaps to death – being licked by a loving huskie.'

'Remember, you never know where that tongue has been.'

'Why would I care? I would be on my way out!'

Paul laughed.

Later, he said, 'You know, in London's day, I doubt if people were dumped. That's why he doesn't describe it. They usually walked behind the sled and the dogs. Or rode on the sled, sitting astride the freight. They controlled the dogs only by word of mouth. Also, as their sleds in those days carried pretty heavy loads, they went quite slowly. So they used fewer dogs and bigger ones.

'Lightweight dogs bred for racing are too stupid for my taste. They are not bred to think. On the other hand, a Malamute from Alaska is too slow. They are very heavy – perhaps 150 lb. And very, very strong; but they can't go fast or far enough. Five or six big Malamutes in a sled could draw, oh, 100 per dog. A lot. The Mounted Police, who wanted to go fast and had heavy loads as well, used dogs of 65–70 lb. They probably used Siberian huskies.'

As we talked, Cathy moved about near the stove, making bread. It was very still in the Wylies' clearing. I glanced out of the window and saw the moon over the tops of the spruces looking amazingly clear and full, the treetops were tipped with silver. In a while the dogs in their clearing began to howl; first one or two, then gradually it was a chorus, as if all of them had joined in.

For a time we listened to them in silence.

I said, 'I wonder what set them off.'

'They just felt like singin', I guess,' said the Wylies' son Peter, looking up from his books.

'You think they're singing?'

'Yep,' he said with certainty.

Paul said, 'Dogs will bark at night if a fox comes near the camp. Or the odd moose.'

'Grizzlies?'

'Well, not now. They're hibernating.'

There is a passage in London's *The Call of the Wild* that describes Buck, the 'Outside' (non-Yukon-bred) dog's joy at meeting nature in the wild, and his first experience of hearing a wolf's call.

Irresistible impulse seized him. He would be lying in camp, dozing lazily in the heat of the day, when suddenly his head would lift and his ears cock up, intent and listening, and he would spring to his feet and dash away, and on and on, for hours, through the forest aisles and across the open spaces. He loved to run down dry watercourses, and to creep and spy upon the bird life in the woods. For a day at a time he would lie in the underbrush where he could watch the partridges drumming and strutting up and down.

One night he sprang from sleep with a start, eager-eyed, nostrils quivering and scenting, his mane bristling in recurrent waves. From the forest came the call (or one note of it for the call was many noted), distinct and definite as never before – a long-drawn howl, like, yet unlike, any noise made by a huskie dog. And he knew it, in the old familiar way, as a sound heard before. He ... dashed through the woods ... and looking out saw, erect on haunches, with nose pointed to the sky, a long, lean timber wolf.

Some nights in the silence that enveloped the forest by Forty Mile River, the howling of the dogs seemed bound to attract the interest of any wolves which might be nearby. I asked Paul if wolves ever joined in the night-time chorus, and if he could tell a wolf-howl from the howl of a dog.

He thought about that for a while. 'A wolf-howl is lower and longer,' he said at last. 'It makes you shiver, as a matter of fact, when you hear it rising and rising; it's so mournful. Unearthly, really. You know I told you how unlikely it would be for a dog to wander off into the forest. Well, the main reason is that wolves would eat him. They're bright. Sometimes wolves are bright enough to send a bitch to lure a dog away from the camp. Once he's outside they tear him to pieces. I know one case where a pack of wolves came into a dog camp and killed two dogs and wounded others. Wolves really are killers. Impossible for a wolf to become a sled-dog; he's too independent. You see, his natural instinct is to travel at night, not in the daytime. The other problem is that wolves like to fight. A friend of mine who tried to harness a wolf with dogs had to tie a tomato-can over his muzzle!'

Sometimes we heard the churr-churr of partridges, and now and again I spotted the fan-shaped imprint of their spread feathers in the snow. Ptarmigan flew through the trees from time to time; and sometimes, where only whiskey-jacks (grey jays) had squawked and fluttered before, small birds of spring were appearing.

'Can Lobbo catch a ptarmigan?' I asked Paul. And he replied, laughing, 'Lobbo's so slow, the ptarmigan would be up and away long before he reached it.'

The tiny claw marks of squirrels could be seen under the trees and once Peter pointed out an actual squirrel, a red one, sitting quite tamely on a branch over Piggy's house. Sometimes I saw the even smaller marks of mice and now and again the pad-marks of a fox.

Then there were the ravens – 'crows' Paul called them – massive birds, which hopped and flapped among the trees where the dogs were. One of them had befriended Paul personally. The reason for this, Cathy told me, was that one day Paul had been driving through the snow and this raven had been sleeping on a stump by the trail. Paul drove past it, deliberately avoiding it, and the raven opened its eyes to realise that a man and seven dogs had passed within striking distance of him while he slept – and hadn't bothered to harm him. He was evidently grateful, and after that, 'Crow' (as Paul named him) came to live in a tree over the dog camp. Later he brought a wife and they hatched young ones, who when they had grown up stayed on as well. Paul was convinced that Crow also entertained his friends around the camp, and indeed there were usually several ravens swooping around the treetops, apparently playing games.

'You know, Crow is clever,' said Paul. 'He likes to tease the dogs. He will wait until a dog is curled up sleeping, and then will cautiously creep up behind him and nip a hair from his back. Painful. The dog will spring up and dive at him, of course, but Crow is always too quick.'

One day Paul took one sled and I took another and we mushed up the Forty Mile towards Alaska. Naturally I was dumped a couple of times; but less than before. I began to think I had learned a little about the knack of balancing on that tiny square of wood at the back of the sled.

As we turned round to go home Crow appeared. He dived, cawing and groaning in the curious way ravens have, and generally gave us a low-level display of aerobatics. Finally, he zoomed over our heads to the camp, and was already waiting in a tree as we drove into it. 'Cronk! Cronk!' he said, loudly snapping his beak.

One morning I was alone with Cathy Wylie. I asked her, when she left this place (she sometimes went to visit her parents in Ontario for a brief period in the summer) what she missed most about it. All I knew was that once she had been a nurse in Dawson City's Nursing Station.

'The quiet? The isolation?'

'That's part of it,' she said, 'but not all. It is difficult to answer. Once I wanted to go to Frobisher Bay, near Hudson Bay. Later I decided to go to Dawson because you can reach it without flying. We did go away once, you know. At first we were lucky to be making $500 a year, trapping. Paul didn't know much about trapping, really, And I was really bushed with all the work in the house, with the chickens, the dogs. So we moved to Saskatchewan. Sold everything up. Began farming down there.'

She smiled. 'Well, we were there all of three weeks. Then I began to think, "What are we doing here? How can people live like this?" There was no real neighbourliness, you see. Everybody was too busy making money, paying mortgages, keeping the banks from taking their homes!'

She smiled and spread her hands. 'So we came back here, took a lease on this cabin and a trapline for $200 a year including taxes and all that. We prefer it out here. Here people are interested in having good friends. As for Dawson, it is, well, half and half. We go there now and again in summer. Some people there come from the south and worry about money, some others I've known for years. So there are good people there.' She paused. 'Well, we like it.'

'You must do,' I said. 'And I don't wonder at it.'

The Wylies sell eggs – they have a lot of chickens – and they clean and sell the marten, lynx and fox skins and the occasional wolverine skin Paul traps. His trapline – his trapping zone, that is – is an area of 1,800 square miles, and he has set 120 traps for marlin; and 24 for the rest – lynx, foxes and wolverine. The law obliges him to visit the traps every five days, although the new traps he uses kill the animals instantaneously. As for moose, he is allowed to shoot only one a year. Last year's carcass was hanging up on a tree near the cabin where the cold acted as a deep-freeze.

'I go off round the traps with a few dogs and old Lobbo for days and days,' said Paul. 'It is much better than Saskatchewan. There, as they say, there are miles and miles . . . of, well, miles and miles. To my mind, Saskatchewan is a good place to be *from*!'

By now I knew that Paul and Cathy had read Jack London's Yukon stories and that they admired them. On the eve of my last day I asked Paul what he thought of Robert Service, the English-Canadian who had lived in Dawson for years and turned out such well-known verses as 'The Shooting of Dan McGrew' and 'The Cremation of Sam McGee' – poems that read to me with the easy, infectious rhythms of an inferior Kipling, although I don't expect everybody to agree with the word 'inferior'. Whatever the *mot juste* is, Service is certainly the poet of the Yukon, the Klondike and the Gold Rush.

Instead of asking Paul point-blank what lines of Service he preferred, I handed him a volume of the collected poems and asked him to mark with a 'P' any lines that particularly took his fancy.

I was not surprised, after what he had told me of his love of remote winterbound valleys like the Forty Mile, to see his marks against the stanza of 'The Spell of the Yukon':

> No! There's the land. (Have you seen it?)
>   It's the cussedest land that I know
> From the big, dizzy mountains that screen it
>   To the deep, deathlike valleys below.
> Some say God was tired when He made it;
>   Some say it's a fine land to shun;
> Maybe, but there's some as would trade it
>   For no land on earth – and I'm one.

'And you, Paul,' I thought to myself, 'are another.'

He said, 'Tell you what, tomorrow's your last day. I'll drive you in the sled to the top of our hill. It's quite high – 2,000 feet or so – and you can see a mass of land from there. It's a great bird's-eye view. I think we'll take fourteen dogs this time, in tandem. And I'll try harnessing Lobbo with little Smithie in the lead.'

The result of this plan of Paul's was one of the greatest experiences of my life.

With fourteen big strong dogs harnessed two-by-two in front of it, the sled shot out of the Wylie camp like a bullet, turned a left-handed corner at top speed with no trouble at all – because Paul was mushing and I was simply sitting inertly in the sled feeling like Napoleon on the Retreat from Moscow. Then we started on the long slog up the steep snowy trail to the top of the hill. Paul's encouraging cries to the dogs of 'Hut! Hut! Hut!' rebounded off the spruces and willows and birch trees lining our route. The dogs' breath rose like dense plumes of mist into air as beautifully clear, sparkling and cold as ever. I was glad to be wearing deep mitts and my balaclava.

Halfway up we paused to give the dogs a rest, and they snapped up mouthfuls of snow like children bolting ice cream at a soda fountain. From time to time the tracks of small animals crossed our trail. And once the great flat footprints of a moose disappeared into the trees nearby, and the smell of him came to us quite distinctly. The dogs smelled him, too, and they turned their heads in interest in the direction of the trees into which his spoor vanished.

'He's probably in there watching us,' said Paul, sniffing. But we didn't stop to look.

By now far below we could see the powdery blocks of ice in the Forty Mile River where it joined the Yukon, the shapes of the old deserted NWMP post among the trees, and the telegraph office behind the church and the miners' cemetery half-buried now under its shroud of white at the point of land where George Carmack had registered his astounding discovery all those years ago.

I could see the meandering Yukon, white and solid, straggling tortuously south towards Dawson, invisible now behind one of the snow-flecked folds in the hills. Further east the Ogilvie Range ran north to south, and behind *that* the even more impressive outline of the Mackenzie Mountains completely blocked the eastern horizon.

What could I say? I looked at the infinite sheets of snow, felt the clear bitter cold on my cheeks – and could only say, 'Phew!' There were no comforting shadows here. There was only the silence. And, in awe, I spoke the phrase aloud: 'The White Silence.'

'Yes,' repeated Paul. 'The White Silence.'

Then the wonder and the break were over and we set off up the hill once more. 'Pick it up, Lobbo! Pick it up, Smithie!' shouted Paul, disturbing a ptarmigan which flew alongside us for a while in his white winter plumage before veering away into the trees.

Paul said, 'Funny seeing little Smithie next to big Lobbo, uh? They get on, don't they?' They'd made a curious pair – one 50 lb., the other nearer 100. They did get on all right; Smithie seemed to lean into Lobbo's huge side for comfort. The other team dogs, too, seemed to favour travelling in tandem. Some of them had special chums among the others. Jack, who I noticed before had taken a shine to Bag, kept glancing behind him to make sure she was following, which interrupted the rhythm of the others, so he had to be shouted at angrily by Paul.

Truk, the white wolf-dog, just in front of the sled, was carrying his tail straight out behind him today – a sign, Paul reminded me approvingly, that he was really working. 'Yesterday he was drawing you and, do you remember, his tail was flying high like a banner? That means he was showing off, only pretending he was working. Today he's serious.'

Near the crest of the hill, the aspen trees suddenly acquired trunks so pale, they might have been bathed by moonlight; or painted pure white by a landscape decorator. It added a touch of something like magic.

And then, all at once, we were at the top, and the dogs, panting, quickly snatched up cooling mouthfuls of snow, and sat or lay down by the side of the trail to rest. Lobbo took the opportunity to bury his whole head in a snowdrift to cool it.

I looked around me at a seemingly endless view I could never have imagined. It was extraordinary. To the west, the mountains stretched far away, clear and white, to Alaska. We could see the white mosque-shaped mountain called Liberty Dome that marks the border of Alaska. And it was nearly 2,000 miles from there to the mouth of the Yukon in the Bering Sea.

Even Paul seemed subdued by the vastness and isolation of the scene.

'Not a single human being in all that we see from here,' he said, as if in wonder. And pointing across the wilderness, he added, 'My trapline stretches all over that.'

I knew he had marked another stanza of Service's 'The Spell of the Yukon', and I could see why. It was the one that went:

> The winter! the brightness that blinds you,
> The white land locked tight as a drum,
> The cold fear that follows and finds you,
> The silence that bludgeons you dumb.
> The snows that are older than history,
> The woods where the weird shadows slant;
> The stillness, the moonlight, the mystery,
> I've bade 'em good-bye – but I can't.

Paul, too, had tried to bid all this goodbye. He hadn't been able to, either. And he had come back to it.

It was almost over. Paul went to inspect the Forty Mile River that afternoon and found that the place where Brian 'Custer' McDonald had landed with me was now under water. The thaw had begun.

I had to go, so Paul prepared another landing-strip on hard ice nearer the junction with the Yukon. Then he talked to Custer on the radio-telephone and gave him the 'gen'. Custer said he'd be there at about nine o'clock the next day to pick me up.

That night in bed, I lay restless with misery at having to leave. I read by the light of Peter's kerosene lamp what Jack London had had to say about the advent of spring in the Yukon:

> The ghostly winter silence had given way to the great spring murmur of awakening life. This murmur . . . came from the things that lived and moved again, things which had been as dead and which had not moved during the long months of frost . . . . The willows and aspens were bursting out in young buds . . . . Crickets sang in the nights, and in the days all manner of creeping, crawling things rustled forth into the sun. Partridges and woodpeckers were booming and knocking in the forest. Squirrels were chattering, birds were singing, and overhead honked the wildfowl driving up from the south in cunning wedges that split the air . . . .
>
> All things were thawing, bending, snapping. The Yukon was straining to break loose the ice that bound it down . . . .

Well, at least the Yukon had not yet broken loose the ice that bound it down. I was glad about that. So far, the ice was still deep and firm. But the thaw was surely coming and then this beautiful pure snow would melt into dirty treacherous slush. The icicles on the cabin's eaves, I saw, were dripping already; and I had heard wedges of snow from the roof falling heavily into the yard. Sadly, I listened to those sounds of the dying of the winter. It was as if not only the snow and ice but the whole character of this remote and beautiful place was leaking away.

It may seem odd, considering my anxiety at coming to this frozen isolated place at all, that now on my last night, lying on the little bed, watching the big spruce tree outside my window silhouetted against the clear starlit sky and the cats, where they huddled nightly for warmth and comfort on the sill outside – that now, I felt a soul-deep sadness to be leaving this frozen remoteness. When I heard the dogs beginning to howl, the melancholy sound made me shiver. I felt an extraordinary mixture of pleasure – and a profound regret. I thought: 'I must have caught Paul and Cathy's disease. Now I understand why they hurried back from Saskatchewan.'

This feeling stayed with me while I packed my bags next morning, drank the mug of coffee Cathy gave me, while Paul hitched Lobbo and six other dogs to a sled. I patted each dog goodbye in turn. Some jumped up; others took my hand in their teeth and shook it. All tension between us had gone; the dumpings were a thing of the past. They barked and whined, drawing their lips back from their perfect, white teeth in wide smiles. They strained to watch us leaving, shifting restlessly across the yellow pee-holes they had drilled in the deep layer of snow. And then we were off, Peter following on another sled. I waved to the dogs, but we were out of sight of the camp in a moment.

Just after nine, as we waited at Forty Mile, we heard the drone of Custer's Cessna and soon the little plane dipped down and made a perfect landing on the frozen river.

I shook Paul's hand and Peter's, and waved to them from the window of the plane. And that was that. In half an hour I was back in Dawson City.

Custer had decided to call it a day with his Cessna – for this year at any rate. This was his last pick-up. The rivers would begin to melt and become treacherous; he would not be able to land with safety in too many places. 'I'm off to my cabin on Henderson Creek,' he said with finality. 'This very afternoon.'

Dawson was in the throes of a festival known as 'Thaw-di-Gras', a celebration of the beginning of the spring thaw – though, of course, I didn't see anything to celebrate in that. It was a weekend – and a good deal of merry-making was in the offing; so I learned when I went to the Eldorado Hotel and met the proprietor, Peter Jenkins, the genial Mayor of Dawson. There were to be fireworks, pancake breakfasts, toboggan races, log-sawing contests, skating, snowmobile races, and egg tossing on the Yukon River. And no doubt other things besides.

Despite the thaw, Dawson was better than it had been in the middle of the previous summer when I had found it seething with tourists. Some hotels were still closed: for example, the one I had stayed in before and in which I had met Dick North and Tom Byrne, the actor who sat in Service's garden in a frilly shirt and read his poems to tourists in the summer months. Diamond-Tooth Gertie's Gambling Hall was closed, too, and the Midnight Sun Hotel.

Still, the Yukon River here remained well and truly frozen over. It was very beautiful under its deep snow, with wiry tufts of an occasional bush sticking out of it here and there, and across its half-mile width a steep cliff of snow-covered spruce that complemented the higher cliff behind Dawson. The Klondike, too, was frozen. But where it met the Yukon telltale patches of water were beginning to show that spring had started to take hold.

I looked forward to visiting the present-day equivalent of the 'Malamute Saloon' – the Snake Pit bar at the Westminster. I wanted once again to meet its owner, the Englishman, Duncan Spriggs, who had more or less dared me to come back in the winter. And I wanted to hear once more the music group led by the Indian fiddler from Yellowknife who played the Turkey-in-the-Straw type bar music I liked and which suited the spirit of Dawson so well.

The bar was open and rowdy enough – on the Sunday night of the Thaw-de-Gras 'a bunch of the boys were indeed whooping it up', as Service had described in the first line of 'The Shooting of Dan McGrew'. Unfortunately, owing to some misunderstanding between Spriggs and the fiddler, the group seemed to have been temporarily disbanded. At any rate, it wasn't playing now. A couple of bewhiskered trappers who had evidently been whooping it up at the bar for some time told me hopefully that the spat, whatever it was about, would be healed in due course. But unfortunately for me the healing would take place after my departure.

I walked round the town anyway. I walked past the 'British Bank of North America' and then along Front Street, to the soaring wooden tower of St Paul's Church. The streets were already being swept of snow and ice, as I climbed sadly up the road to the Robert Service cabin – there would be no poetry readings there now. Its small compound was still under snow and the cabin itself looked romantic behind the screens of silver tree trunks. Jack London's cabin and the

London museum where I had found Dick North were also under a thick carpet of white, with only the Canadian flag hanging from the museum to lend a splash of red to the background of leafless, silver-trunked trees that ringed it.

This London cabin was, as I have said, the twin of the cabin in Oakland, California; London was one of the many who had found gold elusive. Well, he found other treasure. After his death, his widow, Charmian, explained things thus:

> I have often heard Jack say that he had no idea of using the Klondike as a literary asset, until his dream of gold fell through and he was bound out of the country, penniless to all intents and purposes. It must have come suddenly to him that the adventure had been sufficient in itself, for he had been smitten with discouragement before leaving home, as to any success in the coveted direction of a writing future. But now, floating half-frozen down the river of defeat, as the grey white Yukon seemed to him in his predicament, his assertive buoyancy of brain could not help reviving what he had seen and done and felt in the year just past. Surely *something* could be realised out of it all, to enhance his chance of making a name, earning a voice in the affairs of men.

When I came to the Red Feather Saloon near the Eldorado Hotel, where I was staying (and which advertised that it would accept in payment 'nuggets and gold dust'), I saw it was closed and empty and so, too, was the blacksmith's shop next door to it and the harness store one door down.

There was a depressing end-of-term feeling about Dawson, despite the hilarity that in this weekend of approaching spring possessed the little town's permanent population of about two thousand – trappers, miners or government servants – as they happily greeted the thaw after the long dark winter. I couldn't share their jolly mood. It would be another three months before the tourists came roaring into town, doubling the population for a few hectic weeks. But, still, I had no doubt they would be coming.

I stayed in Dawson for a day or two, and then managed to get a seat on a small plane to Whitehorse. There, before leaving the Yukon behind me, I had dinner with Dick and Andrée North, and told them of my unforgettable experiences with the Wylies – not neglecting to confess to Dick, to his great amusement, of my regular 'dumping' by the dogs. Of course, I thanked him for helping to arrange the whole adventure.

Later, in Vancouver and New York, I would reread my volume of London's Yukon stories. I found them absolutely right: the dogs, the silences, the whiteness, the bitter cold — he had got all of it perfectly. His stories took me back to Forty Mile, and with a feeling of terrible loss I saw again the Wylies' little cabin in the snow under the spruces. I vowed to go back. In my imagination I revisited the mountain top behind the camp and saw once more the seemingly infinite expanse of snow-covered hilltops that stretched away westwards into Alaska or eastwards to the great barrier of the Mackenzie Mountains.

Now in my Whitehorse hotel room I took out copies of the photographs I had taken at the dog camp — and had had processed that day — and, with a large whiskey at my elbow, slowly went through them.

There the dogs were: Lobbo, standing massive on top of his crate, ears pricked forward, strong legs braced, his wide solemn bearlike head turned towards the cabin looking out for his master, Paul; Buck, standing as if he were posing for the judges in a dog show, turning back over his shoulder the handsome head with its clear beautiful black markings; Big Jack, looking at the camera with a sort of coy awareness as he lay resting by the trail, his muzzle flecked lightly with snow; and the gigantic puppy, Lurch, huge and feathery, standing impatiently in his harness, his mouth open as usual to whine an angry protest at the unnecessary delay that he felt was being unfairly forced on him.

I put out the light and stared at the ceiling. I thought of Paul Wylie, the expert musher and trapper, one of those specialists I like and admire so much.

I thought of the dogs as I would always remember them: in the snow, among the wintry trees, in their element. And tonight — now! — in the perfect, clear starlit silence, they would be pointing their noses to the sky, as Jack London had seen, and howling long and wolf-like, as their wild ancestors had done.

And, as London had said, their melancholy cadences rising above the spruces would voice what to them was the meaning of the stillness, and the cold, and the dark.

of Dickens or Shakespeare attracted me – or perhaps I sense in him some bizarre connection with Corina, the old grey mare outside the Plaza Hotel in New York. I really don't know. It is just one of those things.

Epilogue

After that I returned to New York, with images still firmly in my mind of the huskies' breath floating like smoke-plumes in the air and of the little cabin under the brilliant stream of the aurora borealis bridging the Yukon night sky.

I made plans to finish this book in Sag Harbor where I had started it nearly two years before while searching for Melville's *Moby Dick*. So I telephoned Ted Conklin, a new friend and the owner of the American Hotel there, and Ted said at once, 'Come on down and stay. Stay until my marriage, if you like. That's in about six weeks' time. If Tara doesn't change her mind.'

I went back eagerly to Sag Harbor. And after six weeks in that little whaling port where Queequeg, the tattooed harpooneer from the Pacific, had first disembarked on American soil, I managed to throw off the magic of the Northland night that Jack London had spoken of: 'the magic that steals in on one like fevers from malarial marshes'. And by the time Ted had married Tara I had finished this book.

It was odd, in a way. John Steinbeck had set off from Sag Harbor with Charley a little more than thirty years before – long before I had thought of setting about myself to tour bits of America's literary hinterland. By now I had seen Steinbeck's birthplace in California, as well as the scenes of some of his most successful books, and I had fallen in love with Montana as he had done. Now, purely by chance, I found I had fallen in love – again, as he had done – with Sag Harbor as well. In fact, if there are three places in the United States I want to return to more than any others they are Montana, Sag Harbor and New York City.

Of course I am fond of Georgia. And wherever they put up a good new statue to General William Tecumseh Sherman – it would have to be a very good one – I suppose I shall have to pay it a visit. I wish I could explain my fondness for that plundering old soldier – the 'scrofulous vulture' of Matthew Brady's photograph – who behaved atrociously to the Indians as well as to the Confederates of Georgia. In any case although what he said and did fascinates, and even sometimes amuses me, was he really one of those men in history one can be *fond* of? Perhaps something to do with his love

291

READ MORE IN PENGUIN

In every corner of the world, on every subject under the sun, Penguin represents quality and variety – the very best in publishing today.

For complete information about books available from Penguin – including Puffins, Penguin Classics and Arkana – and how to order them, write to us at the appropriate address below. Please note that for copyright reasons the selection of books varies from country to country.

In the United Kingdom: Please write to *Dept. EP, Penguin Books Ltd, Bath Road, Harmondsworth, West Drayton, Middlesex UB7 ODA*

In the United States: Please write to *Consumer Sales, Penguin USA, P.O. Box 999, Dept. 17109, Bergenfield, New Jersey 07621-0120.* VISA and MasterCard holders call 1-800-253-6476 to order Penguin titles

In Canada: Please write to *Penguin Books Canada Ltd, 10 Alcorn Avenue, Suite 300, Toronto, Ontario M4V 3B2*

In Australia: Please write to *Penguin Books Australia Ltd, P.O. Box 257, Ringwood, Victoria 3134*

In New Zealand: Please write to *Penguin Books (NZ) Ltd, Private Bag 102902, North Shore Mail Centre, Auckland 10*

In India: Please write to *Penguin Books India Pvt Ltd, 706 Eros Apartments, 56 Nehru Place, New Delhi 110 019*

In the Netherlands: Please write to *Penguin Books Netherlands bv, Postbus 3507, NL-1001 AH Amsterdam*

In Germany: Please write to *Penguin Books Deutschland GmbH, Metzlerstrasse 26, 60594 Frankfurt am Main*

In Spain: Please write to *Penguin Books S. A., Bravo Murillo 19, 1° B, 28015 Madrid*

In Italy: Please write to *Penguin Italia s.r.l., Via Felice Casati 20, I–20124 Milano*

In France: Please write to *Penguin France S. A., 17 rue Lejeune, F–31000 Toulouse*

In Japan: Please write to *Penguin Books Japan, Ishikiribashi Building, 2–5–4, Suido, Bunkyo-ku, Tokyo 112*

In Greece: Please write to *Penguin Hellas Ltd, Dimocritou 3, GR–106 71 Athens*

In South Africa: Please write to *Longman Penguin Southern Africa (Pty) Ltd, Private Bag X08, Bertsham 2013*

BY THE SAME AUTHOR

Slow Boats to China

Ancient steamer in the Aegean, cargo dhow to Karachi, Filipino kumpit through the pirate-infested Sulu Sea . . .

It needed twenty-three agreeably ill-assorted vessels and seven months to transport Gavin Young by slow boat from Pireaus to Canton – seven months crowded with adventure, excitement and colour. His account of a fantasy come true memorably distils the people, places, smells, conversations, ships and history of the places he encountered in a quite exceptional book.

'An unusual and fascinating book' – Hammond Innes in the *Guardian*

'Storms, fleas, pirates, bad food and bureaucrats . . . Mr Young suffered what he did to entertain us' – Anthony Burgess in the *Observer*

BY THE SAME AUTHOR

Slow Boats Home

The story of an extraordinary journey by boat from the China Seas to England, via the South Seas, Cape Horn and West Africa.

'I am decidedly envious of Gavin Young and his *Slow Boats Home*, successor to his highly entertaining *Slow Boats to China* ... a fascinating, memorable book' – Eric Newby in the *Guardian*

'Like *Slow Boats to China* this is likely to become a classic of travel' – Francis King in the *Spectator*

'A truly charming book' – John Ryle in the *Sunday Times*

'Vivid, stylish account of his year-long voyage from China to Britain via the Pacific and Cape Horn' – Graham Lord in the *Sunday Express*

BY THE SAME AUTHOR

Worlds Apart

For *Worlds Apart*, Gavin Young has written a collection of journalistic pieces that are elegant, vivid and compassionate and show his acute understanding of the varied worlds in which we live.

'Young is a born raconteur. His writing is full of visual impressions and touches of sensibility. He is driven more by people than by seats of power. But it is difficult to be a compassionate journalist without appearing soppy or sentimental. Young often achieves it. One finishes *Worlds Apart* exhilarated, moved, angered and enthralled: a tribute to its quality' – Jon Swain in the *Sunday Times*

'Some have to travel dangerously and it had better be Gavin Young to tell us about it' – Anthony Blond in the *Spectator*

BY THE SAME AUTHOR

Beyond Lion Rock
The story of Cathay Pacific Airways

In 1946 Roy Farrell and Syd de Kantzow's beloved, battered wartime DC-3 touched down in Shanghai for the first time. On board was a cargo of morning coats and toothbrushes from New York, forging the first post-war supply route across the treacherous eastern Himalayas. The international airline that seven million passengers a year now know as Cathay Pacific was born.

Gavin Young, acclaimed bestselling author of *Slow Boats to China* and *Slow Boats Home*, tells the swashbuckling story of an empire of the air – a thrilling, action-packed adventure that began in an age closer to the era of Biggles and biplanes held together by wire and safety pins than to our own.

'Pioneers like Farrell and de Kantzow would have had plenty of time to enjoy the dawn over Kangchenjunga. Would they think of us with envy or contempt, cruising seven miles up with hundreds of passengers, air-conditioning, in-flight concerts, movies, hot four-course meals with an elaborate wine list and all mod cons? . . . All this in forty years! Could the world really have changed so much and so fast?' – Gavin Young

'A rumbustious story, told warts and all . . . as an aviation tale, it is riveting' – *Financial Times*

BY THE SAME AUTHOR

In Search of Conrad
Joint Winner of the 1992 Thomas Cook Travel Book Award

'Part mariner's log and part detective story, it brilliantly evokes the Far-Eastern landscapes fixed forever in our imaginations by Conrad's novels. But above all Young makes us realize that the world Conrad described nearly a century ago is still there . . . the most pleasurable and exciting book I have read this year' – J. G. Ballard in the *Daily Telegraph*

'Young's passion for Conrad and his stories blazes from every porthole' – John Carey in the *Sunday Times*

'Young has produced a unique travel book . . . a fascinating, detailed (and serious) study of [Conrad's] novels in an original way . . . it is also a compulsive account of his own experience as an investigative traveller' – Norman Sherry in the *Guardian*

'Young has an eye for atmosphere; he is marvellous on Singapore as her past impinges on the present, myriad streets stalked by ghosts from the nineteenth century . . . *In Search of Conrad* is both scholarly and enthralling – always vivid, and often a hoot to read . . . better still it may set you to reading Conrad again' – Ian Thomson in the *Independent*

'Gavin Young has managed to write something rare in recent literature – a happy book about the Third World which also has the ring of truth' – Jonathan Raban in the *Independent on Sunday*